Latin American Nationalism

NEW APPROACHES TO INTERNATIONAL HISTORY

New Approaches to International History covers international history during the modern period and across the globe. The series incorporates new developments in the field, such as the cultural turn and transnationalism, as well as the classical high politics of state-centric policymaking and diplomatic relations. Written with upper level undergraduate and postgraduate students in mind, texts in the series provide an accessible overview of international diplomatic and transnational issues, events, and actors.

Published:

Decolonization and the Cold War, edited by Leslie James and Elisabeth Leake (2015)
Cold War Summits, Chris Tudda (2015)
The United Nations in International History, Amy Sayward (2017)

Forthcoming:

The History of United States Cultural Diplomacy, Michael L. Krenn
International Cooperation in the Early 20th Century, Daniel Gorman
The International LGBT Rights Movement, Laura Belmonte
Reconstructing the Postwar World, Francine McKenzie
International Development, Corinna Unger
Women and Gender in International History, Karen Garner
The Environment and International History, Scott Kaufman
The United States and Latin America in the Contemporary World, Stephen G. Rabe
The History of Oil Diplomacy, Christopher R. W. Dietrich
The Nineteenth Century World, Maartje Abbenhuis
Global War, Global Catastrophe, Maartje Abbenhuis and Ismee Tames

Latin American Nationalism

Identity in a Globalizing World

JAMES F. SIEKMEIER

Bloomsbury Academic
An imprint of Bloomsbury Publishing Plc

B L O O M S B U R Y
LONDON · OXFORD · NEW YORK · NEW DELHI · SYDNEY

Bloomsbury Academic

An imprint of Bloomsbury Publishing Plc

50 Bedford Square
London
WC1B 3DP
UK

1385 Broadway
New York
NY 10018
USA

www.bloomsbury.com

BLOOMSBURY and the Diana logo are trademarks of Bloomsbury Publishing Plc

First published 2017

British Library Cataloguing-in-Publication Data
A catalogue record for this book is available from the British Library.

ISBN: HB: 978-1-4725-3600-6
        PB: 978-1-4725-3599-3
        ePDF: 978-1-4725-3602-0
        eBook: 978-1-4725-3601-3

Library of Congress Cataloging-in-Publication Data
A catalog record for this book is available from the Library of Congress.

Series: New Approaches to International History

Cover image © John Bulmer/Getty Images

Typeset by Integra Software Services Pvt. Ltd.

To find out more about our authors and books, visit www.bloomsbury.com.
Here you will find extracts, author interviews, details of forthcoming events,
and the option to sign up for our newsletters.

To Catherine

CONTENTS

LIST OF FIGURES

LIST OF TABLES

LIST OF MAPS

SERIES EDITOR'S PREFACE

New Approaches to International History takes the entire world as its stage for exploring the history of diplomacy, broadly conceived theoretically and thematically, and writ large across the span of the globe, during the modern period. This series goes beyond the single goal of explaining encounters in the world. Our aspiration is that these books provide both an introduction for researchers new to a topic, and supplemental and essential reading in classrooms. Thus, *New Approaches* serves a dual purpose that is unique from other large-scale treatments of international history; it applies to scholarly agendas and pedagogy. In addition, it does so against the backdrop of a century of enormous change, conflict, and progress that informed global history but also continues to reflect on our own times.

The series offers the old and new diplomatic history to address a range of topics that shaped the twentieth century. Engaging in international history (including but not especially focusing on global or world history), these books will appeal to a range of scholars and teachers situated in the humanities and social sciences, including those in history, international relations, cultural studies, politics, and economics. We have in mind scholars, both novice and veteran, who require an entrée into a topic, trend, or technique that can benefit their own research or education into a new field of study by crossing boundaries in a variety of ways.

By its broad and inclusive coverage, *New Approaches to International History* is also unique because it makes accessible to students current research, methodology, and themes. Incorporating cutting-edge scholarship that reflects trends in international history, as well as addressing the classical high politics of state-centric policymaking and diplomatic relations, these books are designed to bring alive the myriad of approaches for digestion by advanced undergraduates and graduate students. In preparation for the *New Approaches* series, Bloomsbury surveyed courses and faculty around the world to gauge interest and reveal core themes of relevance for their classroom use. The polling yielded a host of topics, from war and peace to the environment; from empire to economic integration; and from migration to nuclear arms. The effort proved that there is a much-needed place for studies that connect scholars and students alike to international history, and books that are especially relevant to the teaching missions of faculty around the world.

We hope readers find this series to be appealing, challenging, and thought-provoking. Whether the history is viewed through older or newer lenses, *New Approaches to International History* allows students to peer into the modern period's complex relations among nations, people, and events to draw their own conclusions about the tumultuous, interconnected past.

Thomas Zeiler, University of Colorado Boulder, USA

ACKNOWLEDGMENTS

Of course, it is a truism to state that writing a book is a solitary affair. But, it is also a truism that it could not have been done without a lot of help from others. First, I would like to thank the Fulbright Commission for awarding me two grants to do research and teach in Bolivia. These experiences opened my eyes in numerous ways with regard to Latin American nationalism, and culture; as well as the impact of globalization. In addition, more recently, I was fortunate to lead two study abroad trips to Bolivia, and was greatly supported by West Virginia University and by the Amizade service-learning organization in this endeavor.

While writing this book, I received a great deal of intellectual stimulation from my colleagues and students, both graduate and undergraduate, at West Virginia University. Better colleagues and students could in my estimation not be found anywhere. In particular, I would like to thank Ken Fones-Wolf for organizing the History Department's Research Presentation group, and the members of that group for offering important commentary early on in the research process. I am also supported intellectually by a looser "imagined community" of friends—some former teachers, some former colleagues, some former students, and others. To Alan McPherson, Jason Parker, Max Paul Friedman, Peter Kornbluh, Bradley Coleman, Halbert Jones, Andy Johns, Ted Keiffer, Erin Mahan, Evan Ward, Mike Weis, Kyle Longley, Tanya Harmer, Stephen Rabe, Lester Langely, Thomas Holloway, Walter LaFeber, David Nickles, Steve Streeter, Clayton Koppes, Sayuri Shimizu, Todd Bennett, Kathy Rasmussen, Doug Selvage, Thomas Fields, Robert McMahon, Josh Esposito, Karina Garcia Esposito, Jordan Lieser, Joel Christenson, Michele Stephens, and Tom Zeiler: heartfelt thanks! I continue to benefit from your commentary and ideas.

Special thanks go to people who read parts of, or all of, the manuscript. Arnoldo De León and Erick Langer took time from their busy schedules to read parts of the manuscript and offer important comments. Also, I would like to thank Thomas Zeiler for planting the seed with regard to me writing this book a number of years ago. Catherine Tall went far beyond the call of duty. She read the entire manuscript and gave me invaluable feedback. (She's glad it's done!)

A good chunk of the research took place while on a short (but intellectually stimulating) sabbatic leave at Oxford University and the London School of Economics. I would like to thank West Virginia University (WVU)

for granting the sabbatical; and WVU and the West Virginia Humanities
Council for financial support. Achivists at Oxford University were very
helpful in finding primary (original) sources. Another place I researched
was the University of Pittsburgh Library. I would like to thank their crack
staff for answering my questions about the collection. While researching in
Pittsburgh, I stayed at the Pittsburgh Friends Meeting House, which very
much facilitated my work—heartfelt thanks to their Meeting. The editorial
team at Bloomsbury Academic, including Claire Lipscomb and Emma
Goode, have been models of collegiality, offering not only good comments
but prodding me to keep at it. I would also like to thank Mani Kuppan and
his staff for excellent copy editing.

While writing this book, my father and father-in-law passed away.
Their influence on my development as a person and as an intellectual has
continued after their passing. And many thanks to my mother and mother-
in-law for their encouragement and support, intellectually and otherwise.
Finally, I would like to thank my wife Catherine, and our daughter Claire,
for their support and love.

NOTE ON USAGE

I will use the term "American" to refer to people in the United States. To vary word choice, in addition, I will interchangeably use the term "North America" for the United States and "North Americans" for people from the United States. Like it or not, it has become standard usage to use "America" for "United States." To vary word choice as well, I will use the terms "Third World," "developing country," and "nonindustrialized country" interchangeably. When I use the term "Latin America," I am referring to territory from Mexico to Argentina, including the Caribbean.

LIST OF ABBREVIATIONS

CIA	Central Intelligence Agency
Fed	US Federal Reserve Bank (equivalent of Central or National Bank)
IBRD	International Bank for Reconstruction and Development (World Bank)
IFI	International Financial Institution
IMF	International Monetary Fund
ISI	Import Substitution Industrialization
MNC	Multinational Corporation
NAFTA	North American Free Trade Agreement
NGO	Non-governmental Organization
OPEC	Organization of the Petroleum Exporting Countries

Latin America

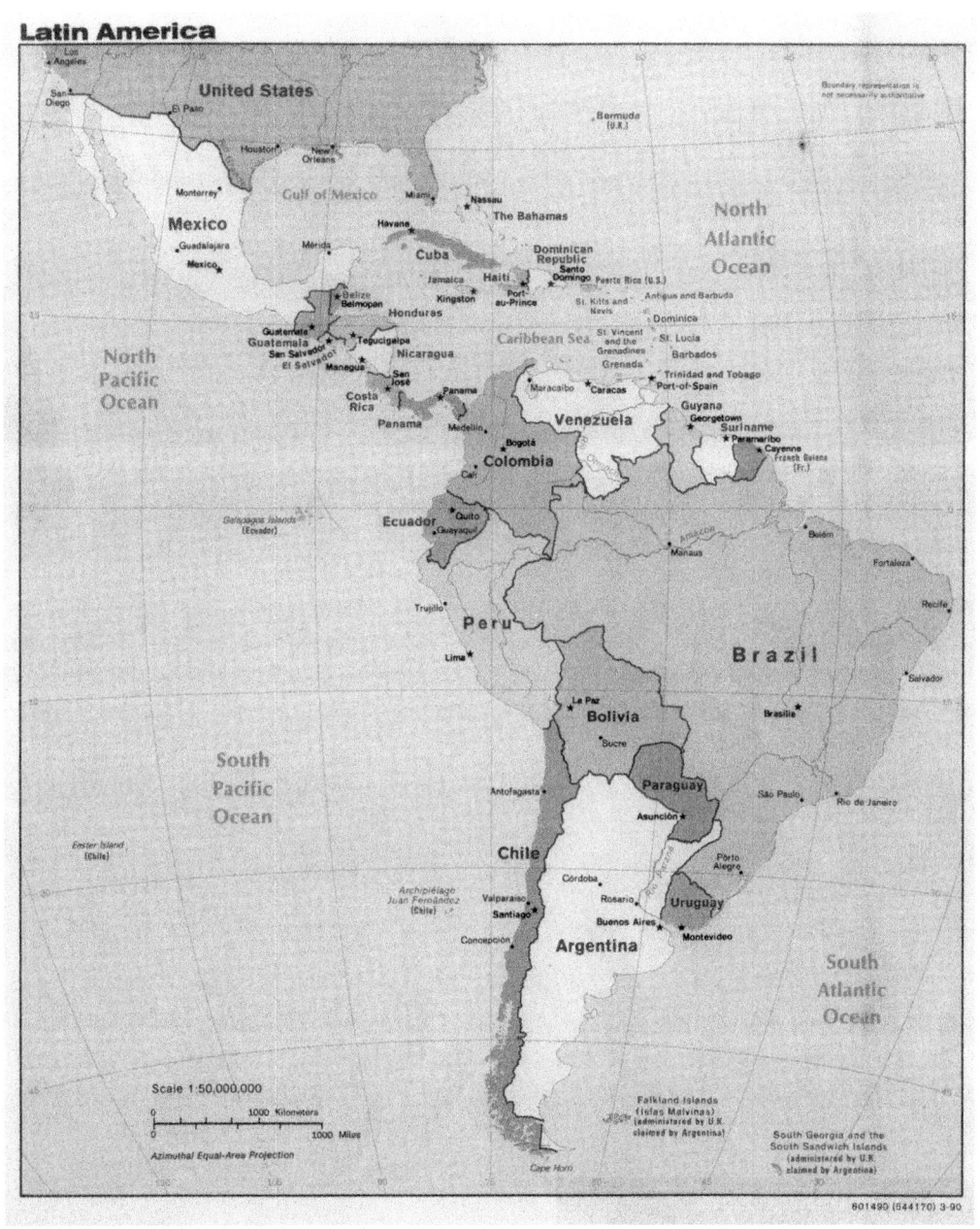

MAP 1 *Map of Latin America.* Source: *Perry-Castañeda Map Collection, University of Texas, Austin, TX, USA.*

PART ONE
Beginnings

Beginnings

CHAPTER ONE

Introduction

*Authorities on nationalism agree on two points: first,
that nationalism as a force is potent, and second,
that nationalism as a concept is difficult to define.*

E. BRADFORD BURNS[1]

"Today, gringo, you drink Bolivian beer!" The man in a street packed with revelers, who shoved a beer in my hand, said this joyfully. Bolivia had just beaten Argentina in a soccer tournament that was a lead-up to the World Cup the following year. Typical of Bolivia on a festive occasion, the streets were packed with revelers. And beating the haughty Argentines—who looked down on the rest of South America as being underdeveloped, nonwhite, and less European (thus less civilized) than they—was especially delicious for Bolivia, a poor nation with a large indigenous population. Indeed, trying to get a handle on something as illusive as nationalism in the late twentieth century was difficult. But, perhaps, soccer and beer were/are some of the more tangible facets of Latin American nationalism.

Does globalization increase the power/intensity of nationalism? Or does it decrease it? Not surprisingly, it does both, in different—and fascinating— ways. This book will examine the complex relationship between these two important phenomena. Although there have been many studies of globalization of late, Latin American nationalism has not been the focus of much scholarly attention. This book will analyze the important intersection between Latin American nationalism and globalization.

As scholar Michael Billig points out, nations have weapons because there is a deeply held belief that some things—in particular, sustaining the nation—are more valuable than life itself.[2] Yet, in most periods of history, nationalism is vague and illusive. Only when patriotic fervor is whipped up by revolution (e.g., during the Mexican and Cuban revolutions) or war (a good example is the 1982 Falklands War) does nationalistic sentiment become clear, distinct, powerful—and inescapable.

Equally illusive is globalization, the other main theme of this book. When defined broadly, it is meaningless. When defined specifically, it does not tell us much about our present-day reality. Nonetheless, situating Latin American nationalism in a global context makes sense, because globalization is increasingly shaping polities at the national level. On the one hand, it seems that globalization and nationalism are antithetical to each other—globalizers would want to tear down national borders, real or imagined. Nationalists, for their part, would want to privilege their own nation at all costs. However, in another respect the two movements are symbiotic. Globalization needs nationalism to ensure that rules are enforced at the "local level." Nations serve that important purpose. In this book, I will discuss two types of globalization. One type, a more general type of globalization, is the increasing network of social, economic, and cultural interactions over time. A second type of globalization is more specific—the US desire to create a world free of barriers to foreign trade and investment (in particular US foreign economic activity).

Much of the literature on globalization has dealt with the industrialized world as well as Africa, Asia, and the Middle East. One reason for the emphasis on Africa, Asia, and the Middle East is that these parts of the world decolonized in the mid-twentieth century, so scholars of decolonization have focused on how these new nations developed while they themselves were part of the international system. Indeed, an entire field of study—postcolonial or subaltern studies—has developed to study this process. Latin America, however, has in general been excluded from this scholarly conversation.[3]

Although Latin America has been largely left out of the conversation on decolonization, economic historians have focused attention on Latin America. This is probably due to the European conquest/colonization of the Americas in the sixteenth century, in which the Americas were vastly changed in economic terms. Also, the Americas, in particular with the export of silver to Spain, vastly changed the world economy, laying the groundwork for Spain's demise, and (as some have argued) laying the groundwork for the industrialization of Europe—with an increased money supply as well as rapid inflation. Although economic globalization is not necessarily the main "driver" of globalization, depending on the time period and/or context, economic globalization was fundamental to the origins of modern globalization since the sixteenth century, and Latin America was fundamental to that process.

Latin American nationalism has also been left out of the scholarly conversation with regard to the increased interest in nationalism since the 1990s. Interest in nationalism has increased since the 1990s with the fall of communism in Eastern Europe, as well as an intensified interest in postcolonial studies with increased scholarly attention being paid to Third

World nationalism. But, even as there have been a number of fascinating, path-breaking studies of Latin American nationalism of late, Latin American nationalism has not been part of the scholarly conversation on nationalism.[4]

In this introduction, first the idea of the nation will be examined. Then, the development of the nation in a globalizing world will be discussed. Should the nation be defined in civic terms—in which the nation decides who is a citizen, based on certain criteria? Or is the nation best defined in ethnic terms, in which only members of a particular ethnic group comprise the nation? The answer is, it depends. However, in Latin America, the civic definition is the definition commonly employed. In the colonial period, many conceived of Latin America as comprised of different nations, based on ethnicity—a "republica de los indios" (Indian republics) and a dominant nation, a European/mestizo (mixed-blood) nation. However, since the twentieth century, most Latin Americans accept the idea that a nation is defined in civic terms.

Although scholars have investigated different types of nationalism in Latin America in recent years, they have focused on the nationalism of what is termed "subaltern groups"—groups that have less power and influence than the middle class or elites. This study, however, will attempt an overall discussion of nationalism—in the context of globalization. The last survey of Latin American nationalism (at the level of the nation as a whole) was published over fifty years ago.[5] Obviously, historical methodologies have dramatically changed in the last half-century. This book will aim to examine the many "nationalisms" in Latin America—nationalism of the political elites, the nationalism of indigenous peoples, and the nationalism of the urban middle and working classes.

Defining nationalism is difficult. At the most basic level, nationalism is about mapping a meta-narrative (a constructed collective memory of a nation) onto a space or place (the sovereign territory of the nation). And what is that collective memory? Cynics might conclude that memory is what we choose to recall. Of course, this begs the question as to who is constructing the national meta-narrative and for what purpose. The beginning of an answer to this question must acknowledge that there is no one national meta-narrative on which there is a deeply held societal consensus. Instead, there are lots of competing national narratives. Different people/groups construct their different versions of national narratives, for their own purposes. And of course, the national meta-narrative is not simply the sum total of the different national narratives who "fight it out" in a level playing field of ideas, with the most persuasive idea automatically winning the day. Instead, those with the most power in society—who control the major means of communication—will have more say in determining the outlines of the meta-narrative than the less powerful. The ultimate purpose of the meta-narrative is to give meaning to a people in a particular space/place and to perpetuate this meaning over time.

In general, definitions of nationalism fall into two categories. First, there are what might be termed "objective" aspects—territory controlled and language used, for example. Second, there are the subjective definitions—involving will and memory, for example.[6] To better understand the subjective definitions, national identity is an important concept. A person's identity is formed of many layers based on family, regional, and national affiliations. National identity has often manifested itself through pride in the accomplishments of the nation—winning soccer matches, for example. Expressions of pride in national identity can be seen when young people serve in their nation's military and thus put their lives on the line. National pride can be a vehicle for people of the nonelite segments of society who exhibit jingoism (excessive pride) as a way of "standing up" to elite members of society. That is, when nonelite members of society come home after fighting in a war, they often refuse to go to their wealthy employers, hat in hand, to ask for increased pay or better treatment. Instead, they demand that a new, more egalitarian nation be formed, in which they are not subservient to their "betters"—and if it means that they fight a revolution to obtain such a nation, so be it. A good example of nonelite military veterans demanding a more egalitarian society would be the Bolivian veterans of the Chaco War against Paraguay (1932–1936). After the demobilization, many nonelite Bolivian veterans refused to accept the hierarchical social system of Bolivia, in which a handful of economic, political, and military elites structured the society solely for their benefit, at the expense of the nonelite majority. These veterans proved to be instrumental in the making of the Bolivian Revolution of 1952.

Identity: Who am I?

Any study of nationalism must consider how much citizens identify with their nation or region—that is, national identity. Different versions of nationalism can be put into two broad, distinct categories to facilitate our understanding of nationalism in Latin America. One category is civic/territorial nationalism—the nation is legally/juridically defined in a specific physical territory, in which there is a common economy, laws, mass public education, shared military/administrative institutions, and a shared civic ideology (including national flag, anthem, and holidays). In turn, the legal system of this nation will decide what the criteria are for allowing "outsiders" to become citizens of the nation. (In addition, they will decide which crimes prove so heinous that a citizen is accused of treason.) A second category is cultural nationalism and is based on culture/ethnicity/genealogy—the members of the nation exhibit a certain "we-consciousness," based on common ancestral descent, common history/memory, and a common culture in the sense that there are unifying customs and accompanying myths. With cultural nationalism, there are sharp distinctions between nations, and there is a primordial aspect to nationalism. It is difficult or even impossible for members of a nation to give up their citizenship and become a citizen of another nation. The phrase "national identity" is normally evocative of cultural nationalism as opposed to civic/territorial nationalism.

One can also discuss regional identity—related to but distinct from the concept of national identity. A Latin American identity was slow in forming, in part because historically each individual Latin American country had its own particularistic experience in fighting and winning its war for independence. Geographical division as well as racial differences within and between Latin American nations proved divisive. And in the case of Brazil, it secured its independence from Portugal not through war but by providing refuge for the Portuguese royal family during the Napoleonic invasion of Iberia in the early nineteenth century. When asked to allow Brazil to convert to a constitutional monarchy, in which the crown had little power, the Portuguese royal family had little choice but to accept. With increased British and US economic activity in the late nineteenth century, Latin American nations began viewing themselves as victims of economic exploitation from abroad. The Latin American reaction to large foreign multinational corporations (MNCs) (backed up by the powerful governments in which they are based) operating in their nations was to put restrictions on foreign economic activity. Thus, economic nationalism proved to be a common thread that drew many of the Latin American nations together and one of the building blocks of Latin American identity. In addition, in the twentieth century, Latin American nationalism got a big boost from the archeological excavations of the early part of the century, which helped to promote the already powerful idea that the pre-Columbian empires were some of the more advanced, and well developed, in world history. Archeology provided a tangible, and convenient, "rallying point" for Latin American nationalism.

Latin American intellectuals have posited a number of different ways one can understand Latin Americans' identity, and, not surprisingly, since these intellectuals closely followed intellectual trends in Europe and the United States, their conceptions of Latin American identity implicitly compared Latin America to its northern counterparts. Further, these intellectuals posited that Latin America was fundamentally superior to the United States. In 1900, Uruguay's José Enrique Rodó was a pioneer in maintaining that Latin America's identity was fundamentally different from the identity of those in the United States and Europe.[7] He viewed the Latin Americans as being a distinct race (a composite of biological, cultural, and political origins) from people in the United States and Europe. He believed what made Latin America distinct was its privileged morality, while the United States and Europe were all about pragmatic utilitarianism—making money by any means necessary, including exploiting the resources and people of Latin America.[8] Using mythological characters and characters from Shakespeare's famous play *The Tempest*, Rodó sharply contrasted the cultures of the United States and Latin America. Ariel, the character that represented cultural refinement, represented Latin America. Calaban, the brutish animalistic character, represented the United States.

Indeed, others had called attention to the cultural differences between North America and the southern parts of the Western Hemisphere, in a less polemical way than Rodó. Legend has it that it was a nineteenth-century French mapmaker who came up with the term "Latin America" because he sought a name that would clearly denote that the culture of the parts of the Americas south of the Rio Grande had a distinct, and more Gallic or Mediterranean culture, as compared to that of its North American counterpart.

This brings us to the concept of national identity in Latin America. In the most general terms, national identity is comprised of what unites a people socially, culturally, and politically and thus marks it as different from another people.[9] Race is central to the formation of national identity. For his part, Jose Vasconcelos of Mexico argued that Latin America, with its large mestizo (mixed-race) population, was superior to nations that were predominantly made up of one ethnicity. Racial mixing led to the harmony of opposites and the creation of a superior mixture of cultures into a new *raza cosmico* (cosmic race).[10] Gilberto Freyre, in his influential *Casa Grande e Favela* of 1933 (published in English *The Masters and the Slaves* in 1946), made a similar argument for his native Brazil. He discussed a deeply imbedded Iberian culture of racial tolerance, which went back to the invasion of the Moors in the eighth century, during which Iberians were forced to deal with a culturally and racially different people. Finally, the important Peruvian thinker Jose Carlos Mariátegui wrestled with why Indians in Peru were in such material misery and how that could be improved. He did not think that racial mixing was a solution. Instead, the Peruvian nation (and Latin America more broadly) was responsible, he thought, for eliminating the economic exploitation of the Indians, by which they would prosper, and could thus become full-fledged citizens of their individual nations.[11]

As such, national identity is shaped by attitudes toward race and relations between the races. Latin American nations, of course, consist of a number of different races and ethnicities. (The topic of racial nationalism will be explored further in Chapter Ten.) There is a scholarly consensus with regard to the definition of race. It is a social construct, which divides people into categories based on a combination of skin color and cultural norms or values. Ethnicity, for its part, is more vague, and a scholarly consensus is illusive. However, most observers would probably agree that language, food, music, religion, and lineage are important factors that would distinguish one ethnic group from another. Yet, it is more complicated. Latinos (people of Latin American descent) in the United States, for example, do not all share commonalities in the categories discussed in the previous sentence; yet many (including some of them) would consider themselves an ethnic group.

It is important to point out that even though national identities are social constructs, they exist because they are useful to societies. Over time, societies forge national identities by means of myths, memories, and traditions, transmitted in the form of popular and powerful symbols. (The Virgin de Guadalupe in Mexico is a good example.) The emerging national identity of a society is hegemonic, in that it presents itself as the only possible identity of a people. Often, too, a glorified nostalgic view of the nation's past is part of this myth-building process. A societal consensus on national origins is important for national identity. Such national identities would not exist if they were not widely accepted. National identity, as such, cannot survive if it is forced upon the majority by a powerful elite. The majority must "buy into" national identity if it is to survive for long.[12] National identity will be powerful and long lasting to the extent it evolves over time to suit the needs of the society. If it is successful in this regard, it serves as a useful framework for a people to unite past, present, and future, giving it a sense of continuity.

National identity is a general and malleable enough concept that it can be a unifying, progressive, modernizing force. However, it can also be harnesses in the name of jingoist xenophobia, as well as authoritarian repression at home. How it operates in individual countries during particular historical epochs is determined by the historical context of each individual nation.[13]

In sum, many express their national identity as a sense of belonging to a particular nation. Some nationalists, often not by choice, are only part of an "imagined community" (in scholar Benedict Anderson's words) and thus do not live physically in their nation. However, many prefer their home to be a specific physical nation made of up a physical territory. Many desire to be emotionally "rooted" in one's own land that provides a sense of belonging—similar to being in a family. Rootedness in one's nation can provide unquestioned acceptance by one's fellow citizens that one cannot get anywhere else.[14] In other words, for some, national identity provides an affirmative, rooted identity. How globalization impacts the degree of rootedness, or the desire for rootedness, is a matter of debate.

The link between nationalism and globalization is clearly evident: without the nation-state system to organize world affairs, globalization would have a very different character than it has. Other than that concept, there is little agreement over the benefits or problems of globalization. The debate over globalization is intense. Proponents of globalization argue that globalization will make individuals' identity more cosmopolitan over time. Others argue that globalization, by creating a homogenized world culture controlled by a small number people in the wealthier and/or more powerful nations, makes people less rooted and want to discard rootedness all together. The argument goes that if people see world culture as tantalizingly appealing, they will lose interest in their local culture and immerse themselves in the acquisitive, materialistic nature of world culture. Then, a fear of the power of globalized world culture will, according to some, create a backlash, in which people will turn to, and even revel in, their local culture. Fearing a loss of cultural distinctiveness in a rapidly globalizing (and homogenizing) world, some people will quickly brush aside world culture and revel in the particularities of their local culture. Given there are a number of examples, or case studies, exhibiting both reactions to globalization, it is a disagreement that will not abate soon.

The construction of nationalism over time

It is important to distinguish between the "nation" and the "state." The nation, in the broadest sense, is comprised of a set of shared ideas, and in particular, beliefs of a people in a specific (if contested) territory. In its ideal form, the state, however, is a set of agreed-upon, governing institutions employed by the nation to achieve its goals. In this book, if I am referring to the nation and state collectively, I'll use the term "nation-state," which combines the lateral construction of nation and the hierarchical one of state.[15]

The effectiveness of states is based on four criteria. First, can they exert effective control over their territory—in particular, ensure public order in the entire state? Second, can they efficiently set up and implement universally accepted "rules of the game" for economic actors to ensure a prosperous economy? Third—and related to the first two—can the state set up and maintain an infrastructure that will allow for the state to maintain control over its territory and facilitate economic growth? Fourth, does the state enjoy a monopoly over the legitimacy of the state apparatus? One way of measuring this legitimacy is to examine how much symbolic power the state can exert—that is, do the citizens readily accept that it should have such a monopoly over its legitimacy over time? Is this acceptance reflected in a high level of civic participation?[16] To understand Latin American nationalism, it is important to realize that the state preceded the nation by as much as a century. Even as the different emergent Latin American nations set up their states in the early nineteenth century, the idea of the nation was weak at first and evolved and strengthened over time.

In a very influential and pathbreaking 1983 book, revised in 1991, Benedict Anderson defined nationalism as an "imagined community."[17] He noted that Latin Americans, along with the United States, were the pioneers in the area of postcolonial nationalism, breaking away from their Iberian "mother countries" in the early nineteenth century. He especially emphasized the role of print media in fostering the development of such a community, in that newspapers in particular allowed for the circulation of—and thus deepening of—nationalistic ideas. However, it is important to ask the questions that flow from this powerful concept. Who is doing the imagining? Do different groups in a particular nation have vastly different visions of nationalism? If so, why? And, what are the different interests/ agendas of the different groups conceptualizing nationalism?

Studies of Third World nationalism in recent years have focused on Africa and Asia in part because of the increased interest in decolonization studies. Not surprisingly, the rapid and dramatic collapse of the European empires in those two parts of the world has drawn the attention of researchers. For their part, Latin American historians have "reimagined" Latin American nationalism in recent years. In a previous generation, Latin American nationalism was conceived of as a "top-down" affair. Now, Latin American scholars have focused their interest on "bottom-up" social movements: indigenous people, women, and other nonelites.

From whence it came? A brief history

The idea of the nation was first conceptualized in war. In the areas of Latin America which the Spanish controlled, wars of national liberation brought the nation into being. Indeed, war represents an opportunity for the creation (and later re-creation) of national identity. Armies of course are composed of peoples of different ethnic, racial, and class background from diverse regions of the nation. The process of forming an army and fighting foster a new, stronger type of national identity.[18]

With the Wars for Independence in Spanish colonial Latin America in the early nineteenth century, and Brazil's independence by the mid-nineteenth century, the elites who directed the independence efforts focused on top-down state building at first. Institutions had to be built, and militaries and police, in particular, had to be created to ensure that as many people as possible in the state's territory were subject to the power of the state. Only after a serious crisis of Latin American states—the Great Depression of the 1930s—did states in Latin America actually build nations. Only with the economic nationalist policies that followed the Depression, including industrialization and urbanization, did Latin American states acquire the resources and, therefore, the ability to create the traditions, myths, and ideas (and effectively disseminate them among their people) to engage in effective nation building.[19]

"Nation building" has become a "hot topic" in academia and the media in recent years. Historians, for their part, have focused their attention on decolonization—the collapse of the European empires in the non-industrialized world soon after the Second World War and the implications of this dissolution of power for the "new nations" of the emergent Third World. Historians of decolonization, in general, have not devoted much effort to examining what might be termed the first major wave of decolonization—Latin America's independence from Spain and Portugal.

Social scientists of all stripes have focused a great deal of attention on nation building in part because the United States, after the collapse of the Soviet system in the early 1990s, thought it could intervene at will in the developing world without the fear that such intervention would "push" the developing world "into the arms" of the Communist bloc. US leaders, thus, saw it incumbent upon themselves to promote US-style nations in the Third World. Such a world of US-style nations, an idea deeply embedded in the US psyche, was the only meaningful pathway to a stable, pro-US world. Nation building, of course, has raised its profile significantly with the US military interventions in Afghanistan and Iraq. This book will examine historically how this process unfolded in Latin America—and how it intersected with globalization.

Differing concepts of nationalism

There are a number of different ways the development of nationalism can be understood. One way is by examining how nations conceive of threats to their sovereignty or in extreme cases their very existence. Nationalism is, on one level, about unifying behind a common threat. Even if deep divisions divide a nation, one thing all can agree on is the importance of unifying in the face of a common threat. Oftentimes, an outside threat can be "channeled" through a local entity. For example, if miners are working for what they perceive as low wages, they might accept the situation if the mine owner is from their nation. But as soon as the mine owner sells the mine to a foreign entity, the mine workers think they are being unjustly exploited—by an outside power. Nationalist sentiment sets in.

The bases of nineteenth-century nationalism can be briefly summarized as various types of national integration: physical integration and social integration. This integration took place on the terms set by the elite. Physical integration meant infrastructure to integrate the diverse regions of a particular country: roads and railroads. Social integration meant forcing native peoples, most of whom lived in the countryside, to speak Spanish or Portuguese. However, by the mid- to late twentieth century, a new vision of the nation challenged this elite-driven version: a pluralistic nation, made up of a variety of peoples, who speak different languages and have different customs.

Of course, different racial/ethnic groups within a nation and citizens from different classes imagine very different types of communities. First of all, there are regions within individual nations (e.g., the highlands and the lowlands); and there are supranational regions (e.g., the Caribbean and South America). Due in part to Latin America's forbidding geography, which has caused subsocieties to develop, individuals often have an intense loyalty to their region. In general, Latin Americans will feel the "pull" of regionalism more at the subnational level than the supranational level. When Latin Americans do feel a loyalty to a supranational region, it is often expressed through identification with a racial or ethnic group. For example, many indigenous peoples in the Andes accept the symbol of the wiphala flag as expressing the yearnings for self-expression through the indigenous nations of the region.

The Latin American economy and society is stratified by social class. Race and racism add another element to the social stratification. Such groupings have a major impact on the expression of Latin American nationalism. Thus, Latin American nationalism is a deeply divided phenomenon. One could talk about two separate nationalisms—one for the elites and one for the nonelites. Elite nationalists were deeply influenced by, and even copied, European societies and nations. With regard to nonelite Latin Americans, until the twentieth century, they had little wherewithal to reach out to their counterparts outside of their region.

Most certainly, nationalism is both particular to an individual society and simultaneously part of a broader worldwide ideology emphasizing the importance of each people (however defined) having self-determination and/or popular sovereignty—the ability to determine their government, and more broadly, their contribution to world society. What is particular to Latin American nationalism?

Latin American nationalism is unique in comparison to the nationalisms of other developing world nations in that Latin America achieved political independence at least a century before it achieved social and economic independence. In other parts of the non-industrialized world, nations achieved political, social, and economic independence (or autonomy) at about the same time—during the wave of decolonization of the European empires after the Second World War. Certainly, for the Third World nations in Asia, Africa, and the Middle East, there was a lag (a couple of decades) between achieving political independence and achieving a modicum of social/economic independence. And it is important to note that both Latin America and other parts of the non-industrialized world have not achieved full economic/social independence—it is a work in progress. However, what makes Latin America unique is that it achieved its political nationalism (in the early nineteenth century) fully a century and a half before it began to achieve a modicum of economic/social independence (in the mid-twentieth century).

The large gap between the achievement of Latin America's political independence and its relative lack of economic development compared to the United States has caused many scholars to wonder why Latin American development lagged compared to the United States and other industrialized nations. One group of scholars, who called themselves *depencistas* (dependency theorists), posited that Latin America remained economically dependent on—even a neocolony of—the industrialized nations long after early nineteenth-century political independence was achieved. Thus, in the mid- to late twentieth century, a school of thought called dependency theory emerged, which argued that only with economic autonomy could Latin Americans be completely independent.[20]

As such, a key aspect of the growth of nationalism in twentieth-century Latin America was economic nationalism, the idea that Latin America governments needed to exert control over key sectors of the economy (especially stocks of valuable, even strategic, raw materials). In some nations, large stocks of valuable minerals such as oil or natural gas were seen as national patrimony to be carefully managed to ensure that the development of this critically important resource was used in a way to foster balanced, diversified economic development of the nation. Some economic nationalists stressed the importance of developing economic self-sufficiency, including stimulating industrialization. Such self-sufficiency would end what they saw as crippling dependence on outside powers, giving the people control over their economic destiny. For that reason, when the various Latin American nations by the early twentieth century sought increased control over their situations, many Latin American people viewed this quest for increased autonomy as "national liberation."[21]

Understanding the evolution of Latin American nationalism is important. Latin American historian Arthur Whitaker noted that in order to understand the evolution of Latin American nationalism over time, it was important to discuss distinct phases or stages. First, in the nineteenth century, Latin American nationalism was focused on political liberalism as imported from Europe. Next, in the late nineteenth-century economic nationalism, the idea that "factor endowments" of a nation's natural resources were national patrimony and thus controlled by the nation-state, began to emerge. Also, cultural nationalism, typified by Rodó's *Ariel*, began to emerge as well. Next, in the early twentieth century, governments began to assume an international role. Then, in the 1930s and 1940s, urban populist movements facilitated the entrance of the urban working and middle classes into the polity. In addition, individual Latin American nations began "playing up" the importance and distinctiveness of their own particular national culture.[22] By the 1960s, there was a moderation of the populist-style nationalism of the mid-twentieth century. Although Whitaker of course could not write about what came after the time period he was writing in, after the 1960s, one could argue, Latin American nationalism was weakened by the neoliberal "revolution" of the 1970s through 1990s. Finally, in a reaction to the problems of neoliberalism, Latin American nationalism increased in power and intensity after 2000.

British historian Eric Hobsbawm, employing what could be termed a "modernist" conception of the evolution of the nation-state over time, was more general in his description of the stages of Latin American nationalism. First, there was the "Enlightenment" stage, in the early to mid-nineteenth century, in which individuals in an agreed-upon space shared a common legal/political system. Next, in the late nineteenth century, the idea of national progress emerged. Progress was defined as modernization and the extension of state power over the entirety of the nation-state's territory. Indeed, the idea of "progress" was so central that only those people who shared the nation-state's conception of it were really considered citizens of the nation. Then, in the early twentieth century, Hobsbawm stated that "popular nationalism" emerged, in particular with the Mexican Revolution, in which everyone was a member of the nation. This idea of "popular nationalism" also applies to the mid-twentieth-century urban populist movements. Modern mass culture—as transmitted by new technologies—was key in forming this newly inclusive national consciousness.[23]

As such, the nineteenth-century, elite-driven, top-down nationalism no longer had a "monopoly" on nationalist sentiment. By the mid-twentieth century, there were, in a sense, competing conceptions of nationalism in the various Latin American nations. A new nationalism of the nonelites raised its profile considerably, with the development of urban populism in many Latin American nations. Although urban populism runs deep in Latin American history, the most prominent urban populists, such as Víctor Paz Estenssoro of Bolivia, Getúlio Vargas of Brazil, and Juan Perón of Argentina, burst on the world stage in the 1940s and 1950s with a powerful message—the nationalism of the nonelites thus became the nationalism of the nation, be it Bolivia, Brazil, or Argentina. Urban populists not only wanted expanded political participation for nonelite Latin Americans, these ubranites also wanted improved public services and economic development for the middle and working classes, and for the poor as well.

Nationalism can be broken down into three areas—political, cultural, and economic. Political nationalism can be defined, on the one hand, as a sentiment/movement that strengthens the politico-military aspect of the nations. Also, political self-determination is part and parcel of political nationalism—popular sovereignty, not unelected monarchical/authoritarian strongmen, should determine the fate of the nation.

Like all cultures, of course, Latin American culture is distinct. The Indian cultures and the mestizo/ladino culture (mixed European and Indian people) that arose from the European conquest of Latin America are the bases of Latin American sociocultural distinctness. In some respects, Latin American culture defined itself as opposed to other cultures—specifically, North American culture. Certainly, the profound influence of indigenous cultures on Latin American nationalism makes it distinct from all others.

Latin American nationalism and the inter-American system

This clash of cultures between Latin America and North America also manifested itself in the economic realm. By the twentieth century, an increasingly important aspect of Latin American nationalism was economic nationalism, discussed above. Indeed, Latin American nationalism cannot be understood unless one examines the collision of Latin American nationalism with the expanding power of the United States in the late nineteenth century. Some background is important here. The United States became an imperial power just as the Latin American nations congealed in the late nineteenth century, after decades of instability and even chaos that flowed out of the destruction of the Wars for Independence in the early nineteenth century.

The two most significant exertions of early US imperialism were into Latin America—the Mexican-American War (1846–1848) and the Spanish-American War (1898). The United States fought the Mexican-American War under the banner of its doctrine of Manifest Destiny: that the United States was destined to control all of North America, which would bring the liberties of US citizens to all who resided there. With its victory, the United States severed about one-third of the northern part of Mexico's territory. As such, not surprisingly, Mexican nationalism has a strong anti-US side to it, as discussed in Chapter Three. The Spanish-American War of 1898 resulted in the United States acquiring two colonies from Spain, the Philippines and Puerto Rico, and the United States placing a protectorate over Cuba.

Fearfully viewing US-landed expansion and commercial expansion (driven in part by growing industrialization, which required inexpensive access to raw materials), Latin American nations made it clear that their "factor endowments" (to use the economists' term) were off limits to foreigners. Moreover, the nation-state, and it alone, had the right to exploit national resources. In the early twentieth century, the Congresses of the countries of the Southern Cone (the region south of the Andes and Brazil), specifically Argentina, Uruguay, and Chile, proved to be the vanguard of the economic nationalism movement. Thus, as discussed above, economic nationalism was born.[24] It was no surprise that economic nationalism proved powerful in the Southern Cone, as Britain attempted to control aspects of the economies of these nations in the nineteenth century.

But by the early twentieth century, it was the United States, not Britain, that Latin America feared. Some Latin Americans fearfully concluded that the United States had effectively created a new Roman Empire in the Americas.[25] Not surprisingly, Latin Americans resisted this imposition of power, driven in part by a desire for Latin America's raw materials and a misplaced sense of Manifest Destiny. Many in the United States concluded that the expansion of US power into Latin American automatically meant progress with a capital "P." A good example of the latter is United States' severing of Panama from Colombia and the subsequent US construction of the Panama Canal. Theodore Roosevelt (TR) stated it directly—since no other nation had the wherewithal to build the canal, and the United States did, it was the duty of the United States to build the canal. Period. Of course, TR, coming from a northeastern old money background, had a sense of noblesse oblige because of his social class—due to his exalted social status, he had an obligation to serve the less fortunate. The noblesse oblige of the northeastern US elite was transformed into the duty of the United States as a whole to spread, by force if necessary, a US version of progress (economic, social, and political) around the globe. Latin America, bordering on the United States, became a laboratory for the US projection of power in the name of progress.

As the Industrial Revolution in the United States took hold in the late nineteenth century, US capitalists looked to Latin America for critically important raw materials, investments in infrastructure, and markets to sell US products being churned out of US factories at an ever-increasing, and alarming, rate. The most important raw materials were oil and metals. Infrastructure investments in railroads (Mexico and Peru were good examples) increased the profits of US businesses. US investors bought up an incredible amount of Mexican land not only for oil and metal exploitation but also for agricultural production. US capitalists' purchases of Mexican land proved to be an important cause of the Mexican Revolution of 1910–1940.

As US economic involvement in Latin America became more and more extensive, Latin American nationalism began to include a strong element of economic nationalism. Some Latin Americans—those on the political left—feared that US economic activity was, at base, economic exploitation. "Vendepatria"—selling the nations' raw materials to foreign investors rapidly and inexpensively, and thus ceding control over critically important resources to foreigners—became a rallying cry.

Latin Americans' concern with stewardship of their nations' resources, particularly their stocks of valuable, nonrenewable resources, for careful, well-planned, long-term use, became palpable in the early twentieth century with the expansion of US (and European nations') power into the region. In response to the growing US and European economic power in the early twentieth century, some Latin American nations nationalized stocks of raw materials and even expropriated the assets of foreign companies. A key early example was Mexico during its revolution, in which it nationalized the subsoil (oil and valuable minerals) with its revolutionary constitution of 1917. Since Mexico was one of the world's biggest producers of oil in the early twentieth century, before Venezuela and Middle Eastern nations began to export significant amounts of crude, this nationalization provoked crises between Mexico and the industrialized nations of the United States and Europe. Powerful MNCs based in the industrialized world owned valuable investments in Mexico and had grown to enjoy the laissez-faire policies of Mexican dictator Porfirio Díaz, who either was in power or controlled the Mexican political system from behind the scenes from 1876 to 1911.

Surprisingly, another trailblazer was poor, landlocked Bolivia. The Andean nation compared to other Latin American nations at the time was wracked by internal dissent, including civil war and political instability. Its leadership proved especially self-serving and inept. Nevertheless, Bolivia expropriated its foreign oil operations in 1937, and in 1952 Bolivia nationalized (with compensation) the three largest, and partially foreign-owned, mining companies that had virtual control over the mining industry. Soon thereafter Guatemala expropriated a large amount of the United Fruit Company's (UFCO) lands in that nation. UFCO had operated in the region since the early twentieth century and, by the 1940s, exerted significant control over not only the Central American and Caribbean economies but also their political systems. Cuba with its 1959 revolution quickly moved to expropriate valuable US investments, in particular oil companies' assets, as well as lands owned by US landowners. Peru nationalized foreign oil company investments in 1970, and Venezuela did the same five years later.

Most of these expropriations offered compensation to the MNC that had lost its investment. However, for Latin American nationalists, it was not primarily about the money. Having control over critically important, and nonrenewable, natural resources was key in this regard. Carefully and appropriately using these resources over time for the economic development of the nation could (theoretically) provide a foundation for the nation's future economic development—a development that (according to the nationalists) would, if done properly, benefit all social classes of Latin Americans.

According to many scholars, Latin American nationalism is an autonomous force. It clearly would exist in and of itself, even if the rest of the world did not exist. As mentioned previously, Latin American nationalism is distinct because of the influence of mestizo (mixed-race people) culture on Latin American nationalism. Because the amalgam of the Indian, European, and African races in Latin America, understanding the culture that emerged from such mixing is key to understanding Latin American nationalism. But, it is important to understand that, due to the clash between Latin American economic nationalism and US interests, Latin American nationalism has simultaneously been strengthened and has an anti-US side to it. Of course, as a "great power," US interests are multifaceted. But one goal has proven to be especially powerful over time: US foreign policy makers have aimed to create a hemisphere open to foreign trade and investment, particularly US economic activity, a goal that stretched back to the late nineteenth century and US interest in "Pan-Americanism." Thus, early on, Latin American nationalism clashed with US-inspired globalization.

The distinctiveness of Latin American nationalism

One reason why Latin American nationalism has not been studied much of late by academics and other observers is that many assume it is not as powerful or potent a force as Asian or Middle Eastern nationalism. Latin

America has not produced a powerful nationalist of the likes of Ho Chi Minh, Mao Zedong, or even a Nassar or Mandela. (Castro is arguably an exception; but his "moment in the sun" was really quite brief.) One reason for the assumption of the relative weakness of Latin American nationalism is that, compared to other Third World areas, its nationalism is older—almost 200 years old—and thus does not have the same intensity of the "newer" nationalisms of Asia and Africa, born in the post–Second World War era. There is, I argue, an unstated assumption held by many that Latin American nationalism is latent most of the time, and only becomes important when "inflamed" by a problem or crisis. Yet, even though nationalism in Latin America is often latent, this book will argue that Latin American nationalism has been, and is, a potent force. How can one measure the importance of Latin American nationalism? I do so in this book by asking two questions about it, and, by the end of the book, proposing tentative answers to these questions. First, what is it about Latin American nationalism that causes it to be an important part of someone's identity—and why has it become a more important part of the identity of Latin Americans of late? Second, how does globalization affect the unfolding process of Latin American nationalism?

Examining Latin American nationalism historically in the context of an historically evolving globalization is I would argue the best way to understand Latin America today. The nation-state in Latin America emerged as a historical compromise, in a sense, between empire and village. During the Spanish and Portuguese empires, from roughly 1500 to the early nineteenth century, the identity of the vast majority of people in Latin America was shaped by their village life and the region they lived in. Then, for a few elites, the imperial overlord in Europe was important for their lives. As the empires crumbled, the nation-state proved an especially useful institution— large enough to allow people to think beyond their village, but not so large that they thought they had no influence over it.[26]

Latin American nationalism is inherently different from its European counterpart. First, Latin American nationalism was a "top-down" project by Europeanized elites from the beginning. Nationalism started as an imposition from above. These elites not only aimed to force Indians and Afro-Latin Americans to speak Spanish or Portuguese but also aimed to impose European-style values—individual free-holding of land, free-market economics, and (arguably more popular) political freedoms. These elites aimed to force their vision of nationalism down the throats of nonwhite Indian and Afro-Latin American peoples, who often resisted this imposition.[27] Second, although there were a number of border wars in Latin American history, Latin American nationalism was not stimulated by long, bloody wars between neighboring countries, as in Europe. And finally, Latin American nationalism is distinct because it includes the concept of indigenous nationalism.

Indigenous nationalism: A parallel nationalism

Starting in the 1930s and 1940s, Latin American nationalism "came into its own" for many reasons. Economic nationalists promoted policies that countervailed against free-market policies to strengthen the various national economies of Latin America. Urban middle-class and working-class people demanded, and were granted, more political participation, as well as the tangible benefits that flowed from such participation, such as improved infrastructure and public services which would provide for better economic well-being for them and their children. Cultural nationalists in different nations emphasized the cultural contributions of their nation, and nationalism became a plurinational phenomenon, embracing Indians and Afro-Latin Americans. Whereas mestizo (ladino in Central America) culture had been derided as a sort of "mongrel" and undesirable mix before the mid-twentieth century, some nations embraced mestizaje as a typically (and uniquely) Latin American cultural trait to be celebrated. Thus, nationalism became an important feature of Latin America by the mid-twentieth century.

In the end, nationalism is a construction by a group of people to legitimize and empower it. The example of Europe is instructive, because early Latin American leaders wanted to copy European nationalism, which was seen as a marker of being a civilized nation. Scholars, leaders, and average people contributed to this construction by emphasizing traditions important to them, traditions that unify them. Scholars studied languages and put them into categories and studied different languages' origins to distinguish different groups from one another. Enthnographers collected and published stories "typical" of the emerging nation. And then, importantly, leaders, who offered protection of their people, invoked the shared culture and shared sacrifices of the people—often to get them to make sacrifices in the present to fend off a threat, perceived or real. As such, in the European context, often a nation emerges slowly over time, and is not "born" at a particular moment.[28] In the Americas, of course, the story is a bit different. With the culmination of struggles for independence from their imperial overlords, declarations of independence were written, as well as national constitutions.

By the mid-twentieth century, the concept of Latin American nationalism had expanded beyond the elite top-down model as conceptualized by the leadership of the new Latin American nations upon independence. By the mid-twentieth century, nationalism included the idea that the state needed to provide for an improved economic well-being of urbanities, who were the majority population in most Latin American nations by that time.

Further, ethnic nationalism came into its own by the mid-twentieth century. Indigenous groups increasingly saw themselves as simultaneously part of an Indian nation (that spanned the borders of a number of states) as well as part of their juridical nation. Afro-Latin Americans, mainly in Brazil and the Caribbean, similarly saw themselves as simultaneously citizens of their particular country of origin but also part of a broader, vaguer Afro-Latin American collective community. As such, the multinational Latin American nation was born. The Indians in a sense lived in a sort of "parallel nation" (parallel to and incorporated in) inside the broader concept of nation (which coincides with the nation-states that make up Latin America). This idea of a parallel nation stretches back to the colonial period, in which there were "republicas de indios" inside Spanish or Portuguese colonial America. However, until the mid- to late twentieth century, the Indians, due to discrimination, did not enjoy the civil rights of other members of the nation-state. How would one define the contours of an Indian nation in Latin America? Indian nations were nations in the sense that they shared customs, a language, and a common lived history. Sometimes, the members of an Indian nation shared a religion and a commonly-agreed-upon concept of race, as well as a specific geographic area.[29] Indians nations did not exert sovereignty as did the nation-state, however.

Significantly, as the rate and pace of globalization has increased, the power of the sovereignty of the nation-state in Latin America has decreased. As such, an opportunity arose for indigenous populations to more powerfully assert their own nation within the broader nation. Thus, globalization proved the handmaiden, in some respects, of the pluralistic or multinational nation (in Spanish, *la nación plurinacional*). Native peoples in Latin America have used globalization to improve their status in their respective societies, which often had denigrated Indians due to their race, ethnicity, or skin color, even as non-Indian members of the different Latin American nations aimed to integrate them into that society—as long as the Indians cast off their native culture. Native peoples in the Americas sought dignity from their societies. The UN Declaration of Human Rights of 1948 was key in this regard. In particular, as indigenous groups began cross-border organizing in the mid-1970s, they became effective at using the machinery of the United Nations to further the interests of indigenous peoples in the Americas. After many years of prodding and consensus building, the UN Declaration on the Rights of Indigenous Peoples was passed in 2007.[30] In a nutshell, this Declaration ensures that indigenous peoples enjoy the full slate of human rights as outlined in the UN Declaration of Human Rights.

Globalization and the wealth of nations

Globalization could not exist without nationalism. Nationalism, at least since the Westphalian system of the seventeenth century, has provided the bases of globalization in at least three ways. First, the expansion of powerful nations, in particular the European powers (including Russia and the former Soviet Union) and the United States, into empires that spanned many nations, has facilitated globalization. Second, transcending state boundaries provides the very definition of globalization.[31] And finally, powerful, multinational organizations that operate as globalizing forces (e.g., MNCs and non-governmental organizations [NGOs]) have used the nation-state system as a springboard for expanding their power.

Globalization is such a big, broad concept that it's hard to get one's mind around it. To make it more understandable, different disciplines focus on different aspects. Economists focus on free trade and investment; political scientists the nation-state and international organizations; and sociologists examine the consequences of increased information flows.[32]

In the most basic sense, it is the growing economic, social, cultural, and political interconnectedness of the world into broader commonalities.[33] Globalization's multifaceted nature is fascinating. In two recent volumes of collected essays by top scholars, edited by Emily Rosenberg, *A World Connecting, 1870–1945*, and Akira Iriye, *Global Interdependence: The World after 1945*, different authors discuss how the formation of the state, empires, migration, economic ties, and cultural connections were influenced by, and influenced, the process of globalization. It is difficult to determine which aspect of globalization is more significant than any other.

The earliest theorists of globalization posited that European economic activity proved to be a crucial catalyst for early globalization. In particular, fifteenth- and sixteenth-century Europe's increasing population helped spur a quest for raw materials, as well as markets for their products. They expanded economically beyond their borders in significant ways, not only enriching Europe's international traders, but leading to increased cultural interaction between Europeans, Asians, Africans, and the Middle East. Immanuel Wallerstein, a prolific and influential scholar, coined the term "world system" to describe this European thrust outward in search of economic gain.[34] Key to understanding the world economic system that emerged from European-based capitalist expansion is that the nations that began the process (the "core") developed quicker than the nations on the so-called periphery. Understanding this core-periphery process is key to understanding the history of globalization. Some authors, who argue that the world system creates dependency of the poorer nations on the wealthy (for industrialized goods and capital), conclude that the core nations practice "neocolonialism" in exploiting the poorer, peripheral nations. That is, the world economic system, after the age of "formal" imperialism (the eighteenth to early twentieth century's "age of imperialism," when the powerful nations controlled territories overseas for their national benefit), was little different from formal imperialism in that in both periods the core simply siphoned off resources for its benefit from the poorer nations.[35] Other authors, however, espouse the idea that globalization benefits all, wealthy and poor nations alike.[36]

It is important to note that the core's drive to expand economically did not take place in a social or cultural vacuum. Once members of the core nations realized how many people lived in the peripheral nations, some of these individuals assiduously worked for the betterment of the needy (or their conversion to Christianity) in the far-flung regions of the world. Some of this interest was in the area of "social betterment" of the nonwhite people of the world—that is, people of European background wanted to spread/impose European culture on the world both for the benefit of Europe and the "recipient nations." Such an impulse was described by renowned British poet Rudyard Kipling as "the white man's burden." In addition, Christian missionary zeal to convert non-Christians fueled a great deal of interest in the peripheral nations.[37]

Although Europe was responsible for the initial thrust to search out raw materials and markets, as time progressed other nations "got in on the act" of the quest for economic benefit. That is, the "core" is not a static concept over time—some nations leave the core and others join it. Because of course the world's population keeps growing, and many desire to increase their economic betterment, economic expansion across national borders continues.

Enter globalization. Globalization has become a hot topic recently. Even though the term goes back only to 1983,[38] it has become a lightning rod of sorts. Some, such as the journalist Thomas Friedman in his popular book *The World is Flat*, see globalization in positive terms. By bringing down borders that separate economies and cultures, international exchange and thus cultural understanding increases. As such, the world will become a more prosperous, stable, and peaceful place. However, others see globalization as a pernicious force that creates economic inequality among nations, and between social classes, enriching the wealthy and creating more poverty. The elected leaders of Ecuador, Venezuela, and Bolivia garner a great deal of support from their people for their antiglobalization stance. Also, globalization, according to its critics, will destroy age-old national, regional, and local traditions central to maintaining the identity of millions of people around the globe, particularly in the Third World.

An important distinction needs to be made between internationalization and globalization. Internationalization represents an opening of national boundaries for the purpose of bringing in products and ideas from other countries which could benefit the host nation. Although non-state actors could help to promote internationalization, they are not the primary "drivers" of it—the nation-state is. Globalization, however, represents a multifaceted integration of economic and cultural attributes of nations. Globalization is driven not only by nations but also by non-state actors. It is a process that operates both within and outside of the nation-state system.[39]

It is hard to pinpoint the origins of globalization. Globalization, which clearly has been going on for centuries, advances rapidly at times and slowly at other times. One could make a case that China in the fifteenth century began an expansionary policy causing a degree of globalization, but its expansionary efforts were tentative.[40] Europe by the fifteenth century, however, began a long-term outward thrust that spurred globalization. But a couple of interesting developments, not investigated thoroughly by scholars, which occurred during the period of Spanish and Portuguese colonization of the Americas, represent early examples of globalization. With the discovery of vast amounts of silver in Upper Peru (now Bolivia) at Potosí in the mid-sixteenth century, the wealth of Spain rocketed to previously unheard of levels. By the seventeenth century, Spain was trading large amounts of silver (to silver-poor China) for silks and other items. The Spanish colony of the Philippines was instrumental in this regard. In addition, Spain drastically reduced its trade with the Ottoman Empire because the Chinese trade superseded it. Thus began the slow decline of the Ottoman Empire.

Often, many view Europe's outward expansion beginning in the fifteenth century as a process by which the Europeans, with little or no outside help, began a long-term process of imperialism. Certainly, Europeans calculated their interests without input from any other source. And certainly imperialism had a very significant effect on the weaker nations it colonized. But, it is important to note that other nations had a major impact on Europe, and their actions help to explain how the European nations grew so powerful by the seventeenth and eighteenth centuries, relative to other nations. One important example is what historian Alfred Crosby termed "The Colombian exchange."[41] With the European explorers reaching out to many nations beyond Europe's borders during the fifteenth century, Europeans spread their goods and ideas while picking up the same from other countries. An example is that most important of commodities—food. Tomatoes and potatoes, among other foodstuffs, were first developed by the Amerindian populations in the Americas. Once the Europeans tasted them, liked them, and began to cultivate them, the availability of food in Europe significantly spiked, allowing for population growth—one reason for Europe's outward expansion. As the population grew, the desire for more trade—and the products it brought in—grew substantially.

Although globalization does not necessarily rest on an economic foundation, clearly economic globalization is very important. As such, one of the key questions of globalization is as follows: why do some nations benefit economically from globalization? And why does globalization affect other nations negatively? Of course, breaking the question down produces other questions—perhaps easier to answer. How do some groups in various nations benefit from globalization? Why does globalization hurt other groups? Because globalization is a capacious concept—to say the least—it is more effective to focus on two of its more important aspects in particular: cultural and economic globalization. Three of the more important "transmission belts" for globalization include migration, various types of economic interaction, and the rise of a global media in which information is increasingly rapidly spread across national borders.

How does globalization influence Latin American nationalism? One must delve deeply into the histories of Latin America and globalization to answer this question. Latin America became integrated into a world trading system, with the creation of the Spanish, Portuguese, French, and British empires extending their systems into the Western Hemisphere just as capitalists within the individual European nations began trading in a more systematic fashion with their counterparts in other European nations. As such, as European imperialists folded Latin America into their increasingly broader trading systems, one can conclude that Latin America as we know it—and Latin American nationalism—cannot be conceived of outside of a global framework.

Does globalization mean the end of the nation as we know it? With the tap of a touch screen, one can transfer information, or capital, in an instant. As such, the institutions that span the globe that facilitate this transfer are becoming more and more prominent in the world today—and more powerful than many nations. Interestingly, both critics and those who celebrate the increasing pace of globalization seem to assume that it is happening both rapidly, and generally, at a similar pace around the globe. However, it is important to note that globalization is not a constant process everywhere. In some places/time periods, it accelerates rapidly; in other places/times periods, it does not.

Even for those who argue that globalization's pace is rapidly increasing, it is too early to write the obituary of the nation. Although globalization is indisputably changing peoples' identities, including national identities, the nation will be with us for a long, long time. As information and people move more and more rapidly across international borders, people become more cosmopolitan for sure—but also fret a feared loss of indigenous culture. The nation is a repository, in a sense, for such culture. The reason why McDonald's was shut out of Bolivia for decades, it is said, was because it refused to use Bolivian potatoes in its french fries. But the issue is deeper. Many Bolivians fear that with increasing (multinational) corporate power in the poor South American nation, elements of Bolivian foodways—a sensitive cultural issue—may be lost forever.

The really fascinating thing about the intersection of nationalism and globalization is that globalization can give tools and opportunities for many subaltern peoples to challenge the prevailing narrative of nationalism. For example, if a Latin American government promotes a top-down form of nationalism, in which the governing elites desire "buy in" from nonelites with regard to the significance of important national symbols and beliefs, nonelites can in effect "bring in" supporters from outside to help them make the case that the society is not serving the needs of the nonelites, and economic, social, and political changes need to occur to privilege subaltern peoples. Examples include how indigenous groups in Chiapas, Mexico and the Andes have used resources from outside of the region/countries, resources obtained because globalization offered these indigenous people the opportunities to voice their grievances more loudly—even to international forums.

Any analysis of the intersection of globalization and nationalism must address the issue of transnationalism. Different from studies on international issues, transnational studies examine how economic and social forces wash over borders, influencing nations from the inside out. MNCs, going back centuries, are one example of potent transnational forces. But, of late, more scholarly attention has focused on international organizations (generally made up of nations) and NGOs (generally non-state actors). NGOs are often reformist—they aim to improve the lives of nonelite people in nations around the world. Often, but not always, they are based in wealthier nations. Often, but not always, they operate in the poorer nations, aiming to improve civil society, the environment, public health, the economic status of the poor, and a great number of other laudable missions.

One way to understand the intersection of globalization and nationalism is to examine how globalization de-centers (breaks down) one's identity, and then helps one to re-center (or construct) it in different ways. So globalization does not, in this line of argument, so much as destroy identity, but force individuals to reconceive of themselves in different ways. Adapting newer, once-foreign ideas/ideology into one's identity would make one more cosmopolitan. The fear that globalization will overly scramble, and even eliminate, one's local- and national-based identity might cause some to try to reconstitute their identity to be more in touch with traditional local and national customs, ideas, and lifestyles.

The key question is as follows—how can one measure the impact of globalization on nationalism? With globalization both fostering and inhibiting nationalism, such measurements will be difficult indeed.

The argument of this book is that Latin Americans have not simply passively accepted the imposition of globalization "from without." Some authors see Latin America as essentially helpless with regard to the imposition of globalization from outside, more powerful, global actors. Far from it. In some cases, Latin Americans have actively shaped the process of globalization. The roots of Latin American nationalism cannot be ascribed to simply reacting against the (outside) forces of globalization, Latin American nationalism has been skillfully used by Latin Americans to counter the more negative aspects of globalization and to protect Latin Americans from the impact of outside forces. And indeed, Latin American nationalism has grown in strength as Latin Americans have seen it as a useful or even necessary force to maintain their economic and cultural betterment and well-being in the face of outside, powerful countries, or entities, trying to control aspects of their lives. During the bulk of the twentieth century, Latin Americans were understandably concerned about, and sensitive to, the growth of US power. US leaders not only coveted Latin America's large stock of natural resources but also wanted to impose their way on Latin American economies and political systems. Such fears fed Latin American nationalism: indeed, Latin American writer Victor Alba once supposedly famously quipped that if the United States did not exist, Latin America would have to invent it. Moving into the late twentieth and early twenty-first century, Latin Americans were concerned with other outside countries and entities (in particular the International Monetary Fund) having inordinate control in their nations.

The irony of Latin American nationalism and globalization

One could argue that no one single region of the world has been for centuries so impacted by, and has itself impacted, the process of globalization as has Latin America. Yet, interestingly, scholars of globalization tend not to focus on Latin America. The focus tends to be on formerly hegemonic (e.g., Britain, late nineteenth century to the 1920s) powers, present-day hegemonic powers (e.g., United States, 1920s–present and China, 1980s–present), and the postcolonial non-industrialized nations in Africa and Asia. In addition, Latin America has not been as important a global "player" in an economic sense since the end of the First World War, which could explain why scholars of globalization have neglected it. This book, then, aims to fill a gap in the literature by first reassessing Latin American nationalism (which has not been examined much of late), while examining the intersection of this nationalism with globalization.

Ultimately, the strength of Latin American nationalism, as it waxed and waned over time, flowed from its interaction with globalization. To the extent that leaders in a Latin American country could promote and maintain policies which would allow their people to benefit from globalization, and shield them from downside risks of globalization, they could build nationalist sentiment.

For those who fear the consequences of the rapidly increasing rate of globalization, one thing in particular that keeps them up at night is the seeming connection between rapidly increasing globalization and economic inequality. Indeed, as globalization accelerates, the number of people in the world (in particular the non-industrialized world) who have unmet needs is also increasing.[42] Although the causality is unclear, it behooves the concerned global citizen to investigate this intersection. Some authors have argued that the process of economic globalization since the Second World War has intensified within the "community" of developed nations and decelerated in the non-industrialized "periphery." Indeed, perhaps it is possible to talk about two "separate worlds": a "cosmopolitan" one of intensifying globalization and the excluded.[43] However, if globalization is defined as a multilayered process of many different aspects, clearly it has become, and will become, a more potent force in most parts of the globe.

Study Questions

1. How would you define globalization? How would you define nationalism?
2. Who or what has the most control over globalization? Who or what exerts the most control over nationalism?
3. How does globalization dilute nationalism? How does globalization stimulate national sentiment?
4. Discuss the origins and development of Latin American nationalism. What are the most important aspects of Latin American nationalism?
5. How would you define Latin American national identity?

For Further Reading

Iriye, Akira. *Global Interdependence: The World after 1945*. Cambridge, MA: Belknap Press of Harvard, 2014.

Micklethwait, John and Adrian Wooldridge. "The Hidden Promise—Liberty Renewed." In *The Globalization Reader*, edited by Frank J. Lechner and John Boli, 11–18. 5th ed. Malden, MA: Wiley-Blackwell, 2015.

Rosenberg, Emily. *A World Connecting: 1870–1945*. Cambridge, MA: Belknap Press of Harvard University, 2012.

Wallerstein, Immanuel. "The Modern World System as a Capitalist World Economy." In *The Globalization Reader*, edited by Frank J. Lechner and John Boli, 56–62. 5th ed. Malden, MA: Wiley-Blackwell, 2015.

CHAPTER TWO

The Wars for Independence against Spain and the Rise of Nationalism

[T]hree centuries of this rule [by colonial Spain and Portugal] necessarily left on [the] American man and his land an indelible mark of intervention from outside America. They also left the seeds of ultranationalism.

DANIEL COSÍO VILLEGAS QUOTED IN SAMUEL BAILY[1]

America is ungovernable; those who served the revolution have plowed the sea.

SIMÓN BOLÍVAR QUOTED IN SHELDON B. AND PEGGY K. LISS[2]

The crumbling of empires in the Americas— states without nations

Simón Bolívar had a dream. After the Spanish were forcibly booted from the Americas, and they were free of its domination, he would form a large, new nation—Gran Colombia, made up of the northern part of South America.[3] It would be a powerful nation and a democratic nation. Gran Colombia never came into existence. Fights between the different geographic segments

FIGURE 2.1 *Portrait of Simón Bolívar, c. 1823. Found in the collection of the Museo de Arte de Lima.* Source: *Fine Art Images/Heritage Images/Getty Images.*
Born in 1783, Bolívar was from present-day Venezuela. Inspired by the ideas of the European Enlightenment, this charismatic leader organized and pursued independence from Spain for the northern South American region, an area stretching from Venezuela to Peru. At the end of his life, he realized the difficulty of forging unity in such a diverse area. He died in 1830.

Table 2.1 Date of independence of North and South American countries

Country	Date	Colonizer
Argentina	July 9, 1816	Spain
Bahamas	July 10, 1973	United Kingdom
Belize	September 21, 1981	United Kingdom
Bolivia	August 6, 1825	Spain
Brazil	September 7, 1822	Portugal
Canada	December 11, 1931	United Kingdom
Chile	September 18, 1810	Spain
Colombia	July 20, 1810	Spain
Costa Rica	September 15, 1821	Spain
Cuba	May 20, 1902	Spain
Dominican Republic	Feb 27, 1844	Spain
Ecuador	May 24, 1822	Spain
El Salvador	September 15, 1821	Spain
Grenada	February 7, 1974	United Kingdom
Guatemala	September 15, 1821	United Kingdom
Guyana	May 26, 1966	United Kingdom
Haiti	January 1, 1804	France
Honduras	September 15, 1821	Spain
Jamaica	August 6, 1962	United Kingdom
Mexico	September 16, 1810	Spain
Nicaragua	September 15, 1821	Spain
Panama	November 3, 1903	Colombia
Paraguay	May 14, 1811	Spain
Peru	July 28, 1821	Spain
Suriname	November 25, 1975	Netherlands
United States	July 4, 1776	United Kingdom
Uruguay	August 25, 1825	Spain
Venezuela	July 5, 1811	Spain

Source: Marco Antonio Pamplona and Don Harrison Doyle, *Nationalism in the New World*. Athens, GA: University of Georgia Press, 2006, xv.

of the proposed nation split it into different countries. Powerful leaders emerged to rule the different constituent parts, forming new countries—states, one could say, without nations. The states were formed relatively quickly, with names now familiar to us: Colombia, Venezuela, Peru, Bolivia, among others. That is, they were "national projects" that emerged over time.

Bolívar and the other liberators of Latin America were very much shaped by the long Spanish colonial project. With the Spanish, Portuguese, French, and British imperial projects in the Americas in the late fifteenth and early sixteenth centuries, Latin American nationalism was born. In what sense exactly? In the wake of the European projection of power into Latin America, some Latin Americans thought Latin American nationalism should imitate European nationalism. Indeed, Latin American nationalism, in part, was a child of the European Enlightenment. The nationalists in the colonies of Spain and Portugal fought for their independence animated by the ideas of intellectuals John Locke of England and Jean Jacques Rousseau of France—that all peoples had the right to determine the form of government they would live under and have the right to political representation in that government.

Indeed, Latin American nationalism was born, as is typical with regard to nationalism that develops as an empire begins to crumble, with the maturation of the colonial economy and society and the development of an autonomous national identity.[4] As the colonies of Spain and Portugal became more wealthy, and more socially stable, not surprisingly they grew more confident in their ability to rule themselves.

Incipient Latin American nationalism was given a boost by the way the Spanish and Portuguese empires crumbled. First of all, in order for the relatively small nations of Spain and Portugal to control vast tracts of territory in the New World, by the mid-1700s they needed to enact drastic reforms. Second, the combination of these reforms proved to be the handmaiden of revolution. The first reform was to assert control in "iron fist" fashion by sending large numbers of Spanish/Portuguese military/bureaucrats to better control the empire. The second reform, enacted mainly in the Spanish colonies, was to loosen up economic restrictions to allow for increased economic production. Such production would make both the imperial subjects and overlords happy, but it had the more profound effect of showing the subjects in the Americas that they could increase their economic well-being on their own, without the "mother country."

Intra-European struggles gave a huge boost to Latin American nationalism. With Napoleon's invasion of Iberia in 1807–1808, and the dethroning of Spain's King Ferdinand, antimonarchist elements in Spain gained support. As juntas, or groups, of Spaniards who resisted Napoleon began to organize, they called for a national convention, or Cortes, to better organize their resistance to Napoleon. This Cortes, which included representatives from Spain's colonies in the Americas, was remarkable in that it articulated a new sense of nationalism in Spain, which reinforced the growing sense of nationalism in Latin America. The 1808 Cortes clearly stated that sovereignty lay in the nation, not the monarchy. It also called for the election of leaders in Spain; however, the Latin Americans who read about this call for democracy in Spain quickly realized that they could apply such ideas to their region as well.

With the rise of the nations that emerged out of the Wars for Independence, in which the new Latin American nations threw off the yolk of Spanish and Portuguese imperialism, Latin America, as a region, was born. The fact that there is no consensus as to the origin of the term "Latin America" as a geographical and political designation is telling. One (older) interpretation stresses that it was a French scholar who invented the term, with Latin Americans then borrowing the term. More recently, scholars have found evidence of the reverse: that Latin Americans themselves invented the term, and Europeans picked up on it, in the mid-nineteenth century. Since Latin American nationalism, and Latin America more generally, is a combination of both European and indigenous influences, it is not surprising that there is no scholarly agreement on the origin of the term itself.[5]

As discussed at the end of the last chapter, many scholars perceive nationalism in Latin America as weaker than the nationalisms of other developing world nations. However, a more precise description would be that Latin American nationalism has the curious nature of being simultaneously weak and yet strongly proclaimed at the same time. To compensate for the weakness of Latin American nationalism, national symbols are strongly emphasized by leaders and writers, such as national flags. Also, Latin American nationalists exerted a great deal of effort to physically integrate their nations by means of railroads and to socially integrate by means of setting up schools in the countryside to teach Spanish or Portuguese to the Indians, as well as European culture as filtered through Latin American elites. Many Indians resisted the imposition of an elite-sponsored educational system that came from the national or regional capital and was imposed on the *campo* (countryside) with no input from *campesinos* (farmers will small holdings).

Probably the most important reason for the weakness of nationalism in the region, at least until the mid-twentieth century, was regional, racial, and social class divisions that were rife throughout the region. Europeanized urban elites who monopolized political and economic power did not consider the Indians to be citizens. Latin Americans of European extraction referred to themselves as *españoles Americanos* (Spanish Americans) or *ciudadanos* (citizens); Indians were referred to as *contributarios* (tribute-payers, and therefore of lower status) although they did not pay tribute (taxes) after the Latin American nations broke away from Spanish control. The label *contributarios* speaks volumes about how, even after Spanish control of Latin America had terminated, Latin American elites did not consider the

Indians a part of the nation: the Indians (at least according to the mentality of the elites) were simply a resource to be exploited.

During the colonial period, inhabitants of Latin America spoke of two separate republics—*república de españoles y república de indios* (the Republic of the Spaniards and the Republic of the Indians). They lived a parallel existence. They lived separate and unequal existences; those of European background forced the Indians to pay tribute, forced taxes, to the Spanish and Portuguese crowns. Tribute, which could be excessive at times, sparked rebellions during the era of Spanish/Portuguese control over Latin America. These rebellions became particularly strong and widespread in the late colonial period. These rebellions were one of the reasons for Latin American independence from their Iberian overlords.

Nationalism in Latin America started out as weak for the simple reason that the Latin American revolutionaries barely began to define themselves as *Americanos* (citizens of a new *patria grande*, independent of Spain and Portugal) when soon they began to draw the lines of new nation-states: Mexico, Central America, and those in South America. In South America, the Liberator Simón Bolívar had a vision that the "northern tier" of South America (Caracas to Lima, including Charcas, or Upper Peru, present-day Bolivia) would be unified as the nation of Gran Colombia. Bolívar thought that only though unity could the Latin Americans form a strong and viable nation that could fend off attackers and adequately protect its citizens. Bolívar's dream, of course, was not realized as geographic boundaries and political rivalries easily overpowered any impulse toward unity. Moreover, in part due to Spanish attempts to reconquer parts of Latin America, nationalism was severely tested early in its infancy.[6]

Unfortunately, the vast destruction of the Wars for Independence in Latin America (1809–1824) and the large amount of loans obtained by the revolutionaries in securing and establishing their new nations created financial dependency on outside creditors. When a Latin American country failed to pay back their creditors, sometimes the nation where the creditors were based used force to coerce repayment of the loans. (One example was the shelling of main port with cannonballs to force it to pay up.) Thus, for many Latin American nations, obtaining individual human and political rights took a back seat to more immediate concerns: the security and economic needs of the people. Because of the fear and destitution of a large portion of Latin American society, not surprisingly, *caudillos* (strongmen) rose up, who, in exchange for loyalty, would provide for basic needs and security. The *caudillos*, of course, tapped into a long tradition of "organic" authoritarian rule in Iberia, going back centuries.

Given the physical destruction wrought by the Wars for Independence, and the social and racial divisions in Latin American society, it is not surprising that elites resorted to a top-down style of nationalism, using Europe as a model. In the late nineteenth century, nearly all Latin American nationalists advocated that Latin America imitate Europe—with regards to its economy, society, and culture, as well as nationalism (at least the elite's vision of top-down nationalism—which differed from the nationalism of the nonelites).

Revolutionary Wars for Independence—1809–1824 and the rise of *caudillos*

Importantly, Latin American nationalism was born in revolutionary war—the Wars for Independence against Spain from 1809 to 1824. To a degree, they were inspired by the example of the revolutionary war in the British North American colonies from 1775 to 1783—the first successful, anticolonial revolutionary war in which a colony freed itself from European control. In addition, it is important to note that Haiti, through revolution, freed itself from French control in the 1790s. Haiti was not only the first successful slave-based revolution ever; it also formed the second (after the United States) republic in the Western Hemisphere.

Beyond the generalization about revolutionary war, however, it is difficult to generalize about the individual experiences of the new nations in the vast, and amazingly diverse, territory from Mexico and the Caribbean in the north all the way to Tierra del Fuego in the south. In Mexico, with its large Indian population, both Indians and mestizos fought for self-determination. Although there were no significant Indian leaders of the revolutionary movement, some of the leadership was mestizo. In much of South America, the elite leadership of the revolutionary wars, nearly all of European background, willingly accepted Indians and mestizos into the lower ranks of the military forces that fought the Spanish. However, after the wars, elites did not want to grant full rights of citizenship to Indians and Afro-Latin Americans who fought in the revolutionary armies. The elite wanted to maintain the social hierarchy of the Spanish and Portuguese empires in the Western Hemisphere.

Interestingly, although Latin American nationalism was born in war, intra-Latin American wars did not shape the emerging Latin American nationalism (as intra-European wars distinctly shaped European nationalism in the nineteenth century).[7] Instead, what shaped Latin American nationalism was (in twentieth-century terms) economic, social, political, and cultural development. And indeed, in the early nineteenth century, there was a tremendous need for development of all types. Latin America emerged from its Wars for Independence (1809–1824) utterly destroyed by years of war against the Spanish. (Brazil, because it achieved independence nearly bloodlessly and with little/no destruction, had a distinct historic experience in this regard.) Thus, the Latin American nations faced an uphill battle to develop both states and nations. First of all, many Latin American nations amassed significant foreign economic debt to finance their Wars for Independence. With independence won, the debt did not magically disappear. Interest had to be paid. Also, a more existential threat loomed. Even after Spanish troops left the continent, they were to return again to try and retake portions of their former empire.

In part because building Latin American nationalism in the nineteenth century involved overcoming key obstacles, many Latin American leaders would conclude that the way to build a strong nation would be to build a strong state. Although it would take more than a century, a key element of Latin American nationalism was how to build independent and strong states and nations economically, socially, and politically. Unfortunately, after the Latin American nations achieved full political independence from Spain by 1824, in the wake of a decade and a half of destructive war, Latin America degenerated into economic, social, and political chaos. Civil wars emerged in a number of nations over the idea of federalism—what sort of power sharing should take place between the capital and the *campo* (countryside). The post independence conflict in Argentina is a good example of this type of conflict.

Nationalism is a project—and a work in progress that changes over time. The project of nationalism proved especially difficult in Latin America for many reasons. One key reason was that colonial Latin American society was rigidly stratified in a *casta* system of racial hierarchy—an aspect of society that remained unchanged with the Wars for Independence. The stratification of Latin American society in the nineteenth century was the result of a double legacy: first, the legacy of Iberian colonialism and second, the legacy of the pre-Columbian Indian Empires (Maya, Aztec, and Inca) and Spanish colonial society. An elite (nearly all of whom were people of European background) controlled political, social, and economic power.

A particularly delicate and vexing problem afflicted Latin America's new leaders, nearly all from the elite strata of society. The elites were in the minority. The majority of the populations of the new Latin American nations were indigenous, of Afro-Latin American background, or of mixed race. Very much in the minority, how could the elites continue to enjoy their economic, social, and political power? First of all, avoiding race wars at all costs was key. Second, the rights of citizens would be nominally extended to nonwhites. But in reality, they most often would not enjoy the same rights of the elite. Since the white elite in Latin American nations viewed themselves as culturally and racially superior to nonwhites, and aimed to instill a love of European culture in the nonwhite majority, elites expected deference to their exalted position in Latin American society from the nonelites.[8] Thus, nonwhites would, in effect, be second-class citizens in their nations. Those who refused to act in a deferential way toward the elites and resisted elite control would be punished, even imprisoned, tortured, or killed. In other words, the elites not only believed in civic and political equality of all races in the new Latin American nations but also believed in social inequality.[9] Therefore, nonelites were locked out and clamored to be considered full citizens of the new Latin American nations. As such, one can talk about multiple "nationalisms" in Latin America—based on social class and race.

Given the physical destruction of postrevolutionary Latin America, the political vacuum, and the social dislocation and societal cleavages, it is not surprising that many Latin Americans in the early to mid-nineteenth century sought strong leaders. They were termed *caudillos* (strong, one-person rule), and their rule was *caudillismo*. Basically, the majority of the people wanted anyone who could provide a modicum of security and prosperity. Oftentimes, such leaders were local leaders who had effective control over a piece of territory. Indeed, such localism bedeviled Simón Bolívar's vision for a "Gran Colombia" discussed above. Democracy, as well as political unity, seemed impossible to many at the time—not just Bolívar.

Given that the Latin American people saw no one else to turn to, *caudillismo* quickly spread across the continent. Did the new Latin American citizenry see *caudillos* as the embodiment of the nation? Or as cynical, power-hungry opportunists? Probably, the average Latin American of the early nineteenth century saw them as a combination of both. In many cases, Latin American citizens resigned themselves to living under the rule of *caudillos*, because if nothing else, *caudillos* offered a modicum of security in a very unstable, almost chaotic, postrevolutionary setting. Latin America at this time was simultaneously trying to rebuild infrastructure while forging new societies, even new cultures.

The historiography (the study of historical interpretations) of *caudillos* has been divided. Some historians view them as power-hungry, corrupt opportunists bent on taking advantage of the post–War of Independence chaos. Moreover, *caudillos* tended to reinforce an already existing localism, making it difficult for nations to coherently address nation-wide problems and build viable national institutions. Other historians view the *caudillos* in a more positive light. On the one hand, the *caudillos* ruled autocratically and stuffed ballot boxes in order to perpetuate themselves in power.[10] However, *caudillos* fulfilled an important function; they provided the populace with short-term security when many Latin Americans felt their lives had hit bottom. With their authoritarian rule, they provided a model for how many late nineteenth century presidents would lead.

Liberals versus Conservatives

During the nineteenth century, the rule of *caudillos* slowly gave way to the building of political institutions, including political parties. Political parties proved a viable way of transferring power from one group to another. Although there were restrictions on who could vote, which limited political participation by poorer nonelites, some Latin American nations had functioning democracies. Scholars put differing amounts of emphasis on the significance of the divide between the two parties, Liberals and Conservatives.

However, nearly all observers would agree that, on paper at least, they offered two distinctly different visions for Latin America. (One reason why some historians view the differences between the two parties as small is that some Latin American leaders self-servingly changed political stripes.)

Conservatives, in essence, thought Latin American society would benefit from an emphasis on the social hierarchy which had existed since pre-Columbian times and was reinforced by the Spanish and Portuguese Empires in the Americas. If each individual "knew" his or her "place," in a Platonic sense of social justice, and did not aspire to a higher social station, the diverse Latin American society would remain unified. In addition to social hierarchy, another "glue" that the Conservatives saw as extremely important was the Catholic Church. Belief in (the Catholic Christian) God would unify the most disparate social groups into an organic whole.

Conservatives saw the divided nature of Latin American societies as potentially dangerous. They feared that the deep social divisions in Latin American society, along the lines of race/social class, could easily cause the nation to disintegrate into a collection of warring factions. Such social divisions were inherently centrifugal forces according to Conservatives. As such, top-town, authoritarian rule was their chosen way of promoting social and national unity. A benevolent dictator would use coercion to keep different social groups "in line" in a not-too-oppressive way. However, in some instances in Latin American history, an authoritarian leader's rule proved so heavy handed it actually created a type of social unity. Social groups that were normally antagonistic banded together (temporarily) to unite to oust the hated dictator.

Liberals, globalization, and the nation

For their part, Latin American Liberals wanted to copy US and Western European society—a key example of "globalization in action" in Latin America during this time period. Liberals imported nineteenth-century European liberalism, with its emphasis on individual rights, to Latin America. Individual rights, including the right to hold private property, were sacrosanct to Liberals, as well as the importance of an educated populace. Only an educated populace would be able to adequately decide who should represent them in representative bodies. And education should be a secular, public education. Liberals feared the power that the Catholic Church had over the educational system in Latin America—and thus feared the power that the Church had over people's minds. In most Latin American nations, only the elite, and some members of the middle class, had access to European culture. For the majority of poorer mestizos, as well as the Indians, they knew little about Europe at this time.

Liberals had great faith in export-oriented economic growth in Latin America. The Liberal leadership in many Latin American nations promoted policies that would foster the export of Latin American products overseas. Of course, the products that fetched the highest prices were those that were unavailable yet desirable to the wealthy nations, such as coffee, valuable metals, and later petroleum. Concomitant with exporting products overseas, Latin American Liberals wanted foreigners to invest in Latin America. Liberals thought that only by making Latin America a propitious environment for foreign capital could Latin America adequately develop economically. Only through increased trade and foreign investment in their nations, Liberals argued, could Latin America build up sufficient foreign exchange to industrialize. With wealth, Latin America could strengthen state institutions and its individual nations as well.

It is understandable how Liberals could have such faith in export-oriented economic growth. By the late nineteenth century, the United States and Western Europe were quickly industrializing. These industrial economies needed metals, oil, and foodstuffs, among other things, for their growing populations. (Because the Middle East did not become a major oil exporter until the 1950s, Latin America was a key source of this critically important resource that the twentieth-century world was becoming increasingly dependent on to fuel its economy.) As Latin American trade with the industrialized world sharply increased in the late nineteenth century, Latin American elites who owned the larger farms and mines greatly benefitted. The other main group that benefitted from this increased trade with the industrialized world was the rising middle class in the industrialized world.

However, there were significant downsides to export-oriented growth. First, the gap between the wealthy and poor widened. The wealthy significantly benefitted from export-oriented agriculture—a system of large-scale farms that produced mainly for the foreign market. The poor, however, barely benefitted from this system. Second, since part of export-oriented growth was making Latin America a friendly environment for foreign investors, some Latin American nations became dependent on foreign investment as the main driving force of the more dynamic parts of their economies. Third, with export-oriented agriculture, the economic well-being of Latin America became tied to overseas markets over which Latin America had little or no control. Such dependency on overseas markets was accentuated if Latin American nations' economic livelihood rested on the sale of a single product overseas, which was known as monoculture. When prices for their exports sank, the economy sank as well.

Liberals, individual rights, and unity

Liberals were ambivalent about granting significant individual, political rights to the populace. On the one hand, some Liberals had a lot of faith in the common person. If the average citizen was well educated (in secular, not Catholic, schools), he or she would be intelligent enough to elect a good leader and actively participate in civic life. However, many Liberals—in particular, the leadership—feared that the "unwashed masses" would never be intelligent enough to be good citizens. With regard to the Indians, Liberals did not think they would ever be equal citizens to mestizos or elites. Liberals thought that Indians needed to be taught Spanish, and Western culture, but did not think they would ever be equal, in citizenship terms, to the rest of the populace. In reality, elections were not "free and fair," open to all, in late nineteenth-century Latin America. Elections were only for the elites and the upper echelon of the middle class. Women and (in many instances) Indians did not gain the right to vote until the twentieth century.

More important than an enlightened citizenry was unity. Liberals thought national unity—top-down unity, imposed from a powerful leadership— to be of utmost importance. They wanted to create integrated, unified nations. Realizing that Liberal reforms, such as individual political and economic rights and freedoms, would be disruptive to social unity, Liberals implemented unifying policies to compensate for the centrifugal forces of individuals in society having increased rights and freedoms.

That meant that they saw infrastructure, in the form of roads and railroads, as very important. That also meant that Indians should be brought into the body politic—on the Liberals' terms. As such, Liberals implemented vagrancy laws, ensuring that Indians would become wage laborers. Also, Liberals pushed for—even using military force to implement this policy— the breakup of Indian communal landholdings into parcels of privately held land. Two motives animated the Liberals in this regard. First, with the breakup of communal landholdings, and their sale in the "free market," wealthy mestizo and elite landholders could buy the most fertile parcels, leaving the less fertile lands to the Indians. Second, Liberals were convinced that privatization of communal Indian lands automatically meant progress and civilization. However, the breakup of Indian communal lands would create so much resentment and anger among the Indians that it would lead to revolutionary sentiment in the twentieth century in parts of Latin America with large indigenous populations, in particular Mexico, Central America, and Bolivia.

A most important European import: Positivism

By the 1870s, Latin Americans, especially the middle and upper classes, had great faith in Positivism. Positivists thought that a rational application of the findings and laws of the natural sciences needed to be applied to society, thus creating a more rational society. Both Liberals and Conservatives shared a belief in Positivism; but Liberals were more entranced with the doctrine than Conservatives. Positivism was espoused by a number of European intellectuals, but the most ardent advocate of positivism, who developed Positivist thought more thoroughly than any other thinker, was Frenchman August Comte. With increasing globalization, of course, intellectual currents flowed more quickly across national borders and even oceans. Positivists argued that Latin America would only develop as a society if they imitated European ways. Positivists also thought that as upper-class and middle-class Latin Americans became more Europeanized, eventually (European-style) progress would filter down to the masses. This "filtering down" process would be facilitated if the population were of European extraction. As such, positivists saw promoting European immigration as promoting progress.

How could the Latin Americans construct viable, stable nations? What are the specific criteria to judge whether they were successful or not with this endeavor? It can be argued that the new Latin American nationalists needed to achieve competency in four major areas in order to build their new nations in a stable, classically republican way. First, they needed to establish legitimacy. Second, they needed to embrace constitutionalism (like North America or Europe). Third, communal aspirations for popular sovereignty needed to be directly linked to the populace's sense of nationalism. And finally, *personalismo*—strong (and hopefully skillful) leadership to keep the centrifugal forces in check—was important. Examples of centrifugal forces are racial/ethnic divisions; geographic divisions, such as the littoral versus the inland mountain regions; and urban/rural splits.[11] The degree to which the various Latin American nations could achieve a degree of competency in these four areas determined how much cohesion and unity they exhibited over time. Nations that successfully "got their act together" in these four areas were generally unified and coherent—such as Brazil and Argentina. Nations/regions that encountered difficulties in these four areas would have a hard time maintaining coherence, and in some cases would split apart into separate national entities, such as the Caribbean or Central America, and remain separated today.

Indians as inspiration and a source of land and labor: The changing, complex relationships between Indians and the nation

For the vast majority of Latin American elites, who were of European background or light-skinned mestizos (people of mixed European and indigenous background) who ignored or denied their Indian roots, the indigenous peoples of the Americas were to be somehow converted into pseudo-Europeans through education and proselytization. Some Indians resisted this imposition. From the point of view of Latin American elites, they had the right to use force against recalcitrant Indians who clearly did not understand that the march of history was to accept the dictates of nineteenth-century European liberalism, imposed from above by Latin American elites.

With regard to the nationalistic "projects" (the different nations that emerged in Latin America after the fall of the Spanish/Portuguese Empires), it is important to note that race and racism were central to the construction of these projects. Creoles (those who were of European background born in the Americas) aimed, at all costs, to preserve and strengthen their position at the top of the new societies forged from the ashes of the former empires. Even as the Creole military leadership led mestizos, Indians, and Afro-Latin Americans into battle against the Spanish, they were wary about promising nonwhites the full rights of citizenship, in exchange for fighting and winning the Wars of Independence. Due to their racism, the Creole leadership did not think the Indians had the intellectual wherewithal to be full-fledged citizens and therefore did not want to give them the full rights of citizenship in the new nations of Latin America.

From the perspective of nonwhite Latin Americans, with the rise of the new Latin American nations in the early nineteenth century, the situation was one of "same mule, different driver." That is to say, the gachupines (literally "tenderfeet," a slang term for Europeans who immigrated to the Americas) with the forced exit of the Spanish, either were powerless or (in most cases) left the continent. As such, the Creoles, leaders of the wars of revolution, were now in charge. However, as they were a numeric minority compared to nonwhites, they were clear about constructing a Europeanized nation that would privilege whites/Europeans in the new nation. As such, nonwhites, until the twentieth century, would be second-class citizens.

There were various methods used to apply force to recalcitrant Indians. For example, their communal lands, through coercion or legal chicanery (using the legal system to defraud Indians of their land), could be sold off from underneath them to individual landholders. If the Indians, who had owned the land for centuries, refused to give up their lands peacefully, the government or the wealthy (new) landowner would use force to compel them to leave. This dynamic was more common in nations ruled by Liberals, as Liberals thought it important to require their nation to accept the ideology of nineteenth-century European liberalism, including the near sanctity of private property. So, Liberals concluded, if the Indians were so backwards as to not understand, or deny, the importance of freeholding, they should be forced off their lands.

But, in some cases, Latin American elites were inspired by the Native Americans' culture of fierce resistance. Just as the Indians resisted the Spanish during the sixteenth-century Spanish conquest, now the Latin Americans were resisting the Spanish to forge independent nations.

The case of the Araucanians (their modern descendants are the Mapuche) in Chile is instructive. During the colonial period, the Araucanians enjoyed considerable autonomy because of their military prowess. Because the Araucanians stopped the Spaniards at the Bio-Bio River during Chile's War for Independence against Spain, they are revered by the Mapuche and Chileans of all ethnic backgrounds.

However, this historical legacy is complicated by a number of things—which show the nuances and richness of Latin American nationalism. First, some Mapuche teamed up with the Spanish against the Chileans in the early nineteenth century. Second, the Chileans in later years dispossessed the Mapuche of their land and tried to get them to shed their Indian culture. Although a number of the Mapuche did assimilate into Chilean culture, they still maintain their Indian culture to the present day.[12] Even as the Araucanians were an important element of the creation of Chilean nationalism, nonindigenous Chileans generally treated them as second-class citizens.

Significantly, however, the relationship between Indian groups and the Latin American nations tells us a great deal about how Latin American elites constructed their nations in different parts of the region. The Araucanians were a relatively small band of Indians who had not developed an intricate, hierarchical society. The situation was much different in other parts of the Americas. The Aztecs, Maya, and Inca were large, well-developed societies; thus, the Spanish conquest encountered a hierarchical society. This proved convenient for the conquerors, as they simply killed the Indian leadership and affirmed that they were the new leaders. Thus, the Spanish quickly and relatively easily obtained control of the entire Indian society, with minimal resistance from the Indians. For their part, the Inca had done the same to non-Quechua speakers when they built the Inca Empire in the fourteenth and fifteenth centuries. Therefore, with the Spanish conquest in the New Spain (Mexico) and Andean region (at least north of Chile), Spain superimposed its own hierarchical society on an already existing hierarchy. With the mutually reinforcing nature of these multiple historical hierarchies, the Spanish idea of assimilation of the Indians was one of dominance.

However, in some countries, the process of conquest proved to be more of a lateral than a hierarchical affair. For example, the Brazilians and the Paraguayans at first made alliances with the different Tupi-Guaraní groups in the lowlands, because it was mutually beneficial to the Indians, Brazilians, and Paraguayans. The Brazilians and the Paraguayans could not subdue the Indians even if they wanted to. They needed alliances with the Indians to fight wars against neighboring countries (e.g., the War of the Triple Alliance, 1864–1870, between Paraguay and Brazil, Argentina, and Uruguay) or to fight wars against other Indians. However, when the Brazilians and Paraguayans did manage to build enough military power to forcibly integrate the Indians into the body politic, they did so.[13]

Conclusion: Top-down nationalism

In the early national period (the early to mid-nineteenth century), the nationalism of the elites in Latin America was (not surprisingly) a top-down project. Elite Latin Americans aimed to impose their vision of nationalism on the indigenous people, and those of African extraction, as well as in the nations in which slavery was an important social institution. Because elite Latin Americans were especially concerned with imposing a European-style society, economy, and culture on nonelite Latin Americans, the rapidly globalizing world of the late nineteenth and early twentieth centuries—with European imperialist projects quickly advancing the process of globalization—facilitated European-style nationalism that Latin American elites were so enamored of.

Scholar Samuel Baily discusses some very important barriers to the elite-driven, top-down conception of nationalism. A very evident one was geography—the extreme topography of mountains and deserts divided the peoples of Latin America within a particular nation. The *personalismo* (personalism) of powerful leaders also inhibited a sense of nationalism that would persist after the leader was gone. Finally, social factors such as strong class divisions, and the Catholic Church, a foreign influence with its control over the educational systems in many Latin American nations giving it significant social power, also inhibited nationalistic sentiment.[14] Latin American leaders, and their people, will be grappling with these factors for centuries after independence. None of these barriers will ever be fully surmounted.

Study Questions

1. What were the main causes of Latin American independence?
2. What continuities do you see from the Spanish/Portuguese colonial experience with regard to independence?
3. What role in the independence process did the nonelite political actors play—those who were not the powerful?
4. How would you describe the nations that emerged from the struggle for independence? Would they be strong nations or weak nations?
5. Even as the new Latin American nations copied many aspects of European nationalism, can you discuss aspects of Latin American nationalism that make it distinct?

For Further Reading

Bolívar, Simón. *Selected Writings 1810–1830*, comp. Vicente Lecuna, edited by Harold A. Bierck, Jr., trans. Lewis Bertrand. New York: Colonial Press, 1951.

Brading, David. "Nationalism and State-Building in Latin American History." In *Wars, Parties and Nationalism: Essays on the Politics and Society of Nineteenth-Century Latin America*, edited by Eduardo Posada-Carbo, 89–107. London: Institute of Latin American Studies.

Collier, Simon. *Ideas and Politic of Chilean Independence, 1808–1833*. Cambridge: Cambridge University Press, 1967.

Wood, James A., ed. *Problems in Modern Latin American History: Sources and Interpretations*, 4th ed. Lanham, MD: Rowman and Littlefield, 2013.

PART TWO

Different National Paths—Brazil, Mexico, the Caribbean, and Central America

Part Three

Different National Paths—Brazil, Mexico, the Caribbean, and Central America

CHAPTER THREE

Two Special Cases:
Brazil and Mexico

*My mother is Japanese, my father is Taiwanese, and my wife is
Korean—I am the best Brazilian of all.*

WILLIAM WOO, A POLITICIAN FROM SAO PAOLO, INTERVIEWED
BY JEFFREY LESSER IN 2001, QUOTED IN LESSER[1]

FIGURE 3.1 *Coronation of Dom Pedro I of Brazil, 1822.* Source: *Unknown.
Accessed via the Library of Congress, Washington, DC.*

FIGURE 3.2 *US General Winfield Scott's invasion of Mexico, 1848.* Source: *Unknown. Accessed via Library of Congress, Washington, DC.*

Introduction

As it is obvious that Latin America is one of the more culturally diverse parts of the world, the journeys toward nationalism have been equally as diverse. As such, this chapter and the next will explore the varied pathways that different nations took toward nationalism. This chapter will compare two of Latin America's diverse giants, Mexico and Brazil, and the challenges they faced in their infancy as nations.

Brazil and Mexico: Different experiments in nation building

Both Mexico and Brazil had to come up with practical solutions for dealing with their size and diversity challenges—that is, their regional, racial, and social class divisions might force the new nations into smaller principalities. For its part, the Brazilian national leadership ceded significant powers to its constituent provinces, creating probably the loosest federation in the Americas (with the possible exception of the United States). In addition, the Brazilian governments were more effective at suppressing revolts, and thus maintaining national unity, as compared to Mexico. Brazil managed to significantly expand its territory because the government did not have to confront or assimilate large, well-organized groups of Indians, as Mexico did have to (e.g., the Maya in the Yucatan).

Mexico, for its part, in its early years was a much more unstable, even chaotic place. National governments shifted with great rapidity between attempts to impose power from Mexico City to more decentralized polities. By the 1830s, rebellions had broken out in a number of parts of Mexico, and the Mexican government/military had a hard time putting them down. A rebellion in the northern province of Texas led to its War for Independence, greatly aided by the United States, and its eventual annexation by the United States (discussed later in this chapter).

South America's giant: Brazil

Up to this point, this book has focused on the rise of nations as Spain's power crumbled and revolutionary movements rose in what came to be known as Latin America. What eminent historian of Latin America Bradford Burns said of Brazilian nationalism could easily apply to the nationalisms of the other nations in Latin America: it's largely based on unbroken territory, a common language, unifying religion, and shared ideological preferences.[2]

However, it is important to note that Brazilian nationalism was distinct in a number of ways from the nationalisms of the Spanish-speaking nations of Latin America. Of course, to fully understand the rise of Latin American nationalism in the nineteenth and twentieth centuries, different national trajectories need to be analyzed. Of course, Spain was not the only imperial nation with holdings in the Americas. Brazil, Portugal's colony, over 8.5 million square kilometers in size, exhibited two features very important to future Brazilian nationalism: its distinctive (huge) size and confidence. Its confidence sprang from its defeats of the French and Dutch attempts to control parts of Portugal's Brazilian colony in the seventeenth century. Moreover, Portugal as imperial overlord, proved very different than Spain: before colonization, the Portuguese crown had centralized power by curbing the power of the elite, in particular by co-opting the power of the wealthier merchants, creating a unified state.

In addition, because the Spanish allowed for the creation of a number of different universities throughout their empire, a number of different centers of intellectual dissent developed. Brazil differed markedly. Portugal allowed for the creation of only one university, the University of Coimbra, at which collectively the intellectuals supported the transfer of power from Portugal to the new country of Brazil in 1822.[3]

In that year, Dom Pedro I, Prince Regent of the monarchy of Portugal temporarily living in Rio de Janeiro, effectively took power from his father, João VI, Portugal's king who was also temporarily decamped in Rio. When João VI quickly left Rio in 1821 to put down a rebellion in Portugal, Dom

Pedro used the opportunity to rally nationalistic support. He thus declared himself the emperor of the new nation of Brazil the next year. Dynastic continuity and legitimacy helped foster political stability.

Finally, because the Portuguese leadership fled to Brazil to escape Napoleon's invasion of Iberia in 1807 Brazil achieved independence. Thus, Brazil "inherited" a unified state without bloody/destructive revolution. As such, Brazil did not have the need to, or feel the need to, create a powerful national government, like other Latin American nations did. Instead, the Brazilian federal system was a loose, power-sharing arrangement between the provinces and the capital.

Because the elite embraced the monarchy from the beginning and the Republic which came after the monarchy came to an end in 1889, it gave the nation and state legitimacy and power early on in Brazil's independence.[4] The monarchy gave way to the republic for a number of reasons. First, with the end of slavery, landowners withdrew their support from the monarchy. Opposition to the monarchy by the 1880s became considerable, especially among the Church and the army, which carried out the pro-republican coup in 1889.[5]

Like other Latin American nations, as discussed in the previous chapter, from its early days as a nation, Brazil wanted to import a positivistic order and progress from Europe and impose it on its polyglot society. Latin American positivism meant that Latin American (and of course Brazilian) elites would apply European social-science, "rational" techniques of organizing a government and society. European culture was seen by Brazilian elites as the most superior in the world, and as such, infusing it somehow across the massive Brazilian geography was key.[6] Europe was important in another way. Globalization, in the form of late nineteenth-century imperialism, proved to be key to the stabilization of the new Republican Brazilian government in the last decade of the nineteenth century. At this time, France and England were carving up Africa. This is known as "formal imperialism"—a powerful country taking territory many thousands of miles away against the will of the area's inhabitants. Then, the imperial nation ran their new territory as a colony of the "mother country." France, England, Russia, Holland, and Japan seemed on the verge of carving up China and did carve up significant parts of Asia, in particular Southeast Asia. (India had been a British colony going back to the late eighteenth century.) But, importantly, a new nation was getting in on the imperial game—the United States. Even as the United States in some ways was copying the European example by wanting to get in on the imperial game, US imperialism was different. It was comprised of the spread of US economic and political interests—known as "informal imperialism."

This new burst of imperialism (in particular US imperialism) had considerable impact on Brazil as it attempted to preserve its new republican government from an attempt by promonarchist forces in Brazil to overthrow the new republic and return to the pre-1889 monarchical system. Whereas Brazilian positivism represented a type of cultural globalization in Brazil in the nineteenth century, in the late nineteenth century a convergence of US and Brazilian economic interests, as well as a shared interest in maintaining a republican form of government in Brazil, represented a new type of globalization: the spreading of US economic and political interests.

The United States as a driver of globalization: US military force helps Brazil maintain its republican form of government

The United States practiced what historians term "informal" or "insular" imperialism. Instead of taking large tracts of land overseas and administering them directly, Washington's leaders instead only took and administered small islands with good ports. After all, holding large tracts of land, with large numbers of people, was a contradiction to some of the hallowed values of the United States ("all men are created equal"). Also, from the perspective of whites in the United States, bringing in large numbers of nonwhite, non-Protestant peoples was undesirable, even dangerous. And then, there was the expense of administering overseas colonies, which US leaders steadfastly wanted to avoid.

US leaders, even as they shunned "formal imperialism," intervened in overseas nations. They did so largely to promote foreign trade. As the US economy in the 1890s sunk deeper and deeper into depression, US leaders looked to new areas for economic activity—Asia and Latin America. When a monarchist revolt seemed on the verge of forcing from power the recently created (largely by means of a bloodless coup) Republic of Brazil, the United States sprang into action. The US Navy was key. First, US leaders believed a larger navy was needed to protect a larger merchant shipping fleet. Second, US leaders argued that a larger navy meant a more powerful United States. Throughout history, so the argument went, a more powerful navy was a sine qua non for building a more powerful nation.

In 1893, US ships positioned themselves in the Harbor of Rio de Janeiro, Brazil's most important port and one of the best in the hemisphere. They positioned themselves in a way to prevent the monarchist rebels from occupying the port. These rebels wanted to "turn the clock back" to the days of the monarchy. With US help, the Republican forces prevailed. US foreign policy was animated by the concern that a monarchist Brazil would be less open to foreign trade than its republican counterpart.[7] Politically, too, the United States was spreading its interest to Brazil: it wanted Brazil to maintain its representative, republican form of government because the United States believed all should have a representative form of government.

The US intervention in the Brazilian dispute of 1893 proved to be one of the more important precedents, or turning points, in both the relations between the United States and Latin American states and US foreign policy.

It signaled that the United States would shift from territorial conquest in Latin America (the 1846–1848 Mexican-American War, discussed below) to an "informal empire" in the Americas.

Another driver of globalization: Immigration

A key aspect of Brazilian nationalism was their rapidly growing export economy in the nineteenth century, especially in the areas of sugar, cotton, and coffee. Expanded exports meant expanded revenues for the national government. Also, large-scale immigration in the nineteenth century expanded the size of the nation. Immigration was promoted by the state as a way of bringing in more laborers and supposedly higher-quality laborers than African slaves.[8] The slavery system crumbled due to its inefficiency, opposition by some powerful Brazilian elites, opposition by Great Britain, and active resistance on the part of some of the slaves, some of whom fled the plantations and set up their own communities called *quilombos* (communities of former slaves) in the Brazilian interior.[9] One reason the state promoted European immigration was to increase the size of the white population ("whitening"). It was thought by elites (most of whom were white) that making the society more European would improve it. Further, Brazilian elites assumed that whites were more efficient workers than black slaves.

Race and racism are at the heart of the nation-building project in Brazil. As it was the republican government that eliminated slavery, it caused the wealthy landowners who were former slave owners to dislike this new government. Indeed, many Afro-Brazilians feared, not surprisingly, that these former slave owners, the most powerful members of the new republican government, would try to reinstate slavery.[10] In later years, a myth of racial democracy would emerge in Brazil (discussed in a later chapter). Such a myth was alluring because it could unify a racially diverse society. Indeed, Brazil was the largest slaveholding country in the Western Hemisphere. Recent literature has shown, however, that Brazilian society is significantly less racially egalitarian than the myth implies.[11]

The intersection of national identity and globalization can be seen very clearly in how Brazilians constructed their version of national identity over time. Like other aspects of Brazilian nationalism, it is distinct from the nationalism narratives of other Latin American nations. Brazil's concept of national identity differs from other nations in the Americas in that it celebrates immigration as constantly improving Brazil. Although the standard national narrative of a number of nations in the Americas asserts that immigrants are improved by their arrival in a new land, in Brazil, the dominant national identity narrative is that *immigrants themselves when they arrive automatically improve* Brazil—as long as the immigrants are white European, or Japanese.[12]

Rapid globalization put Brazil's government under significant strain. However, Brazil managed to maintain national unity in the face of such strains. Significantly, Brazil has successfully walked a fine line between federalism and centralization. In the early period of the republic, up through 1930, federalism was a loose-fitting garment. The provinces of course enjoyed this freedom. Although there was unrest, the Brazilian government successfully put down the uprisings. Then, in response, there was centralization. Mexico, for a number of reasons, not least because of the French invasion in the mid-nineteenth century, has had a harder time forging a political and social consensus with regard to the degree of federalism versus centralization.

Mexico: The (short-lived) doomed empire, and chaos

In Latin America, it is very important to understand how long a shadow the colonial past cast on the modern day. Colonial Latin America was very socially and culturally diverse. It was made of people of African descent, as well as indigenous peoples, a variety of mixed-blood peoples and (white) Europeans. Those who were part European and part Indian were mestizos (ladinos in Central America). Those who were part European and African/ Indian) were zambos (pardos in Brazil). There were two main groups of white Europeans. First, there were creoles (those of European extraction, but born in the Americas) and second, gauchupines.

The case of Mexico is instructive. Once Mexico threw off the colonial yoke of Spain and became independent, it had a hard time maintaining social and political unity. Mexico, reflecting the regional and social class and racial diversity of many Latin American nations, was thus subject to extreme centrifugal forces. Could the center hold? As it turns out, only with a consistently powerful central government could Mexico maintain its national unity. Instead, Mexico, in its early national period, shifted back and forth from centralization to federalism, accentuating the already existing centrifugal forces. Indeed, centrifugal forces, in which different regions or states in Mexico have demanded and fought for increased autonomy from the central government, have characterized Mexican history from the beginning, and in particular in the early years of the Mexican nation when it lost Central America, Texas, and then its northern frontier in the Mexican-American War with the United States (1846–1848). Because Mexico's historical trajectory is so different from that of the other Latin American nations, it bears scrutiny as a separate entity.

The early years of Mexican history were characterized by economic and political crisis, so much so the nation almost fell apart. Although in many Latin American nations the early years of independence were characterized by bitter struggles between Conservatives and Liberals, in Mexico these struggles were particularly divisive. Conservatives wanted to preserve a paternalistic, hierarchical society, reflective of the colonial era. In a sort of Platonic fashion, each social group would understand the importance of hierarchy in general and their particular place in it. Conservatives feared "rocking the boat" by introducing social reforms that could lead to significant social change and maybe disorder and violence. In the Conservative vision, there would be a strong leader in a sense "keeping everyone in their place" to ensure that the system functioned with little conflict.

Liberals, for their part, wanted to enact sweeping social changes to, at least in the long run, convert Mexico into an economic/social/political entity similar to Great Britain or the United States. Economically, Liberals wanted to break up the communally owned Indian lands and promote freeholding. They saw an increase in export-oriented agriculture and promoting exports of valuable raw materials (in particular minerals) as a way of earning significant amounts of foreign exchange, so Mexico could industrialize. In addition, Liberals wanted Mexico to become a representative democracy. As such, the deep changes that Liberals called for could, in the short run, be destabilizing. As such, Conservatives saw Liberal ideology as particularly dangerous.

Wounded nationalism

Upon its independence from Spain, Mexico was one of the largest Latin American nations. Mexico inherited territory from present-day California in the northwest, to Panama in the south. Because its geographic and cultural diversity was more pronounced than Brazil's, Mexico would have a harder time maintaining its national unity than Brazil. As with Brazil, the forces of globalization accentuated already existing centrifugal forces. Chiapas in the far south was culturally more connected to Guatemala than the rest of the country. It would have been difficult for even a competent, efficient federal government in Mexico City to effectively govern such a large space before such unifying institutions such as railroads and a national press existed. Unfortunately for Mexico, its early governments were not known for their competency or efficiency: in fact, just the opposite. Wracked with political division, the post-1824 governments could not deal with the economic disaster wreaked by the war against Spain. Given the power of these centrifugal forces, in which social cleavages along the lines of ethnicity, race, class, and region caused Mexicans living in the far-flung regions of the nation to demand more autonomy, it was not surprising that Mexico seemed on the verge of disintegrating.

In Mexico's North, during the colonial period, limited means of communication and transportation meant that it was only loosely connected with the rest of the country. Only a very small part of Mexico's population lived in the wide expanses of mountainous desert in the North. The different

Catholic orders set up missions to forcibly bring Christianity to the isolated Indian groups on the country's northern frontier. These tireless, dedicated churchmen attempted to bring Catholicism (and Spanish culture as well) to many of the Indians. The missionaries attempted to care for large numbers of Indians who contracted dangerous diseases. Many died from these diseases. The missionaries also encountered resistance from the Indians. Bloody Indian uprisings proved difficult to put down. Such resistance caused many in Mexico to wonder if it was worth the effort for the missionaries to continue their efforts. Indeed, as support for their endeavors from the Church and the state dried up by the late eighteenth century, a number of these missions were closed. As such, Mexico's northern territories were not closely linked, politically or culturally, to the rest of the country. The battles between Liberals and Conservatives for the heart and soul of the young Mexican nation were particularly bitter because both sides thought that if the other side triumphed, it would mean the end of the Mexican nation. As such, the stakes were particularly high. This partisan strife was combined with the incompetent, power-hungry leadership of Santa Anna, who was president eleven separate times over the course of thirty years, taking power in coups and in turn being deposed in coups, led to disaster.

When the Mexican government in Mexico City in 1835 decided to centralize power in the federal district, it led to political crisis. Significant trends in globalization, in particular immigration from the United States, accentuated already exiting centrifugal forces, which caused Mexico to lose a significant amount of territory. Mexicans on the edge of the Mexican nation, for example in Texas and the Yucatan, had become used to significant autonomy. When the decree came down from Mexico City that their autonomy would be curtailed, these regions erupted in rebellion. The situation in Texas lent itself to separatism, as the Mexican government had tried to control its far-flung province by inviting in immigrants from the United States as long as they promised to convert to Catholicism and give up their slaves. The immigrants did not adhere to these stipulations. When Texas erupted in rebellion in 1835, they felt little allegiance to Mexico and particularly disliked Mexico's attempt to suppress the rebellion. When the Texans defeated Mexico's attempts to "keep them in the fold," they forged their own nation, from 1836 to 1845. With an undeveloped economy, and lacking basic infrastructure, the Texans did not have sufficient resources to run their own nation. As such, when offered the opportunity to be annexed by the United States in 1845, they accepted. Indeed, this decision is not surprising, since a majority of the Texans were of US extraction.

When the United States absorbed Texas, against the will of Mexico, it was in the interests of the leadership of Texas (which was nearly all white). However, Mexico, not surprisingly, saw the annexation of Texas to the United States as an act of war. With its absorption into the United States, the United States inherited a border dispute between Texas and Mexico. President James K. Polk, a member of the Democratic Party, saw this as an opportunity. The Democratic Party was the party of landed (westward and southern) expansionism. As the population of the United States grew, the thirst for land grew with it. The Democratic Party's vision for the United States was to build a society of small, individual landholders (the vision of Thomas Jefferson, founder of the Democratic Party). The idea of Manifest Destiny, that the obvious future of the United States was to take over all of North America, was not only about land hunger. Advocates of Manifest Destiny, for their part, saw that expansion of US society as bringing the benefits of US liberties to the inhabitants of North America. More generally, advocates of Manifest Destiny saw the landed expansion of the United States as spreading the benefits of US-style progress—economic and political liberties—to the entire North American continent. Finally, adherents of Manifest Destiny thought that God had destined the United States to occupy all of North America (including Mexico). Although adherents of Manifest Destiny thought that the non-American inhabitants of North America would automatically benefit from the extension of US power over the continent, such was not the case. In reality, Mexicans and indigenous people did not end up enjoying the same liberties as other Americans. As such, they resisted US rule. Not surprisingly, many of these nonwhite peoples were treated as second-class citizens and resisted US rule over them.

Texans claimed that their southern boundary was the Rio Grande (or Rio del Norte). The Mexicans claimed that the boundary was to the north—the Rio Nueces. As such, the territory between these two rivers was in dispute. (It appears that the Mexicans were correct—virtually all extant maps at the time put the border at the Rio Nueces.) President James K. Polk, in the spring of 1846, with visions of Manifest Destiny dancing in his head, provoked a war with Mexico by sending US troops into the disputed border region in south Texas, reputedly to protect the border. Then Mexican troops, perceiving this audacious move for what it was—an invasion—fired on the US troops. Declaring "American blood has been spilled on American soil," Polk asked for a (controversial) declaration of war from the US Congress. Indeed, the Mexican-American War (1846–1848) proved to be one of the most controversial in US history. Most of Polk's opponents perceived Polk's actions for what they were—an attempt to provoke a war with Mexico, so the United States could invade Mexico and force Mexico to give up a great deal of its territory. To Polk's opponents, it was a war of conquest, which flew in the face of hallowed US ideas embodied in the Declaration of Independence and the Constitution. In 1848, after US troops had invaded the eastern port of Veracruz, and marched west to eventually occupy Mexico City, Mexico sued for peace in order to get the US troops out of their nation as quickly as possible. One reason for Mexico's decision to sue for peace was that Indian groups in Mexico were using the opportunity of the war to more forcefully assert themselves, including militarily. Some Mexican officials feared that these Indian uprisings could eventually get "out of hand," threating the Mexican state itself. The war ended with the Treaty of

Guadalupe Hidalgo, requiring Mexico to give up about half of its northern territory (which was sparsely populated) to the United States.

Mexican nationalism was wounded, but at the same time stimulated, by its disastrous war with the United States. One of the more famous stories of Mexican history is the *niños héroes* (literally, the boy heroes)—cadets from Mexico's military academy, who jumped to their deaths from Chapultepec Castle in Mexico City instead of being captured and possibly humiliated in some form by the United States. These heroic young men epitomized national sacrifice and are still revered today.

From US invaders to French invaders

However, the Mexican-American War was only one example of wounded nationalism. In 1862 Spanish, British, and French troops occupied Mexico in an effort to force it to make good on payments of interest on Mexican government bonds that were in arrears. It was common in the nineteenth and early twentieth centuries for the leadership of economically and militarily powerful nations to use direct military force to compel (weaker) nations who had sold bonds to investors/creditors in their country to forcefully coerce these weaker countries, who had fallen behind on paying the required interest on their creditors' investments (i.e., the bonds), to pay up. First, the powerful, creditor country threatened to attack a major port of the weaker, debtor country, unless it quickly found a way to start paying on the bonds in arrears. If that was insufficient, the powerful, creditor nation would simply occupy the weaker, debtor country's customs house and collect duties on exports or imports. Then, these collected funds would then be sent to the bondholders. In some cases, if a weaker/debtor nation fell into arrears, powerful/creditor nations would use it as an excuse to expand their power into the weaker/debtor nation in imperialistic fashion—which is what happened in Mexico from 1863 to 1867.

One reason why the European nations decided to intervene militarily was they surmised that the Mexican government would put up little resistance. Indeed, Mexico was wracked by civil strife, even bordering on civil war, perpetrated by Liberals and Conservatives who sharply differed on education and religious policy, among other disputes. Mexico's weakness, however, also prevented it from making any serious attempt to repay their European creditors. As such, all except the French gave up on their attempts to compel payment on bonds held by their investors, and withdrew their troops.

However, the French decided to beef up their contingent of troops and invade Mexico (its main port, Veracruz) with the vision of setting up a French colony in Mexico. Napoleon III had visions (delusions?) of grandeur, in essence setting up another Napoleonic empire, trying to revive the glory of France under the leadership of his famous uncle Napoleon I, but this time it would be in Mexico. Two members of the Austrian monarchy, Maximillian and Carlotta, were asked by Napoleon to lead this new empire. Mexican resistance to this French invasion proved to be another important example of wounded nationalism. Headed up by Liberal Benito Juárez, who later became the first full-blooded Indian to lead Mexico, Liberal rebels beat back the French invasion. An important battle, which Mexico lost but caused it to fight harder later on and eventually to triumph, was the Battle of Puebla on May 5, 1862 (cinco de mayo, or May 5). The Mexican forces were led by General Porfirio Diaz, who would later become Mexico's longest-serving president and leave his significant stamp on Mexican history. (Although celebrated more often outside of Mexico than in Mexico itself, "cinco de mayo" would become an important, nationalistic holiday for Mexicans.) With the capture and execution of Maximillian, and the resulting expulsion of the French, Mexico would heal its wounds and work to unify itself. Indeed, after years of bitter political struggles and foreign invasions, the end France's brief rule in a sense provided a useful "rallying point" for Mexican citizens, stimulating Mexican nationalism. As such, Mexican nationalism has a stronger anti-foreign (even xenophobic?) side to it as compared to other nations' sense of nationalism.

Mexican nationalism is significantly different than the nationalisms of other Latin American nations in other ways as well. Because of multiple foreign invasions, Mexico built up one of the stronger states/militaries in the region as a way of safeguarding national security. Moreover, there was a unifying cultural symbol that characterized Mexican nationalism from the beginning—Our Lady of Guadalupe, a mixed-race version of the Virgin Mary.[13]

In the late nineteenth and early twentieth centuries, Mexican leaders, exemplified by Porfirio Díaz, who led the country for nearly one-third of a century, aimed to implement at least some aspects of the Liberal vision— private property-holding and a laissez-faire policy toward foreign investors. Such policies aimed to build up Mexico's economy and thus its national strength. In some parts of Mexico, for example the Yucatan, in the late nineteenth and early twentieth centuries, a friendly environment toward outside investors helped transform one of the poor parts of the country into one of the richest. However, the emphasis on private property holding, which at times caused a forcible dispossession of Indian lands, skewed the distribution of income toward the wealthy, laying the groundwork for the Mexican Revolution.[14] As will be discussed in future chapters, the Mexican Revolution spurred a renewed interest in Mexican nationalism, in particular economic and cultural nationalism.

For its part, Brazil's trajectory as a nation proved to be happier than Mexico's because the powerful Portuguese-speaking nation would easily win conflicts with its neighbors. Mexico, however, was in a very different situation—bordering the powerful United States. It was unfortunately, supposedly, "so far from God—and so close to the United States." (This phrase is widely attributed to Díaz, the late nineteenth-century Mexican leader.) However, Mexico and Brazil are similar in that they both have a diverse ethnic makeup and are spread across a wide geographic area, which makes it difficult to maintain national cohesion over time.

Study Questions

1. Discuss the reasons why, and the process by which, Brazil became independent—what are the most important aspects of the process?
2. Discuss the reasons why, and the process by which, Mexico became independent—what are the most important aspects of the process?
3. What aspects of Brazilian nationalism make it a distinctive case? What aspects of Mexican nationalism make it a distinctive case?
4. Often, the Caribbean is described as an area with a divided, or fractured, nationalism. Discuss the three most important reasons why Caribbean nationalism is fractured.
5. Often, the Caribbean is separated from the rest of Latin America with regard to studying/understanding nationalism. Can you give one reason why this separation is warranted? Can you give one reason why the separation is not warranted?

For Further Reading

Brading, David. *The Origins of Mexican Nationalism*. Cambridge: Centre for Latin American Studies, 1985.

Burns, E. Bradford. *Nationalism in Brazil*. New York: Praeger, 1968.

Domingues, José Maurício. "Nationalism in South and Central America." In *The SAGE Handbook of Nations and Nationalism*, edited by Gerard Delanty and Krishan Kumar, 541–54. Thousand Oaks, CA: SAGE Publications, 2006.

Joseph, Gilbert. *Revolution from Without—Yucatan, Mexico, and the United States, 1880–1924*. Cambridge: Cambridge University Press, 1982.

Mallon, Florencia. *Peasant and Nation: The Making of Postcolonial Mexico and Peru*. Berkeley: University of California Press, 1995.

CHAPTER FOUR

Fragmented Nationalisms: The Special Cases of Central America and the Caribbean

And I shall remember the long hard years of the modern beginning and that it was the little people, the poor, the humble, and the seeming weak who first began to blow on the still living but small and hidden flame of freedom and blew till it soared like a torch and all the land began to light up around us .... So out of the past far away and the past near at hand is born the present, in which a people coming to maturity and nationhood can look back and give praise, look around and give thanks, look forward with prayer and in humility but with confidence and strength.

NORMAN W. MANLEY, CHIEF MINISTER OF JAMAICA, IN A BROADCAST ON NOVEMBER 10, 1957, QUOTED IN FRANKLIN KNIGHT[1]

Introduction

The cases of Central America and the Caribbean provide difficult questions for the student of Latin American nationalism. Indeed, do the Central American nations and the Caribbean nations represent one nationalism? Or do they represent many? Nationalism is a complication/fragmented affair throughout Latin America—but especially fragmented in Central America and the Caribbean. The two case studies are quite different: Central America was a relatively unified entity for a few years, the Caribbean never was so. But both are similar in that there have been nationalists in both areas that have tried to construct/reconstruct a type of regional nationalism—to no avail. As such, they provide excellent "case studies" of the diffuse—but important—nature of Latin American nationalism.

Globalization and fragmentation in Central America and the Caribbean

The fragmentation of nationalism in Central America and the Caribbean proved to be the result largely of geography, language, and ethnicity, as well as cultural differences and political strife. The "otherness" that different groups saw in outsiders proved more powerful than any unifying features. The fragmentation of the Caribbean was overlaid by the fact that different European nations conquered different islands. This fragmentation has proved to be stubbornly enduring, despite the efforts of some over the years to promote different sorts of confederations or unions in the two regions. However, it is important to note that the process of globalization also hindered, or even prevented, such unions/confederations. Globalization inhibited any sort of Central American or Caribbean political unity from forming. Different European nations, and later the United States, set up lucrative sugar plantations in the Caribbean and banana agribusiness empires in Central America. As such, multinationals moved into the Caribbean similar to the way they did in Central America. The outside imperial powers could use divide-and-conquer techniques to control the situation. If one nation complained about the terms by which a small nation would allow a large (foreign, multinational) economic enterprise (based in a powerful, industrialized nation) to exploit the resources of that nation, then the large enterprise could simply say (with the implicit backing of its nation) that they were getting a better deal than the country next door was getting, so they better be happy with what they got.

Divide-and-conquer techniques similarly increased the control enjoyed by the large multinational companies (MNCs) with regard to labor policies. Large foreign enterprises could employ large numbers of workers from the host nation and offer them better wages and working conditions than those offered by local companies. In effect, the labor movement was therefore divided, and thus weakened.

More than in other parts of Latin America, with the possible exception of Mexico, Caribbean nationalism formed around the desire to rid the country of imperialism, or, more generally, of foreign influence. Such influence was first and foremost economic. By the mid-twentieth century, for example, foreign multinational corporations controlled a good chunk of Jamaica's bauxite (raw material for aluminum). Jamaica's desire for control over this critically important (and valuable) resource strongly animated their desires for national independence. For example, Jamaican nationalists were animated by a desire to eliminate British power from their country, which they successfully did by 1962.

The Caribbean

For its part, the Caribbean was never a unified entity. From the beginning, different ethnicities and the isolation of the various islands conspired to keep the Caribbean a fragmented polity. Most importantly, because different European imperial powers ruled different islands, there was no way for the Caribbean to coalesce as a nation or any other political unit for that matter. It is also important to note that the more important of the Caribbean islands have been "pawns" in a competitive—and bloody— imperial game. For example, the control of Havana Harbor (Cuba) was exchanged between Britain and Spain in the mid-eighteenth century, because it was well placed and the best harbor in the Caribbean. Control of the Caribbean was important for the Spanish, because they shipped their silver mined from South America and Mexico through the Caribbean. For the British, Caribbean islands provided a significant amount of income from sugar production and export.

Two special cases: Haiti and Cuba

Two countries in which foreign influence had a particularly important formative influence on the nationalism of the host nation are Haiti, which was controlled by the French for about 175 years, and Cuba, which was controlled by the Spanish nearly four centuries, from the early 1500s to 1898 when the United States, very much helped by Cuban independence fighters, exerted informal control over the island nation until Fidel Castro's 1959 Revolution.

The case of Haiti is especially important in understanding the Caribbean's different path toward national liberation. Haiti is unique for a number of reasons, but only two will be highlighted here. First, Haiti was a French colony—it was the most important one by the late eighteenth century. (The French lost all of their non-Caribbean North American imperial holdings when they lost the Seven Years' War to England in 1763.) Second, Haiti was more subject to the forces of globalization than other nations—both economically and culturally. Because it was such a lucrative sugar-producing colony for the French, the French imported a large number of slaves to work in the sugar plantations. As such, African cultural influence in Haiti was more pronounced than that in other Caribbean nations.

Haitian nationalism is a different strain from many other Latin American nationalisms. To start with, it achieved nationhood early. It was the second nation in the Western Hemisphere to free itself from imperial control, in 1803. Also, a key difference between Haiti and the rest of Latin America is that its imperial overload was France; indeed, Haiti was France's principal colony in Latin America. Most importantly, Haiti freed itself from imperial control by means of a successful slave rebellion, the world's only example of a successful slave rebellion leading to the formation of a nation.

France's main reason for keeping Haiti was its revenue from sugar production. However, the human cost of sugar production was tremendous. Slaves were literally worked to death, and then more slaves were imported from Africa. When Haitian slaves successfully expulsed French power, it sent shock waves through the slave-holding nations of the Americas. Many decide to end slavery altogether. Indeed, with the exception of Brazil and Cuba, all of the Latin American nations gave up slavery by the 1850s. Although there were a number of reasons why the Latin American nations gave up slavery by the 1850s, the fear of a large slave rebellion *a la* Haiti was one reason the Latin American nations gave up the odious institutions. (In Latin America, slavery was never as economically important as it was in the United States. In the mid-nineteenth century in the southern United States, slavery fueled one of the wealthiest economies not only in the hemisphere but in the world.)

Because Haitian slaves were treated so poorly, the dreams of the Haitian revolutionaries were to create a postrevolutionary, nonexploitative society. In this regard, Haitian nationalism was not successful. Even as the French overlords were forced out, a wealthy class of mulatto plantation landowners proved to be exploitative of a low-paid, poorly treated workforce. Politically, as well, even as some of the Haitian revolutionaries dreamed of a postrevolutionary democracy, Haiti's political culture devolved into authoritarianism. Because the postrevolutionary society did not create an egalitarian economic system, nor a stable middle class, it is not surprising that the political system degenerated into authoritarianism, with the small elite supporting the authoritarian leader, who kept the poor majority "in check."

Haiti's slave rebellion was the first successful slave rebellion in the history of the Western Hemisphere and the second Western Hemisphere nation (after United States) to throw off the yolk of European power. Haiti is significant considering Haitian cultural nationalism contains a large number of what scholars call "African survivals"—elements of African culture. Unfortunately for the Haitians, their country has been one of the poorest and most politically unstable of all the Latin American nations. With the US occupation (which US leaders implemented largely because of political instability on the island) from 1916 to 1933, Haitian nationalism contained a strong streak of anti-US sentiment.

Cuba

Similarly, foreign intervention helps to explain the prominent element of antiforeign (in particular anti-US) sentiment in Cuban nationalism. If the Caribbean is a special case with regard to Latin American nationalism, Cuba is a special case within the special case. Cuba was the last Spanish colony to give up African slavery in 1889. And it was the last of Spain's colonies (along with the Philippines) to break free of Spain's imperial control. Cuban independence fighters against Spain managed to secure the exit of Spanish power, only to cruelly have their victory snatched from them by their powerful neighbor a mere ninety miles to the north of the United States. The United States set up a protectorate to control Cuba. Thus, Cuba became subject to one of the more important drivers of globalization in the late nineteenth and early twentieth centuries—the intensification of imperialism by the world's powerful nations, exerting their control over the less powerful nations.

Fidel Castro's (leader of the 1959 Revolution) intense anti-Americanism flowed directly out of the Cuban experience. A number of prominent US leaders, going back to the late eighteenth century, coveted Cuba, mainly because it was so close to Florida and had great economic potential. As tensions within the United States rose to a fever pitch in the mid-nineteenth century, a number of people in the antebellum South, the few decades leading up to the US Civil War of 1861–1865, thought that Cuba would be a fine addition to the United States because at the time it was a slave-owning colony of Spain. Thus, Cuba's addition to the United States would add to the ranks of the "slave states" in the South in their competition with the North. Cuba was riven by a bloody civil war in the late nineteenth century over the issue of independence, and the United States declared war on Spain because the Spanish could not control the mushrooming human rights disaster on the island. Moreover, US leaders had imperial visions (see Chapter Eighteen, on inter-American relations). Such visions were fueled lucrative investment and trade opportunities on the island. A number of US investors (now, they would be termed "agribusiness") on the island had amassed a great deal of wealth investing in sugar plantations, selling the product mainly to the large and growing US market. Indeed, in the late nineteenth and early twentieth centuries, Cuba, along with Mexico, provided the most lucrative business opportunities for US overseas businessmen.

With the Spanish-American War, the United States, for the first time emerged as imperial power. However, the US empire that emerged out of the Spanish-American War of 1898 was very different than the European empires of the eighteenth and nineteenth centuries. As opposed to directly owning and controlling vast tracks of land overseas, the US government would control only small amounts of strategically placed land overseas—Puerto Rico, the territory on which the Panama Canal was built (discussed in Chapter Eighteen), and the Philippines. Generally, these strategic "pinpricks" of land had good ports to serve as refueling stations for the US Navy and Merchant Marine. This type of empire is termed by scholars as an "informal" empire, which means that the imperialist country (in this case, the United States) would exert control by means of economic and culture influence, not direct, political-military influence/control (This concept was discussed in the previous chapter). This vision of "informal empire" was expertly, and tirelessly, promoted by US leaders, including most famously by Adm. Alfred T. Mahan of the US Navy. Mahan wrote how no great nations had become great without building up its navy. Mahan also discussed how a more powerful US Navy was necessary in the late nineteenth century to protect US commercial ships that were increasingly active in seeking economic opportunities overseas. Because of the economic difficulties faced by the United States with the depression of the 1890s (the worst in US history up to that point), many US leaders, as well as US citizens, thought that the economic salvation of the United States lay in accumulating more wealth through increased overseas activity. From the point of view of many US leaders, the choice was stark: either the United States expand its economic activities overseas or face social conflict, even social upheaval and eventually socialism or communism at home.

Interestingly, and importantly, there was a convergence of thought between US leaders (business leaders and foreign policymaking officials) regarding the export of US products overseas. Both Latin Americans and US officials (and citizens) thought exporting US surplus products was imminent. US leaders, of course, saw selling the large amounts of products rapidly churned out by US factories as instrumental for preventing a contraction of the US economy and the concomitant social and political strife. For their part, the Latin Americans feared that such an influx of goods would damage the nascent industries in their economies and wanted to keep the mountain of US surplus goods out.[2]

US policy in the Spanish-American War of 1898 inevitably fomented the growth of Cuban nationalism while at the same time causing that nationalism to be a powerful anti-US phenomenon. When the United States forcibly expelled Spain from Cuba, a brief conflict supposedly termed a "splendid little war" by the Secretary of State John Hay, the United States made it clear that it did not want to absorb Cuba as part of the United States. Indeed, considering Cuba's large Catholic and nonwhite population, the leadership of the United States (of elite, white, Anglo-Saxon stock) did not want Cuba to become part of the United States because this political elite thought, in blame-the-victim fashion, that bringing Cuba into the United States would only bring in increased racial strife, something that US leaders wanted to avoid at all costs. In the post-Reconstruction US South, white, racist antiblack groups, most notably the Ku Klux Klan, used coercive intimidation to prevent blacks from enjoying the full array of their rights as US citizens (civil rights). Up until the present day, some nonwhites in the United States still do not enjoy all of their civil rights. In the last decade of the nineteenth century, the number of lynchings of blacks by whites rose to very high levels. As such, US leaders did not want to bring Cuba into the United States, with its large black population, fearing that such a decision would create a new wave of violent racial strife.

However, US leaders were insistent that the United States refuse to offer official diplomatic recognition to the Cuban independence forces. These US officials feared that an independent Cuba might be too weak to repel future possible imperialistic incursions by the British, or worse, the Germans. Instead, US leaders placed a protectorate over Cuba. Cubans were incensed, and thus, Cuban nationalism in the twentieth century had a strong strain of anti-American sentiment built in (see Chapter Eight on left-wing nationalism).

Race, nationalism, and globalization in the Caribbean

In understanding Caribbean nationalism, it is important to realize that for the Afro-Caribbean population—the majority of the population in many Caribbean nations—the idea of national liberation was, from the beginning, very different from the rest of Latin America. Slave rebellions were not that important to the development of Mexican, Central, and South American nationalism. However, slave rebellions proved to be an important feature of Afro-Caribbean history. As such, national liberation in the Caribbean was tied up in two significant movements. The first was antislavery and the second was the struggle for political equality and economic justice for Afro-Caribbean people.[3]

Physiologists have concluded that the biological differences of people of different skin colors are nonexistent. Instead, race is a powerful social construct. However, just because race is a social construct does not mean that it is unimportant. Indeed, race and racism have been used for centuries to justify slavery, withholding civil rights, and postslavery forms of economic exploitation of nonwhites.

The determination of who constituted an Afro-Caribbean or black person in the Caribbean is different from a number of other nations which the reader is probably more familiar with, for example, Europe and the United States. As such, it is important to describe how race is conceived of differently in different nations so as to best understand Caribbean racial identity.

In the early twentieth-century United States, before US citizens self-identified their race on census forms, many used the "one-drop" rule to determine if someone was black. If they had anyone in their family tree of African descent, going back as far as it was possible to reckon, then she or he was black. However, in the Caribbean the construct of race was conceived differently. Instead, individuals were categorized as different races based on cultural attributes: values, traditions, customs, lifestyle, way of speaking, and dress. It is important to note that this cultural construction of race does not mean that the Caribbean proved less racist than other parts of the world. Indeed, in the Caribbean, Afro-Caribbean or black culture was considered inferior, and nonblacks concluded that black Caribbean people could progress if they discarded their culture as quickly as possible and picked up European manners, modes of speech, types of dress, and ultimately, values. What was European or white was automatically good; what was black was automatically antimodern and antiprogress. Whites viewed non-European ethnic groups in the Caribbean, such as Indians from the Asian subcontinent and the Chinese in a similar fashion.

In the late twentieth and early twenty-first centuries, there has been more intermingling of the different races and cultures of the Caribbean's different ethnic groups. Mixed-race marriages are more common and socially acceptable, and there are increasingly more expressions of tolerance toward those of different races. Although the different Caribbean nations are more tolerant toward including nonwhite and mixed-race people, racism in the form of a racial hierarchy remains. Whites enjoy sitting atop the racial hierarchy; the next rung down is mixed-races persons, and persons of African descent remain at the bottom. This hierarchy is perhaps more subtle than its nineteenth-century variant but no less powerful. There is an expectation on the part of many whites, as well as light-skinned mixed-race people, that white/European culture is superior and nonwhites must give up the individual attributes of their different ethnicities to climb up the racial hierarchy and to advance economically. Thus, the dominant culture in the Caribbean remains a variant of European/white culture. In the view of the white/light-skinned, mixed-race group, which has predominant power in the Caribbean, if nonwhites fail to assimilate into the dominant culture, they will be denied access to power and economic opportunities, and they will be denigrated as antimodern and antiprogress. As a response to this racial hierarchy, a type of Afro-Caribbean nationalism has emerged, in which people of African descent in the different Caribbean nations assert that African culture and heritage is of equal value to European cultural traditions.

Central America

Although observers often put economics and religion in separate categories, this would not be a good practice for understanding colonial Latin America. Not only was the Church a powerful economic entity, it was an important driver of early globalization in Latin America. The vision of Church officials in the colonial period extended to economic globalization, in that it was a Catholic priest in the early seventeenth century who was the first known person to propose a canal across the Central American isthmus. Although not built until 1914 by the United States, the idea of a canal crossing the "narrow waist" of land (Chilean poet Pablo Neruda's term) would fire the imagination of many for centuries. Indeed, one of Central America's main characteristics with regard to globalization is that globalizers aimed to figure out the easiest route across the rugged terrain of the area.[4]

Central America was initially unified with its independence from Spain in 1823, but parochialism proved to be strong enough to overwhelm the fragile Central American nationalism. Central America, as with the rest of Latin America, has a society deeply divided in numerous ways. Since social unity was tenuous at best, national unity also proved weak. Centrifugal forces, due to ethnicity, race, and most significantly geography, pulled at the Central American nation until it broke into the five nations of Central America (between 1838 and 1840) that remain today. Central America's division into five smaller nations (Guatemala, Honduras, Nicaragua, El Salvador, and Costa Rica) proved problematic, as powerful outside entities (and the driving forces of economic globalization).

Although Central America was less buffeted by the forces of globalization in the nineteenth century as compared to the Caribbean, trade in primary source products that were plentiful in Central America but rare elsewhere, such as dyes and hardwoods, was brisk with European and North American buyers. By the early twentieth century, globalization came to Central America in full force, because of MNCs that produced bananas and sugar. One early example of an outside power exerting its force over Central America was the US effort to support Panamanian nationalists in successfully achieving its independence from Colombia. Then, in return for US efforts to obstruct Colombian attempts to put down the Panamanian revolution, US officials demanded that Panama give the United States access to a strip of land in the center of Panama to build a canal: the Panama Canal.

In addition, MNCs, starting in the early twentieth century, began to have a major impact on Central America's economy, society, and politics. The United Fruit Company (UFCO, or United Fruit) in the early to mid-twentieth century, could play one Central American nation against another. For example, if one country offered tax incentives or other inducements to United Fruit, the country next door could offer more lucrative benefits, thus minimizing UFCO's tax burden. Such tax revenues for the Central American nations were important, providing critical resources they could have used for infrastructure development and other needs. For this and other reasons, there have been efforts by the individual Central American nations to reunify themselves. These efforts have come to naught. In the early 1960s, the Central American nations formed a Common Market of their own, to much fanfare. (Supranational regional organizations will be explored in Chapter Twelve.) But agreement quickly broke down between the nations on how to "divvy up" investment/production in a way that would be coordinated and avoid duplication. That is, it would not be a good use of resources to have multiple countries produce the same product, which would only lead to bitter price competition and probably bankruptcy of the industry. As it turned out, the trade agreements Central American nations made with the United States proved more significant on Central American–focused trade harmonization efforts.

Central America has been known for two main things. First, it has been dependent on the export of foreign products and import of foreign capital, and it has had a large poor population. These phenomena are linked. Second, it has one of the largest indigenous populations in the hemisphere, in particular in Guatemala. Given the large indigenous population, similar to the Andean nations, there are parallel nationalisms, or nationalisms within nationalisms. That is, the Indians exhibit a dual nationalism, being citizens of both the nation-state in which they reside and their particular Indian tribe or group. The Indians' sense of their own particular nationalism of course serves as a vehicle for transmitting important aspects of their culture and history to the younger generations. Indian nationalism serves another purpose as well—to build a sense of strength through solidarity to demand that mestizos and elites treat them with a sense of dignity. Until the late twentieth century, Indians were effectively treated as second-class citizens by non-Indians; and discrimination of Indians still exists. Therefore, Indian nationalism serves as a way of building networks among different Indian groups to press their respective governments to bring such discrimination to an end.

All in all, because Central America has not been unified since the early nineteenth century, its sense of nationalism (as a unified nation) has atrophied over time. The subtitle of the standard history in English of Central America, by R. Lee Woodward, is "a nation divided." However, the brief period (about fourteen years) in which Central America was a unified nation recedes into the ever more distant past, it does not make sense to talk about a unified, meta-Central American nationalism.

Because of historic geographic, social, and racial divisions, nationalism in Central America and the Caribbean is probably the most fragmented in all of Latin America. But, it is also the most complicated and interesting. Even as those outside of Central America and the Caribbean by the mid-twentieth century viewed nationalism there as quiescent, in some countries, in particular Guyana, Cuba, and Nicaragua, nationalism would become very important to outsiders, in particular the United States.

Study Questions

1. What are the factors that foster Central American nationalism? What are the factors that weaken Central American nationalism?
2. What are the factors that foster Caribbean nationalism? What are the factors that weaken Caribbean nationalism?
3. Discuss the similarities between the two different regional nationalisms: the Caribbean and Central America. Then, discuss the key differences between the two nationalisms.
4. What is unique about Haitian nationalism? On the other hand, how is the Haitian experience similar to the experience of other Caribbean nations?
5. Discuss how globalization has impacted nationalism in the Caribbean and in Central America.

For Further Reading

Allahar, Anton. *Ethnicity, Class and Nationalism: Caribbean and Extra-Caribbean Dimensions*. Lanham, MD: Lexington Books, 2005.

James, C.L.R. *The Black Jacobins—Toussaint L'Ouverture and the San Domingo Revolution*, 2nd ed. New York: Vintage, 1989.

Knight, Franklin. *The Caribbean: Genesis of a Fragmented Nationalism*, 3rd ed. New York: Oxford University Press, 2011.

LaFeber, Walter. *Inevitable Revolutions—United States in Central America*, 2nd ed. Norton, 1993.

Perez, Louis. *On Becoming Cuban: Identity, Nationalism, and Culture*. Chapel Hill: University of North Carolina Press, 2008.

Woodward, R. Lee. *Central America: A Nation Divided*, 3rd ed. New York: Oxford University Press, 1999.

Consolidation of Nationalism as US Influence Supplants European Influence

CHAPTER FIVE

The Consolidation of Liberal Oligarchical (Top-Down) Nationalism in the Late Nineteenth Century

The new American states were all unprecedented social experiments into which were amalgamated the cultures, races, and political traditions of both settlers and indigenous peoples. The societies that arose from those experiments are still in search of solid identities today, still extracting and refining the ore that will be their legacy to civilization.

JUAN GONZALES[1]

Today the nation is what Rupert Emerson refers to as the "terminal community," that is, "the largest community which, when the chips are down, effectively commands men's loyalty, overriding the claims both of the lesser communities within it and those which [cut] across it or potentially enfold it within a still greater society."

RUPERT EMERSON, QUOTED IN SAMUEL L. BAILY[2]

Consolidating nationalism from above, part I: Importing European culture

For the elites and the members of the middle class who imitated the elites, nationalism in late nineteenth century Latin America meant strong leadership (usually of the Liberal political party) and an emphasis on exporting primary materials abroad and importing as much European culture as possible. According to the elite leadership of the Latin American nations, only if a Latin American nation excelled in all three areas could nationalism—at least the elites' conception of nationalism—thrive. In the late nineteenth century, the power of the Europeans in the world was at an all-time high, as European imperialism reached its apex. So, it was not surprising that the Latin Americans wanted to imitate the Europeans.

The "Europeanization" of Latin America in the late nineteenth and early twentieth centuries took many forms. For example, Simon I. Patiño, who by the mid-1920s controlled about one-half of Bolivia's tin exports, and was one of the wealthiest men in the world, built a mansion in his hometown of Cochabamba, Bolivia—importing European building materials and European (mostly French) architects and artists. It is essentially a monument to how important it was for Latin America's elite to imitate European culture.

In a sense, nationalism of a European type was "implanted" in Latin America by Europeanized Latin American elites. These elites saw European-style nationalism as equivalent to progress. European-style nationalism was formed by means of an economic "revolution" in the sixteenth and seventeenth centuries, when a feudalistic-style economy became a market-based economy, including a transnational free-market system. (In a feudalistic system, there are a few very large landholders and many landless workers who work on large estates. Relationships are determined by the traditional control that the large landholders have over workers that live/work on their large holdings. In a free-market system, there are more landholders. However, in Latin America often there are a few very large landholders and a number of small landholders.) In addition, the growth of centralized administrative systems (in both the civilian and military sectors) facilitated the growth of nationalism. Finally, in the cultural and educational sphere, there was growth of a national intelligentsia, trained in increasingly prominent educational institutions that were increasingly funded not by religious orders but instead by the state. This intelligentsia was key for spreading the ideology of nationalism to the far-flung areas of the state through a state-run educational system.[3] Certainly, the indigenous peoples of Latin America had no choice in the matter and resisted in various ways, choosing to maintain their traditional way of life and worldview. In some cases, when there was economic benefit at stake, the elites forced them to participate in the newly powerful Latin American nations of the late nineteenth century.

Consolidating nationalism from above, part II: Foreign investment and trade

As discussed in Chapter Two, nineteenth-century political life was split into the Liberal and Conservative camps. Although Liberal ideology called for a decentralized federal system of power-sharing and representative government, by the late nineteenth century a number of Liberals had become authoritarians. Because Liberals thought inviting in foreign capital to stimulate economic development in their nations was of extreme importance, they created propitious environments for such investment. As economic globalization became more prevalent in the late nineteenth century, driven in large part by new, wealthy, and politically powerful multinational corporations (MNCs), Latin American nations saw an opportunity. Although some in their nations benefitted, the foreign investment (the majority from MNCs) mainly benefitted a handful of wealthy citizens, thus increasing the already wide gap between the wealthy and the nonelites. In addition, there was a fear among a number of Latin Americans that Liberals, by allowing foreign capital to control key sectors of the economy (e.g., mining and oil), were essentially selling the national patrimony at fire sale prices to foreigners. Thus, allowing in a great deal of European investment was socially destabilizing.

Mexico's authoritarian Liberal leader Porfirio Díaz for about one-third of a century proved a master at using economic policy to create a great deal of wealth as well as at maintaining political stability in a rapidly changing society. He used "pan y palo" techniques—bread and the stick—to create order and stability that capitalists at home and abroad liked. The "bread" was the crony capitalism of Díaz's Mexico. If businessmen really wanted to prosper, working with Díaz would rapidly facilitate their becoming wealthy. For example, for businessmen (nearly all of them from abroad, representing MNCs) to drill oil in the oil-rich nation, they had to obtain a "concession," or official government permission, from Díaz's government. Without such permission, no government sanction, and of course no government protection, of these oil wells would be forthcoming. Thus, political connections were important if businessmen really wanted to prosper. Díaz's decision to "lock out" of his patronage system large swaths of the middle class (and of course the working class and poor) would come back to haunt him. Many concluded that the "system" (economic and political) was "fixed," and could only be overturned through revolution. Díaz's "stick" was his notoriously repressive rule. He routinely intimidated and threw into prison, his political opponents, defanging his political opposition. Moreover, many, if not the majority, of Mexicans in the late nineteenth and early twentieth centuries feared that foreign entitied were controlling some of Mexico's most important natural resources. Such fear helped to fuel the Mexican Revolution, as discussed in Chapter Seven.

Increased foreign trade in the late nineteenth century affected Latin America in a way similar to that of the large influx of foreign capital just discussed. The benefits of foreign trade tended to flow to the wealthiest in Latin America, exacerbating an already wide gap between the wealthy and the nonelites.[4] Further, some Mexicans feared that Mexico's increased dependency on selling goods overseas for its economic livelihood would prove to be an Achilles' heel should economic difficulties overseas force foreigners to stop purchasing Mexican goods. With the Great Depression of the 1930s, discussed in the next chapter, Mexico, along with the rest of Latin America, suffered when the bottom dropped out of the global economy and foreigners did not have money to spend on purchasing Mexican products.

The late nineteenth century in Latin America was one of the time periods in which foreign trade did increase economic growth. As the industrialized world demanded more and more of Latin America's products, whether metals or oil for its factories, or foodstuffs to fill the stomach of the industrial countries' growing population, Latin American trade with Europe and North America boomed, creating a surge of wealth—termed by some as the "dance of the millions." This surge in wealth proved socially destabilizing in some ways. The benefits of such growth flowed mainly to the wealthy, increasing an already large gap between the wealthy and nonelites. However, the wealth provided government leaders with resources. Through more efficient taxation systems, some of the foreign exchange earned from exports funded the growth of state institutions. Such institutions helped unify the nation. In tangible terms, now the state had the funds to improve and build infrastructure (roads and railroads) and educational systems.

Even as economic growth could build the power of the state in the short run, it did not produce nations that were unified in the long run. Divisions along the lines of social class and ethnicity persisted. In some nations, such as Mexico, such divisions resulted in social strife and even revolution. However, another thing that hastened the revolution in Mexico was the development of an authoritarian state.

Consolidating nationalism, part III: Imposing private property on all

For foreign investment and trade to flourish, there had to be a free-market economy based on private property holding citizens. Authoritarian Liberal leaders aimed to create such an economy and society. The best example of a Liberal leader who became authoritarian was Porfirio Díaz in Mexico. With Porfirio Díaz's consolidation of power in the late nineteenth century, Mexican nationalism—the elite conception of it—grew in power and importance.

Mexico, like a number of Latin American nations, had been a collage of a number of "patrias chicas" (small republics). There was not much of a sense of overall Mexican "nationhood." As such, to create a national unity—and a sense of nationalism—would be a tall order. Díaz, in many respects, was successful—at least for a few decades. Arguably, however, Díaz's top-down nationalism helped to create the conditions for the Mexican Revolution of 1910–1940.

Some resisted the top-down policies. Díaz used the "palo" (stick) to maintain order on his regime's terms. Díaz, of course, was not the only Latin American leader to use the stick to maintain order. In the late nineteenth and early twentieth centuries, the militaries of the various Latin American nations came into their own, providing the force to maintain Liberal authoritarian rule. For example, since Liberals wanted to break up communal Indian landholdings, provoking Indian resistance, the army was instrumental in carrying out the (private property) wishes of the Liberal oligarchs. A private property system was not only considered progressive: it was also instrumental to the export-driven agricultural model of the oligarchs. Liberal oligarchs also wanted to ensure that "mano de obra" (the labor force) was malleable to the needs of the elites—that is, that strong, independent unions did not form that could challenge the state. A more pliable labor force, of course, benefitted the owners of large corporations in Mexico, including MNCs. Forcing a private property system on the Indians, to their detriment, was socially destabilizing.

Liberals also wanted to socially integrate Indians into the body politic. Social integration meant bringing indigenous peoples into the body politic on the terms of the elite. These peoples would be educated in state-run schools and speak the official language (Spanish or Portuguese), whether they wanted to or not. The Indians would also be forced to learn Western culture and history. If there was significant resistance to the top-down integration projects, these various integration projects would be carried out by force.

Consolidating nationalism from above, part IV: Positivism and "progress"

Given the dislocations and social conflict caused by Liberal policies, it was not surprising the Liberals embraced authoritarianism as a way of increasing the power of the state and the nation. In addition, Díaz was fulfilling the dream of the nineteenth-century positivists in Latin America. Latin American Liberals embraced positivism as the only way of producing order and progress in Latin America. Indeed, positivism proved to be one of the most enduring and important aspects of Latin American politics and society.

Positivism, developed by European intellectuals in the mid-nineteenth century, was the doctrine that free-market economic growth, coupled with the rational (scientific method, by means of social science, a new field at the time) application of carefully thought out government policy to social problems, could create a stable society of happy citizens. In turn, the power of the Latin American nation would also increase, which would give it more leverage in negotiating with other nations. Latin America would become culturally and economically advanced, joining the industrialized powers of the world.

The only way, positivists argued, to foster progress for the entire society was to apply the scientific method to society. The scientific method, which until the late nineteenth century was confined to the natural sciences, called for coming up with carefully thought out hypotheses and rigorous collection and analysis in order to produce accurate and replicable findings. So, the positivists concluded—why not apply natural science techniques to society? Thus, social science—the Latin American variant of it—was born. With the careful application of social science to social problems, whether it was poverty, lack of education, or social divisions leading to conflict, order was valued above all else. Positivists were concerned with social order and economic prosperity above all else. Indeed, social order was viewed as a key determinant of economic prosperity. Businessmen would not be willing to invest funds in productive enterprises if they feared that social disorder would destroy their investment. As such, many positivists were uninterested in democracy—because it might lead to disorder. It is no surprise, then, that the slogan on the Brazilian flag is "ordem e progreso" ("order and progress"), the two most hallowed ideals of the positivists.

FIGURE 5.1 *Brazilian flag. The caption says "order and progress."* Source: *Public domain.*

Consolidating nationalism from above, part V: The military

The top-down authoritarian Liberalism in late nineteenth-century Latin America was, as noted above, socially disruptive. Authoritarian leaders justified their top-down rule by concluding that only a firm hand from above could keep the individual nations together as cohesive units. A more organized and efficient military served these authoritarian leaders well.

Since positivism was a European import, it was not surprising that Latin Americans would look to Europe for a key institution that would provide for social stability: a more organized and powerful military modeled on the European militaries. In the mid-nineteenth century, the Latin American militaries were small, underfunded groups. However, there were two major developments that caused the Latin American militaries to become more powerful by the late nineteenth and the early twentieth centuries.

First, some men from the *campo* (countryside), in particular Indians, joined national guards as part of a broader political movement. For example, in Mexico in the late 1850s, with the "Liberal Revolution," national guards were formed to fight the Conservative opposition. These national guards, sometimes providing a political counterweight to local elites, helped to infuse a sense of nationhood in people from the countryside. In Peru, national guards formed to fight the Chileans in the War of the Pacific, which occurred during 1879–1884.[5]

Second, the Latin American militaries, by the early twentieth century, obtained resources from European and US militaries. As governmental resources were limited in many Latin American nations in the early twentieth century, Latin American nations gladly accepted outside support for their militaries. Many Latin American militaries were trained and funded first by European countries and then by the United States. The United States began sending military advisors to Latin America largely in response to the fear that Europeans might be using military aid to extend their influence into the Western Hemisphere. Going back to the Monroe Doctrine of 1823, in which the United States called a halt to the expansion of European influence in the Americas, the United States has been concerned with any growth of European influence in Latin America.

Such concerns reached high levels once German and Italian fascist governments began sending their military trainers—and thousands of dollars of military materiel—to some (strategically located) Latin American nations. As such, US military aid first began to flow to Latin America in the early 1920s in the form of military advisors to the various Latin American militaries (termed "military groups" or Milgroups). Later, the US government gave direct US military assistance, or materiel, to the militaries in the region. Such assistance was first given to counter what the United States saw as (fascist) European designs on the Americas. Later, US leaders viewed building up the Latin American militaries as a way of "immunizing" the Latin American nations against communism.

Conclusion: Looking back, and looking ahead

In sum, Latin American nationalism in the late nineteenth and early twentieth centuries went through probably its most significant change. To understand this transformation, it is important to understand the historical context of Latin American nationalism going back to its early nineteenth-century roots. Second, it is important to understand the impact of globalization on Latin American nationalism.

With regard to historical context, the sociologist Gino Germani set forth what he terms six stages of nationalism. First, there were the revolutions and wars for national independence in the early nineteenth century. Second, anarchy and caudillioismo followed, as well as civil wars in some countries. Third, there were unifying dictatorships, attempting to promote positivism as a means toward progress: economic, social, and political. As the nineteenth century was a period in which globalization was happening rapidly, it is not surprising that the Latin Americans imported this important concept from abroad. Also, as the Latin American nations began to export more and more commodities abroad, it increased the wealth of the Latin American nations. Such wealth was controlled (at first) by dictators. However, not surprisingly, the nonelite Latin Americans, once they saw the tremendous wealth created by commodities exports, wanted democracy and a more equitable sharing of the wealth.

Fourth, by the early nineteenth century, representative "democracies" with limited participation, normally of elites, began to appear. Fifth, there were representative democracies with limited participation. Sixth, there were representative democracies with near total representation.

In the early twentieth century, Latin America embarked on the transition from representative "democracies" with limited participation to representative democracies with enlarged participation. This was the era of Latin American populism, which had a tremendous impact on the expansion of Latin American nationalism. This development will be examined in the next chapter.

Study Questions

1. What is positivism? How did it impact Latin America in the late nineteenth century?
2. How did the increasing pace of globalization affect Latin America in the late nineteenth century?
3. Discuss the major political parties in Latin America in the late nineteenth century. What are their most important attributes?
4. What were the most important changes in Latin American nationalism in the late nineteenth century?

For Further Reading

Galeano, Eduardo. *Open Veins of Latin America—Five Centuries of the Pillaging of a Continent.* New York: Monthly Review Press, 1973.
Loveman, Brian. *For la Patria—Politics and the Armed Forces in Latin America.* Lanham, MD: Rowman & Littlefield Publishers, 1999.
Ocampo, José Antonio and Juan Martin. *Globalization and Development—Latin American and Caribbean Perspective.* Santiago: UN Commission for Latin America and the Caribbean, 2003.

CHAPTER SIX

Latin American Nationalism in the Early to Mid-Twentieth Century: New Conceptions of Nationalism Spring Up

We want neither the barbarism of the gaucho *nor the barbarism of the cosmopolitan. We want a national culture to be the source of national civilization, and an art that will be the expression of both phenomena.*

RICARDO ROJAS, ARGENTINE NATIONALIST OF THE EARLY 20TH CENTURY,
QUOTED IN SAMUEL BAILY[1]

Introduction

As discussed in Chapters Two through Five, Latin American nationalism from its beginning after the Wars for Independence in the early nineteenth century was essentially a top-down, elite-driven process. Although the vast majority of the soldiers who fought for their independence were Indians, Afro-Latin Americans, and nonelite mestizos, they did not have much say in how the new nations of Latin America were constructed. However, nonelite Latin Americans, by the early twentieth century, played a major role in a new construction of nationalism; they were the impetus behind a new, more inclusive Latin American nationalism.

There were two main challenges in the early twentieth century to top-down, elite-sponsored nationalism that caused Latin American nationalism to become more inclusive. One was the rise of indigenous nationalism in the 1910s and 1920s. These nationalists, nearly all of whom were Indian,

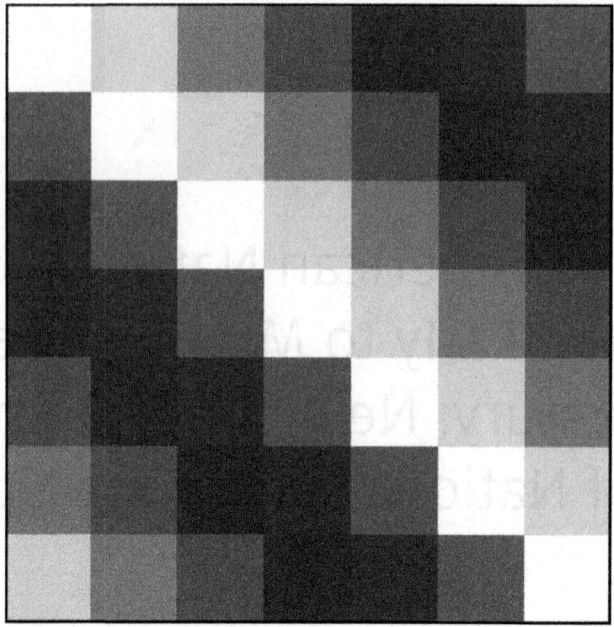

FIGURE 6.1 *Wiphala (flag of the Andean indigenous peoples)*. Source: *Public domain.*

aimed to forge a more inclusive vision of nationalism. The second was urban populism, which had roots that went back to the turn of the twentieth century but really did not flower until the 1940s. The majority of the urban populists were white or mestizo. As such, not surprisingly, they clung to some of the positivists' pro-European bias, in particular with regard to racism. National identity was key for both of these "counternationalist" movements. These movements aimed to create different "imagined communities" in Latin America. As these challenges welled up from the nonelite majority, Latin American politics changed from their nineteenth-century situation as being a struggle between (elite) Liberals and Conservatives to a struggle between the political left (nonelites) and the political right (some members of the middle class and elites). Left-wing nationalism will be explored in Chapter Eight and right-wing nationalism in Chapter Eleven.

First, indigenous or "Indian nationalism" will be discussed. There was an important cultural side of indigenous nationalism. The US, European, and Latin American mestizo urban elite "discovery" of and fascination with the Indians in the 1910s and 1920s facilitated the rise of indigenous nationalism. Newly discovered archeological sites proved key in this regard. (Ironically— or perhaps tellingly—they were discovered by non–Latin Americas. Since early forms of Latin American nationalism were top-down affairs in which the ideas were imported from Europe, perhaps it is not surprising that it was non–Latin Americans who were the archeological trailblazers in Latin America.) In the second decade of the twentieth century, archeology provided fertile ground for the growth of an "Indian nationalism." The pre-Inca ruins at Tiawanku, in the Bolivian altiplano (high plain), sparked interest not only in the ancient Indian civilizations but also in the plight of Indians within Bolivia. They were first systematically excavated by an Austrian archeologist, Arthur Poznansky, in the early twentieth century. More well known is the famous Inca ruins at the so-called Lost City of the Inca, Machu Picchu ("discovered" by US anthropologist Hiram Bingham in 1912), which helped to foment interest in Indian cultures in Latin America and around the world. Peruvian nationalists, in particular Indians and mestizos, began to see Peru's Inca heritage as central to their sense of Peruvian nationalism.[2]

Increasingly in the 1920s, mestizos who had not set foot outside of their cities began to venture into the countryside, curious to better understand the Indians. They were simultaneously aghast at the dreadful living conditions of the Indians as well as fascinated by what they saw was a culture that seemed both "exotic" and close to nature. Indeed, most of the Europeanized elites of Latin America's cities, and the mestizos as well, saw themselves as superior to the Indians as "civilized" and the Indians as "primitive" or "savage." The fact that nearly all Indians lived in small villages, or in the countryside, and did not have many physical possessions, and in some cases lived off the land, reinforced an already existing, powerful idea in Western civilization—the

FIGURE 6.2 *Picture of Araucanian Indians, Chile.* Source: *Columbus Memorial Library, Organization of American States, Washington, DC.*

idea of the "noble savage." That is, the only way that Indians have ever lived, and could and should live, is in a state of nature. The "noble savage" idea portrays the Indians as having no or minimal culture. In addition, so the "noble savage" argument goes, Indian culture, what little there is of it, is unchanging over the millennia.

Indigenous/Indian and mestizo nationalism: The case of Mexico

Revolutionary Indian nationalism burst upon the Latin American stage with the Mexican Revolution of 1910–1940. One important aspect of the revolution was that the Mexican people had chafed under the dictatorial regime of Porfirio Díaz for too long. (Díaz's regime was discussed in the previous chapter.) The resistance to Díaz was divided along the lines of geography, social class, and ethnicity. But, eventually, the resistance to Díaz's regime proved strong enough to force him from power. A second important aspect of the Mexican Revolution was resistance to foreign landownership and foreign investment in the country. Many Mexicans perceived that foreign landholders and large foreign investors (the oil industry is a good example) had too much control over Mexican government policy. Díaz's government, this argument went, was overly concerned with bringing in foreign investment, which served the needs of Díaz and his supporters but not that of the majority of the Mexican people.

Although the Mexican Revolution was a vastly multifaceted and complicated event, discussed in more detail in the next chapter, one important strain was indigenous or Indian nationalism, especially in southern Mexico. Emiliano Zapata (part Nahua Indian and part Spanish), from the state of Morelos in the south-central part of Mexico, became world famous as an Indian revolutionary, who lead a mestizo-Indian army to regain access to lands that had been taken by mestizos, either through legal chicanery or force. The followers of Zapata, many of whom were Indians, were termed "Zapatistas." As such, Zapatista nationalism was a form of Indian nationalism.

Zapata had little interest in governing all of Mexico; he mainly fought for his people's access to land. The focus of his movement was on the dispossessed, a large number of who were Indian. Over the years, large haciendas, through legal chicanery or coercion, had expanded at the expense of the smaller landholders, including communally owned Indian landholders. Dictator Díaz allowed for and facilitated the large hacienda owners, his political base, to either buy land inexpensively from formerly communally held Indian community lands or simply take it outright. Not only did the growth of the already large hacienda owners please Díaz's constituency; Díaz saw private property ownership as modern and forward thinking and communal Indian ownership as inefficient and backward.

However, not only economic issues animated the Indians. Indian cultural nationalism in early twentieth-century Mexico became a very important part of the Mexican national psyche, and entered the worldwide stage as well, with a flowering of Mexican art with indigenous themes. The most famous indigenous nationalist artist was not an Indian at all—Diego Rivera. Indian nationalist art divided the world into a Manichean division between Indian and European. The divide between the two is stark—a very "revisionist" view. Europeans are portrayed as excessively greedy conquistadores or outside, foreign investors, or large landowners. Indian cultural nationalist artists depicted Indian society in utopian terms—well-developed, well-organized Mayan and Aztec civilizations. This Indian cultural nationalism was a form of cultural resistance against the top-down, mestizo nationalism of prerevolutionary Mexico. The legacy of the Mexican Revolution would prove lasting. Later revolutionaries in the 1990s, in Chiapas, a mixed coalition of Indians and mestizos, would borrow Zapata's name and call themselves the Zapatistas. The Zapatistas would, through the use of instantaneous, global communications, have a worldwide following in the late 1990s and early twenty-first century.

Such indigenous nationalism was a response to the European-imported positivism, which, at its most racist, viewed the Indian past as an albatross around the neck of Latin America. How these nationalists viewed their past tells us a great deal about their worldview. Indigenous nationalists in Mexico were very proud of the accomplishments of the Maya and Aztec empires. Artists, in particular muralists, depicted these former empires in a very positive light while at the same time portraying the Spanish as greedy, bloodthirsty imperialists. One of the important Mexican revolutionary intellectuals, José Vasconcelos, came up with the concept of the "cosmic race." He articulated what many mestizos in Mexico—and other parts of the region—had thought for centuries: mestizaje had created a unique culture in Mexico. Vasconcelos, who served as Minister of Education in Mexico during the revolution, viewed the cosmic race as essentially the harmonization of opposing forces. He believed that mestizaje as a process will over time work out racial differences.[3] In addition, in this conception of mestizaje, mestizos combine the best attributes of the Indian and European races. As such, it represented not only a new, innovative culture; it was also superior to both European and Indian cultures.

Latin America's most potent indigenous nationalism—the case of the Andes

In the nations of the Andes, Indians in the mid-twentieth century began to make it clear that they were unwilling to accept second-class citizenship status. Indians could not even enter certain (white/mestizo) parts of Latin

American cities. Racism in the Andean region prevented Indians from pursuing certain careers and even deprived them of justice before the law. Most Indians were poor. Moreover, Indians in this part of Latin America historically resented the fact that whites and mestizos in essence demanded that they either downplay or even deny their Indian past as the only "ticket" to full-fledged citizenship status in the nation. Until recently, the educational systems of the Andean nations did not include information on the Indian past although the Indians were a significant portion of the population. Moreover, until recently, Indian languages were not taught in the schools. Until the mid- to late twentieth century, whites and mestizos assumed that their nation could not progress until the Indians basically gave up their culture. The Indians demanded that their culture be given the same status as European culture.

As a means of advancing social, political, and economic gains, Indians began to emphasize that they were part of a separate nation within the broader national unit (Ecuador, Peru, Bolivia, or whatever Andean country where they lived). Indians who felt they were part of a separate indigenous nation within the broader national unit were members of two nations simultaneously. Indigenous congresses were held in the 1940s in some Andean nations. Such efforts proved successful in reducing anti-Indian discrimination.

Indigenous nationalism has, as one of its roots, the ill treatment of Native Americans not only by the state but by multinational companies (MNCs) as well. An early example was the large British companies that invested in rubber production in the early twentieth century in Peru—in particular Inambari Pará Rubber Estates, the Tambopata Rubber Syndicate, and the Cerro de Pasco Mining Company. By paying Peruvian authorities a nominal sum under the table, Indians could be forced into what only could be called a type of slavery in which physical abuse was common.[4] The Peruvian organization Asociación Pro-Indígena (Indian rights organization) protested this ill treatment, even employing help from transnational organizations, such as the British-based antislavery society, to get the word out with regard to this horrible treatment of the Indians. One of the first human rights activists who operated on multiple continents, Roger Casement, concluded:

> These [Indians] are not only murdered, flogged, chained up like wild beasts, hunted far and wide and their dwellings burnt, their wives raped, their children dragged away to slavery and outrage, but are shamelessly swindled into the bargain. These are strong words, but not adequately strong. The condition of things is the most disgraceful, the most lawless, the most inhuman I believe that exists in the world today.[5]

Indian nationalism, thus, can only be understood in a global context.

In some parts of nineteenth-century Latin America, Indians were the backbone of the economy—in particular with regard to providing labor and tribute (forced taxes paid to the state).[6] As immigration from Europe and Asia increased, the centrality of Native Americans to economic production was no longer so clear. However, as Indians were gradually stripped of their social and political rights in the late nineteenth and early twentieth centuries, and their culture denigrated, they no doubt remembered how central they were to the nineteenth-century economy. As such, by the mid-twentieth century, not surprisingly they had grown tired of second-class citizen status in the region and organized an Indian rights movement. This movement aimed to secure social justice/equality and political rights.

Ecuador and Bolivia as case studies

As in a number of Latin American countries in 1992, the quincentenary of Columbus' voyage to the New World, indigenous peoples in Ecuador used the anniversary as a way of protesting centuries of exploitation. Going back to the beginning of the national period, Ecuadorian elites associated themselves with the glory of the Indian past to legitimize their rule. Indeed, going back to the earliest years of Latin American nationalism, Simón Bolívar and Jose Antonio Sucre arranged, with the support of criollo elites (those of Spanish background), for Indians dressed as Sun Virgins to crown the two liberators as heroes. During Ecuador's early years, elites and mestizos portrayed the Indians as either descendants of "noble Inca" or savages. In either case, they (according to the elites) needed to accept the mores of Western civilization before they could progress. For their part, Indians in the nineteenth century resisted the top-down nationalism of the criollo elites by maintaining aspects of their traditional culture.

When compared with Ecuador, Bolivia has not only a larger indigenous population but also a richer Indian tradition. With regard to the rise of indigenous nationalism, Bolivia is extremely important since it has one of the largest indigenous populations in Latin America. As a percent of its total population, Bolivia is one of the "most Indian" nations, along with Guatemala. Not surprisingly, indigenous nationalism has played an important role in twentieth-century Bolivian history. Globalization played a role in the rise of this indigenous nationalism, with the consequences of the Chaco War of 1932–1936 between Paraguay and Bolivia proving key in this regard. Although the major antagonists were Paraguay and Bolivia, other South American nations played a role in the war, while US officials and others in the United States carefully observed the war. A number of observers (this perception was quite widespread in Bolivia) feared that multinational oil companies had prodded both nations toward war, and these companies' only interest was controlling the oil-rich lands of the Chaco region. There was little evidence of such meddling, but the perceptions were real. Also, outside nations attempted to mediate an end to what seemed to be senseless slaughter.

The Chaco War proved to be a major crisis in Bolivian nationalism because Bolivia lost about one-third of its territory to its neighbor, substantially redrawing the map of South America. However, it also greatly stimulated indigenous nationalism. The widely held, and largely accurate, perception of the Chaco War was that incompetent Bolivian political and military leadership caused the deaths of many nonelite mestizos and Indians, the "cannon fodder" of the war. Bolivians of all ethnicities concluded that major social change—even a revolution—would be necessary to prevent such a future debacle. However, a separate, but very important, strain of Bolivian nationalism—indigenous, or Indian, nationalism—was stimulated by the Chaco War. For many Indians, fighting, and seeing their Indian compatriots become casualties in a losing effort led by incompetent leaders, was the last straw. From the perspective of the Indians, they had been systematically abused by mestizos and whites: the white/mestizo elites had economically exploited the Indians, treated them unjustly, and excluded them socially. Now they were cannon fodder in an unnecessary, lost war. Until the Bolivian Revolution of 1952, some Indians, called pongos, were legally bound to the haciendas they worked on. Basically, they were serfs. So, Indians began to organize to fight for basic human and political rights. A big part of their mission in organizing was not only to coerce mestizos and elite whites in Bolivia for better treatment by Bolivian civil society; it was also to get the white/mestizo majority to realize that Indian culture was not inferior to European culture.[7]

Indian nationalism, however, was not the only "bottom-up" nationalist surge in the early to mid-twentieth century. Urban populists, made up of the urban working and middle classes, demanded more political say, and elites ceded some political power to them. (Urban populism is discussed below.) The two, new bottom-up forms of nationalism reinforced each other in synergistic fashion. In the early to mid-twentieth century, in part due to the populists' inclusion of the urban working and middle classes as part of the national project of the various Latin American nations, Indians began to resist the elite-constructed national project of the nineteenth century. Often working in barbarous conditions in the countryside, and living on starvation wages, they began to demand to be treated as equals to whites and mestizos. Asserting a separate Indian national identity, separate from their Ecuadorian national identity, was central to this struggle.[8]

Populism, nationalism, and globalization

Argentinian Juan Perón was the most well known of the Latin American populist leaders. Born in 1895, he entered the military and quickly rose through the ranks, participating in a 1943 coup which brought in reform-minded group of leaders. Peron ran for president in 1946, and, helped by the support of his charismatic wife Eva, became the hero of Argentina's urban

FIGURE 6.3 *Populist leader Juan Perón, President of Argentina, 1946–1955, 1973–1974.* Source: *Hulton-Deutsch/Hulton-Deutsch Collection/Corbis via Getty Images.*

working and lower middle classes. Although the military ousted him from power in 1955, he returned from exile in late 1972 to lead Argentina again, until his death two years later.

Indigenous nationalism was not the only bottom-up challenge to top-down, elite-driven nationalism. A second type of revolutionary nationalism that would cast a very long shadow on Latin American history was the rise of urban-based working and middle-class populist nationalism. It was termed "Populist" because before the rise of such governments, Latin American nations were largely run by the elites, and in most cases, the elites' basis of power was their large landholdings in the campo. Populist leaders' support, however, lay in the urban working and middle classes. The two most well-known, and probably best, examples are Juan Perón in Argentina and Getúlio Vargas in Brazil. Although populists generally shied away from terming their movements revolutionary as such, the profound changes they provoked, and implemented, caused such a tremendous change in Latin American economics, society, and politics that one could conclude populism was revolutionary.

Although these two figures did not rise to power until the 1930s, populism in Latin America largely took the form it did because of two key, early twentieth-century events that rocked Latin America, in particular economically, clearly displaying that it did not have a great degree of control over its situation. The first of these events was the Great War (later known as the First World War). The second event was the worldwide Great Depression of the 1930s. The First World War resulted in the severing of economic ties between Europe and Latin America, causing great economic pain in the region. As economic ties between Europe and Latin America were quickly dissolved, it seemed that Latin America's economic, social, and political stability would dissolve as well. Latin America's debilitating dependence for selling primary or raw materials to the lucrative European market, as well as Latin America's dependence on Europe for both investment and physical capital for Latin America's economy, was clearly shown. Although the Latin American economies recovered in the 1920s, there was a distinct difference in the post–First World War situation; increasing economic ties with the United States would become more important than such ties had been with Europe.

Stock market speculation proved to be the catalyst for the biggest economic downturn in world history, later known as the 1930s Great Depression. However, because the Depression was a complicated, multifaceted, long-lasting event, it is not surprising that there were many causes of it, not just the collapse of world financial markets. For decades, in tandem with industrialization, economic inequality around the world had grown. That meant that working-class and lower-middle-class people did not have the disposable income to buy the increasing large mountain of products churned out by an increasingly productive capitalist system. Although businessmen realized that they needed to facilitate the easy purchase of consumer goods through innovative techniques (company financing of "big-ticket" items such as cars increased demand) in order to keep consumers buying such items at a rapid rate, such innovation was not enough to reduce inequality. Another set of causes of the Depression can be found in the reaction of the world's central banks. It did not help that the world's central bankers (including the US central bank, the Federal Reserve) decided at this very inopportune time to restrict the flow of money and credit to the industrialized world's economies—thinking that "sound money" would somehow provide a security blanket to economies in peril. Instead, as central banks around the globe crimped money and credit, the world's economies spiraled ever downward. Thus, governmental financial policy abetted the problems of the real (nonmonetary, noncredit) economy, reinforcing the downward trend in the economy.

Before the Great Depression, much of Latin America was imbedded in the world economy. Countries like Argentina (beef and foodstuffs) and Brazil (coffee), for example, were more intricately connected to the world economy than others. In fact, Argentina's world trade was one reason why, before the First World War and its interruption of trade between Europe and the Western Hemisphere, Argentina was one of the world's wealthiest nations, and Buenos Aires was considered the Paris of the Western Hemisphere. In 1900, per-capita gross domestic product of Argentina was only slightly less than that of France.

With the Depression, Latin American nations suddenly were cutoff from supplies of industrialized goods, both goods for factories and finished products for (middle-class and elite) consumers. Although the Latin American nations knew before the Depression, on some level, they were dependent on the industrialized nations for key items, in the 1930s it became painfully evident. In turn, as the Latin American economies soured, social and political conflict sharpened. In fact, all but three of Latin America's nations experienced a nondemocratic (often violent) change of government in the 1930s, in part due to the deepening worldwide economic crisis.

The Latin American response to the Depression was both logical and nationalistically brilliant. Many Latin American nations decided to implement statist (government directed) economic policies, including Import Substitution Industrialization (ISI). Latin American nations would increase tariffs, both protecting infant industries and promoting foreign investment in their economies. With high tariffs, industrial world capitalists would invest "behind the tariff wall." A second part of ISI was that the nation would control key sectors of the economy (e.g., railroads, utilities, airlines, some heavy industries) to ensure they were vibrant contributors to the economic system.

National control over these key sectors was given a boost with two extremely important events in the history of globalization—the Second World War and the rapid decolonization of the European empires, exhausted from their bruising battles in the Second World War. These most important of mid-twentieth-century events reinforced each other, as the resource-exhausted European nations after the Second World War had a hard time paying the costs of maintaining their empires. During the Second World War, the Latin American nations greatly increased their stock of foreign exchange. During the war, they sold large amounts of primary products at high prices to the Allied wartime powers—products necessary for the Allies to win the war. Simultaneously, Latin American nations could not spend this exchange on world markets, since the war had caused world trade to sharply decline. With this mountain of foreign exchange, some Latin American nations bought foreign-owned key industries in their nations, so they could control these key sectors of the economy. For example, after the Second World War, the British sold their (decrepit) railroad system to the Argentine government. Although the railroads were in need of repair, the Argentines were happy to now control a key sector of their economy.

Scholar William Robinson summed up the varied strands of ISI very well in a recent book. Instead of using the term "ISI," he uses the term "developmentalist capitalism," a term only a bit less cumbersome than "Import Substitution Industrialization." This form of capitalism, which became quite common after the Second World War in a number of developing world nations, "involv[ed] a much greater role for the state and the public sector; mass social mobilizations growing out of anti-colonial, anti-dictatorial, national-liberation movements; and populist or corporatist political projects." The term "corporatism" means, in this context, that some Latin American states, in particular during the "high tide" of ISI, attempted to unify the politics and society of their nations by establishing a degree of government intervention and even control over segments of society and the economy—for example, labor unions and business organizations. By establishing "official" labor unions and business organizations, the government could exert a degree of control over these sectors of the economy.[9]

ISI made virtually everyone in the Latin American nations happy. As such, it is not surprising that ISI proved to have a great deal of staying power—all the way up to the 1970s. ISI, along with the nationalization of key industries, formed the bedrock of many Latin American populist governments in the 1940s and 1950s, two of the key examples being Perón's Argentina (1946–1955) and Vargas' Brazil (1930–1945, 1951–1954). Working-class people and unions realized that ISI meant, at least in the short run, a growing economy and therefore more job security. Businessmen enjoyed the high tariff walls, not wanting of course to compete with more efficient foreign producers. Riding this wave of economic prosperity for all were charismatic leaders such as Perón and Vargas. All in all, a stronger economy meant a stronger nation—and average Brazilian and Argentine people appreciated both the stronger economy and nation, embodied in the forceful leadership of the populist movements of the 1940s. Although ISI would cause conflict with the United States in the postwar period, and ultimately ISI would begin to unravel in the 1970s, it proved to be a useful and important policy for Latin American nationalists from the Great Depression until the 1970s. Indeed, it is important to note that ISI represented a new departure in political economy, building up the power of the various Latin American nations. Thus, ISI could be termed a nationalist-populist doctrine of political economy.

Conclusion: The new nationalisms of early to mid-twentieth-century Latin America

Indian nationalism along with mestizo nationalism would prove to be a very important movement in twentieth-century Latin American history. Because of the political exclusion of Indians in the region, the bonds of Indian nationalism facilitated the organization of diverse Indian groups. These groups have demanded political equality and strive for a more economically egalitarian society. With regard to mestizo nationalism, since mestizos form the majority population in most Latin American states, mestizo nationalism has greatly "broadened the base" of Latin American nationalism.

Urban populism, like mestizo nationalism, very much broadened the base of Latin American nationalism. ISI not only was a response to the economic, social, and political crises of Latin America. It was also an economic nationalist policy. Economic nationalists argued that the only way the Latin American nations could fully benefit from their nations raw materials was for the nation to control it. Further, economic nationalists concluded the only way for a Latin American nation to develop economically and diversify its economy was for that nation to put controls on outside economic activity, including nationalizing key industries. This powerful formulation of Latin American nationalism, economic nationalism, would come into direct conflict with the US vision of economic globalization—an open world for US commerce everywhere.

Study Questions

1. What are the key differences between "top-down" nationalism and the "bottom-up" forms of nationalism discussed in this chapter?
2. What are the key differences between urban populism on the one hand and Indian/Afro-Latin American nationalism on the other?
3. How did indigenous and mestizo nationalism change Latin American nationalism as a whole?

For Further Reading

Castro-Klarén, Sara. "The Nation in Ruins: Archeology and the Rise of the Nation." In *Beyond Imagined Communities: Reading and Writing the Nation in 19th Century Latin America*, edited by Sara Castro-Klaren and John Chasteen, 161–95. Baltimore, MD: Johns Hopkins University Press, 2003.

Conniff, Michael, ed. *Populism in Latin America*, 2nd ed. Tuscaloosa, AL: University Alabama Press, 2012.

Gotkowitz, Laura. *Revolution for Our Rights—Indigenous Struggles for Latin and Justice in Bolivia, 1880–1952*. Durham, NC: Duke University Press, 2007.

Langer, Erick and Elena Munoz, eds. *Contemporary Indigenous Movements in Latin America*. Lanham, MD: Rowman & Littlefield Publishers, 2003.

Lee Anderson, Jon. "The Distant Shore—In Peru, a Killing Brings an Isolated Tribe into Contact with the Outside World." *New Yorker* 92 (Aug 8–15): 40–51.

Rockwell, Elsie. "Schools of the Revolution: Enacting and Contesting State Forms in Tlaxcala, 1910–1930." In *Everyday Forms of State Formation—Revolution and the Negotiation of Rule in Modern Mexico*, edited by Gilbert M. Joseph and Daniel Nugent, 170–208. Durham, NC: Duke University Press, 1994.

Vasconcelos, Jose. *La raza cosmica. The Cosmic Race*, 2nd ed. Baltimore, MD: Johns Hopkins University Press, 1997.

CHAPTER SEVEN

The Eagle and the Nationalists: The United States Responds to Economic Nationalism in Latin America during the Great Depression

If the criteria of the International Monetary Fund had governed the United States in the 19th century, our own economic development would have taken a good deal longer. In preaching fiscal orthodoxy to developing nations, we were somewhat in the position of the prostitute who, having retired on her earnings, believes that public virtue requires the closing down of the red light district.

ARTHUR SCHLESINGER, JR., QUOTED IN DUNCAN GREEN[1]

Economic nationalism is the common denominator of the new aspirations for industrialization. Latin Americans are convinced that the first beneficiaries of the development of a country's resources should be the people of that country.

LAURENCE DUGGAN[2]

US versus Latin American nationalists: Clashing visions

The European imperial surge in the late fifteenth and sixteenth centuries (discussed in Chapter One) provided an important impetus to globalization. European expansion continued, little by little, into almost all corners of the globe—until the First World War sapped the resources of many European nations and put a halt to further imperialist expansion. Indeed, in response to seemingly inexorable European expansion in the eighteenth and early nineteenth centuries, US president James Monroe issued one of the more important pronouncements of US foreign policy: the Monroe Doctrine of 1823. Although many history textbooks have characterized the doctrine as stating that Europe must have a "hands-off" policy toward the Americas, North and South, in reality the Monroe Doctrine, in a more limited fashion, called for the containment of already existing European influence (in particular, colonies) in the Americas.

Another imperial surge occurred in the late nineteenth century with the industrialization of the European powers. With industrialization, there was a two-pronged drive to globalize. First, with growing industries and populations, the European nations needed raw materials, and foodstuffs, from abroad. Second, as industrialists became increasingly efficient and productive, the European nations increasingly sought markets overseas as a means of combatting economic gluts that could lead to economic downturns. Even as many European nations were expanding their "formal" empires overseas—increasing the size of their colonies and adding new ones—they were also extending their informal empires. This was of special significance for Latin America. Even as the Latin American nations retained their political sovereignty won at the cost of a large amount of blood and treasure with the Wars for Independence against Spain in the early nineteenth century, by the late nineteenth century, their economic sovereignty was being undermined. At this time, as the economic power of the European nations grew and reached out to Latin America, these nations, or multinational companies (MNCs) based in these nations, controlled significant portions of the Latin America economy.

A number of Latin American nations were on the receiving end of a "neocolonial" relationship with a more powerful European nation or the United States. Neocolonialism is different from "formal" imperialism. "Formal" imperialism means that a powerful nation establishes political control over territory overseas against the will of that territory's inhabitants. Neocolonialism, also referred to as "informal imperialism," uses economic and cultural techniques to expand the power of a powerful nation to unwilling inhabitants of foreign nations. The reasons for such expansion include desire for control over key resources or to expand foreign markets. The expansion of foreign markets was often due to a desire to improve the economic situation at home for the powerful nation; improving the economic situation, it was thought, would foster political and social stability. Significantly, the host nations did not simply accept the powerful nation's neocolonial extension of power. Often, they resisted such an imposition. Sometimes, they accepted parts of the economic and cultural attributes of the powerful nation while putting their own stamp on such cultural influences.

Neocolonialism had a profound impact on the social structure of Latin America. As the growing middle classes of North America and Europe increasingly enjoyed consuming products from Latin America, such as bananas, coffee, and sugar, and as their industrialized economies relied more and more on oil, some of it imported from Latin America, the export-driven sectors of these economies became more and more lucrative (see Chapter Five). The elites of Latin America who controlled the export-driven segments of the economy grew rich and had a greater incentive to extend their land holdings further and further into the country. As these elites bought up, or simply expropriated, more land from poorer farmers who thus lost their small holdings to the large landowners, there were more landless people in Latin America. (Many of the poorer farmers were Indians.) With more landless people, there was a larger pool of available labor to work on the growing haciendas of the elite who made more money by exporting products overseas. As this pool of labor expanded, wages fell, which suited the large hacienda owners. However, as the ranks of the landless peasants grew, and as their wages stagnated or fell, they could not feed their families.

A good example is in the Yucatán Peninsula of Mexico, where MNCs based in the United States owned large tracts of land they used for growing hemp—a very important product for making rope, a critically important product for the rapidly industrializing United States. As the foreign-owned hemp plantations acquired more and more land from small Yucatan farmers, resentment against the United States grew, which eventually burst into open rebellion during the Mexican Revolution.[3]

By the late nineteenth century, two other up-and-coming nations became imperial powers—Japan and the United States. (US foreign policy toward Latin America will be further discussed in Chapter Nineteen.) Although many US citizens do not see the United States as an imperial power, by 1898 it had become an extra-continental power, adding Hawaii, the Philippines, Guam, and Puerto Rico to its list of colonies. In its imperial drive, the United States was animated by the abovementioned factors—search for (inexpensive and plentiful) raw materials and for markets overseas (Asia, in particular China, was a goal).

One of the most influential scholars of US naval power, Admiral Alfred T. Mahan, in the late nineteenth century, wrote a number of articles arguing that the US government needed to increase the size and the power of the US Navy. He argued that a more powerful navy was important because throughout history, all powerful nations had had powerful navies. He also concluded that US overseas commerce needed to expand overseas in order to keep the US economy productive. And to protect a larger merchant marine, a larger navy was needed. To ensure that the larger merchant marine and navy had way stations and coaling stations, the United States needed to have access to overseas ports. To control such ports, the United States needed to take a few, small colonies overseas.

The US acquisition of the Panama Canal Zone in 1903 was another territorial position, and the construction of the Canal also aided US overseas commerce as well as made a two-ocean US Navy more efficient at protecting US interests overseas. Significantly, too, after the US victory against Spain in the Spanish-American War of 1898, the United States placed a protectorate on Spain's former colony, Cuba. The protectorate meant that Cuba would not be able to control its foreign policy and would have to abide US intervention to protect its citizens and property in the island. The protectorate would significantly increase anti-US Cuban nationalism.

Arguably, the US acquisition of colonies overseas was a form of "informal empire" or "insular imperialism." US leaders did not think that controlling large amounts of territory overseas, as the Europeans were doing with the "carving up" of Africa for example, was a good idea. US leaders did not want to absorb large numbers of nonwhite, Catholic people that many whites in the United States saw as racially inferior. Nor did US leaders want the expense, or the burden, of controlling large tracts of land overseas.

Instead, Washington officials supported the idea of an "open world" for US commerce and investment overseas—ideally in every corner of the world. Expanding US commerce, facilitated by owning strategically placed forts overseas, would eventually lead, it was thought, to such a world. Indeed, the famous "Open Door Notes" of 1899 and 1900 set forth a framework by which the United States could maximize its foreign trade and investment— without using (expensive) military force to achieve its goals. As "formal" imperialism came to a head in Africa in the late nineteenth century, US officials intensified their drive to promote a world open to US commerce, investment, and influence.

First battles of globalization and nationalism— the United States confronts economic nationalism in Latin America: Bolivian and Mexican oil

The US desire for an open world appeared to be coming to fruition in the 1920s. After the First World War, the world economy surged. As the capital of world finance moved from London to New York during the First World War, careful observers realized this represented an important shift in power and a significant change in the recent history of the world. US capitalists were extracting resources in, and investing in, a dizzying number of nations around the world. US products were even being consumed in faraway places such as Southeast Asia and South America. US movies were particularly popular in Europe, and baseball was becoming popular in nations such as Cuba, the Dominican Republic, Nicaragua, and Japan. Argentine author Manuel Ugarte proclaimed in 1925 that the United States was becoming, in effect, a "New Rome."[4] And, it is important to note that US economic foreign policy in the early twentieth century, an open world for the private sector, in particular US commerce and investment, was in its interests but not in the interests of the developing world. As the Arthur Schlesinger, Jr., quote at the beginning of this chapter indicates, US economic development in the nineteenth century was very much a function of high tariffs to protect US "infant industries" that could not compete with more efficient foreign competitors. But, by the early twentieth century, the United States was focused on taking down the barriers to foreign trade around the world. US leaders conveniently ignored the historical fact that high US tariffs were important to US economic/industrial development, even as Washington leaders, in the early twentieth century, hypocritically railed against such barriers to trade and investment should *other* nations implement such barriers to US exports and foreign investment.

US concern for improving its relations with Latin America in the 1920s was largely because US capitalists were trading and investing in Latin America more and more. In 1914, direct US investment in Latin America was $1.6 billion; by 1928 it was around $5.2 billion, about 30 percent of the total of such investment.[5] Interestingly, just as Latin America was becoming a very valuable economic asset to the United States, US-Latin American relations hit probably their worst nadir in about a century. Interhemispheric relations had soured due to repeated, and long-term, US military incursions into some Central American and Caribbean nations. To improve US relations with its southern "neighbors," the United States proclaimed the "Good Neighbor Policy" of the 1930s. US leaders, led by President Franklin D. Roosevelt, stated that the United States would not intervene militarily in Latin America. Latin American leaders, who had been calling for such a policy for decades, were extremely happy.

The Good Neighbor Policy, however, could not reconcile the clash behind US-sponsored globalization—the concept of an open world—and Latin American economic nationalism. Economic nationalists aimed to control key aspects of international economic activity in their country to ensure that such activity benefitted the host nation. Washington officials not only feared that economic nationalist policies would lead to inefficient Latin American economies. They also feared that Latin American nations could hurt the US economy by limiting or even closing off parts of Latin America's economy to US MNCs' economic activities. This clash of US economic and cultural expansion ran directly into Latin American nationalism. As Latin

America implemented Import Substitution Industrialization (discussed in the previous chapter), it simultaneously strengthened already existing economic nationalist ideas, which stretched back to the Mexican Revolution, if not further. Although a number of examples could be cited, two of the best are the oil expropriations in Bolivia and Mexico.

Economic nationalism in Bolivia

Landlocked, poor Bolivia proved to be a trailblazer in what was to eventually become a region-wide movement toward economic nationalism. There were unfounded but widespread rumors that US-based Standard Oil in Bolivia and the Anglo-Dutch multinational Shell Oil in Paraguay had provoked the Chaco War of 1932–1936 (discussed in the previous chapter). But such rumors proved to be powerful. The Bolivian government nationalized Standard Oil's holdings in 1937. Bolivian officials, in a sense, feared that the open world desired by the United States would create a world economic system in which the industrialized nations would disproportionally benefit from ever cheaper raw materials while the developing world would, in an open (economic) world, rapidly sell off its "national patrimony" (i.e., the subsoil minerals and oil), leaving no national wealth for future generations. In addition, Bolivian nationalists saw the expropriation of the foreign oil company's reserves as a way of asserting national control over a resource, the sale of which would be used to diversify and develop the nation's economy. It is important to note that the Bolivian expropriation of an entire industry was the first such expropriation in Latin American history and proved to be a model for future leftist nationalists in the years to come.

Not surprisingly, Standard Oil officials petitioned the US State Department to compel Bolivia to compensate the MNC. State Department officials obliged, and negotiations between the company, the Department, and Bolivian officials resulted not only in compensation for the company, but Bolivia received a promise of $25 million in economic assistance from the United States—an important precedent. It was perhaps the first significant US economic assistance offered to a developing world country (not counting US colonies and Cuba, which was a protectorate of the United States from 1898 to 1933).

The Mexican Revolution

The year after Bolivia's expropriation, a more significant and much more well-known expropriation occurred in Mexico—one of the world's biggest oil producers. Mexican oil production for world consumption went back to the early twentieth century. Porfirio Díaz's top-down, export-driven nationalism had called for Mexico to export as much as possible in order to earn foreign exchange—increasing Mexico's economic power. With the outbreak of the Mexican Revolution, bottom-up nationalists reversed Díaz's formulation. They thought that foreign control and sale of oil meant that only foreigners would benefit from Mexico's oil. They wanted the Mexican government to control Mexico's subsoil. The revolutionaries saw it as "national patrimony" to be carefully husbanded for future generations of Mexicans, not sold off willy-nilly to the highest bidder. Also, national control meant that the Mexican nation could use the proceeds from sales of oil to develop and diversify its economy.

The Mexican Revolution was a long, complicated affair. The revolution featured the rise of prominent Mexican revolutionary figures. Two of the more important ones were Francisco "Pancho" Villa and Venustiano Carranza who contributed to Mexican nationalism during the revolution. As their supporters were largely mestizo, their form of nationalism could be termed mestizo nationalism. Between the three figures of Zapata (discussed in the previous chapter), Villa, and Carranza, Mexican nationalism was a very diverse and complicated concept. Villa, a poor farmer from Mexico's north, fought to create a more egalitarian Mexico where lower-class Mexicans could have access to land and become well educated. Carranza, who also hailed from Mexico's north, wanted to create a strong Mexican nation.

Carranza used two main techniques to build the power of the nation. First, he organized the writing of a new constitution that he hoped would simultaneously grant increased rights to Mexican citizens, foster improved well-being among the citizenry, and build up the power of the Mexican state. Second, as a specific way of building up the power of the Mexican state, he nationalized the Mexican nation's subsoil (mineral and oil deposits). Written into the new Mexican Constitution during the revolution in 1917 (Article 27), the nationalization of the subsoil was in some ways continuous with the Spanish colonial tradition. In Spain, the royalty controlled the subsoil, granting concessions (if it wanted) to those who would exploit it (not just for individual gain but for the nation's benefit). For Carranza, with the nationalization of the subsoil, Mexico would have the resources to build a strong nation as well as to promote economic development and diversification which would benefit all Mexicans.

As such, Carranza proved a very important figure in the development of left-wing nationalism because he helped to push through the 1917 Constitution, which called for increased government intervention in the economy and society for the betterment of all. Previously, few Latin American governments had not intervened in the economy or society; laissez-faire ruled the day. Termed by one historian as "social constitutionalism," the 1917 Mexican Constitution was an inspiration to future left-wing nationalists in Latin America. Among other things, the new Constitution called for land and educational reform. Educational reform wrested control of the educational system from the Catholic Church while at the same time causing Mexican schoolchildren to view themselves as part of a new, revolutionary Mexican nation.[6]

How did Article 27 work in practice? Foreign multinational oil companies were not denied access to Mexico's oil, but they had to pay more for a concession to drill for oil. In a series of agreements, Mexico and the foreign oil companies decided that the companies would not have to pay the increased taxes on their pre-1917 concessions, only on post-1917 concessions. These agreements left nationalists unsatisfied that Mexico had sufficient control over its critically important oil supplies. During these years, the Mexican government's leadership's nationalist fervor was waning, and a desire to keep foreign oil companies operating in Mexico was increasing. However, in 1934, one of the more radical Mexican (and Latin American) governments came to power, that of Lázaro Cárdenas. He implemented one of Latin America's most thorough land reforms. Then, partly in response to a drawn out labor conflict between the multinational oil companies and their Mexican workers, in 1938 he nationalized the entire oil industry of Mexico. Cardenas had accepted the argument of the nationalists that only by full control of the Mexican economy could the Mexican nation ensure that it would fully benefit from Mexican oil reserves.

Conclusion: A new US foreign policy helps to stimulate Latin American economic nationalism

Nationalism, as this book argues, has many facets to it. Some are inward looking; others are more outward focused. Even as Latin American nationalists in the late nineteenth and early twentieth centuries were focused on economic, social, and cultural development as key aspects of their nation development, they were not ignoring the outside world. As US influence in the Western Hemisphere significantly grew in the late nineteenth and early twentieth centuries, Latin American economic nationalism grew as a sort of "shield" against a more assertively expansionistic United States. The scholar Nelson Werneck Sodré back in 1960 succinctly summed up the motivations behind economic nationalism when he said,

> Because now foreign economic forces are the greatest obstacle to our development and [as] their internal allies decline in power, they no longer hold the nation in tutelage. For any country with a colonial post, with an economic structure subordinated to foreign interest, to create

itself nationally is to accomplish a task in many ways similar to that would the European nations accomplished at the dawn of the Modern Age with the defeat of feudalism and the advance of capitalism. What for them were feudal relations, restrictions on development, are for us all that still remains of the colonial past. Nationalism presents itself as liberation.[7]

By the early twentieth century, the "foreign economic forces" that Werneck Sodré referred to were largely US-based companies and Latin American-US trade. In sum, Latin American economic nationalism was in response to a very important turning point in US foreign relations. Starting in the late nineteenth century, US foreign policy makers turned away from landed expansion, which they had been pursuing from the beginning, and instead promoted the economic and cultural expansion of the United States. This turn says a great deal about the process of globalization in the late nineteenth and early twentieth centuries and beyond. In stark contrast to the European powers that had recently carved up Africa (in a burst of landed imperial expansion in the late nineteenth century) for themselves, adding millions of square miles of territory to their empires, no longer would the United States seek to increase its power by territorial conquest. Although a number of late nineteenth- and early twentieth-century US leaders made this point publicly, Woodrow Wilson, in an influential speech on US policy toward Latin America in 1913, during the first year of his presidency, made the point very clearly.

As Washington shifted to promoting its economic and cultural interests overseas, Latin Americans viewed this as a tactical change, not a change in underlying expansionary US motives. That is, Latin Americans saw more continuity than change in US foreign policy. The United States would still be attempting to influence the situation in Latin America; it would simply use different means to do so. For their part, the Latin American nations aimed to strengthen their economies by means of a combination of Import Substitution Industrialization and economic nationalism. US leaders, starting in the post–Second World War period, would make a more concerted effort to coerce Latin America to "buy into" its vision of an open economic world.

Study Questions

1. What are the key sources of economic nationalism in Latin America?
2. What did the economic nationalists aim to achieve?
3. How does economic nationalism relate to nationalism as a whole?

For Further Reading

Gonzales, Michael J. *The Mexican Revolution, 1910–1940*. Albuquerque: University of New Mexico Press, 2002.

Joseph, Gilbert M. *Revolution from Without: Yucatan, Mexico, and the United States, 1880–1924*. Durham, NC: Duke University Press, 1987.

Lehman, Kenneth. *Bolivia and the United States: A Limited Partnership*. Athens: University Georgia Press, 1999.

Pike, Frederick. *FDR's Good Neighbor Policy: 60 Years of Generally Gentile Chaos*. Notre Dame, IN: Notre Dame University Press, 1995.

Smith, Robert Freeman. *The United States and Revolutionary Nationalism in Mexico, 1916–1932*. Chicago: University of Chicago Press, 1972.

Wood, Bryce. *The Making of the Good Neighbor Policy*. New York: Norton, 1967.

PART FOUR

Nationalism and Modernization

CHAPTER EIGHT

Reviving the Populist Dream: Rise of Left-Wing Nationalism after the Second World War

They would have overthrown us even if we had grown no bananas.

JOSÉ MANUEL FORTUNY QUOTED IN PIERO GLEIJESES[1]

Introduction

The study of nonindustrialized world economic development, after falling out of favor in the 1980s and 1990s for a number of reasons, mainly because of the perceived, and real, failure of the Cold War–era US-led and Soviet-led modernization schemes for the Third World, has roared back to assume a position of importance in policy circles and academic venues in the twenty-first century. The post–Cold War interest in globalization spurred interest in Third World development, and the 9/11 attacks further intensified interest.

For a number of reasons, general surveys of nonindustrialized world economic development position Latin America as either the first chapter or the last chapter. Because, historically, Latin America obtained its political independence from its imperial overlords before the rest of the developing world, some authors address it first. An important observation is that even as Latin America achieved its independence in the early nineteenth century, the new, generally elite Creole (born in Latin America of European background) leadership did not alter the social and economic systems very much.

As discussed in Chapter Two, from the perspective of the nonelite classes in Latin America, when the Latin American nations gained independence in the early nineteenth century, the situation was "same mule, different driver." That is, the political revolutions in Latin America in the early nineteenth century were not social revolutions. As such, with regard to social/economic development, the region had not yet sufficiently developed its socioeconomic system to allow for a relatively equitable distribution of wealth.

Other authors put Latin America at the end. In part, this decision is due to the decades-long interest in decolonization of postcolonial societies—the "new nations" in the Middle East, Africa, and Asia after the decline and fall of the European empires after the Second World War.[2] (The process of decolonization started a bit earlier in the Middle East.) As such, Latin America does not easily "fit" into this postcolonial "model." The main reason is that there was long lag between political independence and the development of the socioeconomic sector (which is still a work in progress). In addition, in Latin America, there have been a number of nations that have achieved "Newly Industrialized Country" (NIC) status, that is, somewhere between lesser-developed and industrialized worlds—Mexico, Argentina, and Venezuela. One nation, Latin America's giant, Brazil, has even made it to a sort of "international club" of influential nations, the BRIC (Brazil, Russia, India, and China) countries. The BRIC countries are more highly industrialized than the NICs. Thus, because of its different historical trajectory to the rest of the developing world, and the wide variety of economic development experiences in the region, Latin America, as a postcolonial, developing region, often defies categorization.

Indeed, sorting out the connections between Latin American nationalism, economic development, and globalization are key to understanding the historical trajectory of the region. Nationalism is perhaps the most nuanced and complicated of these issues.

There are two main threads of nationalism in Latin America: right-wing nationalism and left-wing nationalism. Right-wing nationalism often aims to exclude nonelite segments of the population in order to maintain a rigid hierarchy with elites (supported by the military) at the top of society. With roots in the Liberal oligarchic tradition of the nineteenth century discussed previously, as well as the 1930s military regimes that were enamored of fascism, this right-wing nationalism had a resurgence with the military dictatorships that plagued the region between the 1960s and 1980s. However, a stronger strain is left-wing nationalism, which aims to liberate the nation from foreign influence and to include the working class and poor majority as equal citizens.[3] This chapter will examine left-wing nationalism while leaving an analysis of right-wing nationalism to Chapter Eleven.

Left-wing nationalism has a complicated genealogy. Some might chart its origins to the Indian rebellions in late colonial Latin America. The Indian rebellions in the Andes, which occurred from 1780 to 1782, in which a number of groups of Indians worked together to control significant parts of the Andes, including the city of La Paz, was an important example of an Indian rebellion. The Mexican Revolution would be one of the more recent origins of left-wing nationalism.

In Europe and North America, many would have a difficult time understanding the concept of "left-wing nationalism," as nationalism is more closely identified with the political right in those two regions. However, in Latin America, left-wing nationalism is an important ideology. Basically, the idea is that the nation has the obligation to use the state to better the condition of the dispossessed or those at the bottom of the social hierarchy.

As discussed in Chapter Seven, the initial Latin American reaction to rising US economic power in the hemisphere was to put in place economic nationalist policies. During the Second World War, however, economic nationalism in Latin America was muted. Most Latin American nations were repulsed by the ultranationalist, or fascist, ideologies of the Axis powers and wanted to contribute the Allied war effort. Most Latin American nations too—and this was reinforced by the 1930s Good Neighbor policy of the United States—thought it best to work with the United States. As such, Latin American nations during the Second World War sold their valuable raw materials—strategic minerals and oil being the key ones— to the United States at or below market rates, although they knew that the United States was desperate for such materials. Instead of asking for the market rate for their exports, Latin American leaders calculated that after an Allied victory, the United States would reward the region with economic assistance for economic development. The Latin Americans were disappointed in this regard. And, thus, the spirit of the Good Neighbor waned in Latin America.

After the war, the United States remembered that Latin American economic nationalism was powerful in the region. And US power, in the hemisphere and the world, was very high in 1945 as the war came to a close. Not surprisingly, the United States aimed to use its power for its long-term self-interest. As such, Washington desired to get the Latin American nations to "buy into" the US vision for the Western Hemisphere—a hemisphere open to trade and investment of all of the member nations. It was an idea (moreover, an ideal) that went back to the 1880s and the US desire to promote Pan-Americanism in the region. Pan-Americanism (at least the US variant) was focused on trying to create an "open hemisphere" for the free flow of goods and investment, something that, due to the declining terms of trade for raw materials or primary products, would benefit the United States more than Latin America. Pan-Americanism did, however, contain the idea that cultural interchange between North and Latin America would be beneficial to both regions.

To implement its vision for an economically open hemisphere, US leaders early in 1945 organized a conference of the Latin American nations at Chapultepec Castle, in the heart of Mexico City's cultural district. US leaders made their case that only if the Latin American nations abandoned economic nationalism (including Import Substitution Industrialization [ISI]) would the region develop into economically prosperous, politically stable, anticommunist, and pro–United States countries. Skeptical Latin American leaders walked a fine line. They did not want to refuse to sign the Act of Chapultepec, thus antagonizing the "Colossus of the North," because they still held out hope that the United States would allocate economic assistance to Latin America. At the same time, the vast majority of the Latin American leaders assembled in Mexico City for the Conference did not "buy into" the US vision for the hemisphere. A number of Latin American leaders feared that an open hemisphere would lead to sharp competition between US producers and Latin American producers, a competition that the United States was poised to win, at Latin America's expense.

Thus, the stage was set for a series of conflicts between left-wing nationalists in Latin America and the United States. Latin American nationalism—at least its left-wing variant—had always had an anti-US side to it, at least going back to the early twentieth century. The already existing conflict between Latin American economic nationalism and the US desire for a hemisphere of open markets was exacerbated by the Cold War. The onset of the Cold War between the United States and its allies and friends, and the Soviet Union and its adherents, significantly increased the intensity of the conflict between the United States and Latin America (at least the leftist nationalists in the region). Two points are important here: first, some US policy makers mistakenly assumed that Latin American economic nationalists were "fellow travelers" with communists. Second, some US policy makers used the perceived threat of communism in Latin America as a way of garnering support among the US bureaucracy, and US public, for a more assertive US antieconomic nationalism foreign policy toward Latin America. During the Cold War, US leaders exaggerated the communist threat in Latin America even though the number of communists in Latin America was small and the communist political parties (outside of Cuba after 1961) in the region were not very powerful. This chapter will examine some of the left-wing nationalist movements in the region, the US response to them, and the global implications of both the movements and the US attempt to contain/quell them.

Guatemala

An early conflict occurred in Guatemala. On the face of it, Guatemala seemed an unlikely place for a challenge to the United States to emerge. Until the Guatemalan Revolution of 1944, US investors, particularly the United Fruit Company (UFCO) based in Boston, Massachusetts, had been welcomed into the country. Also, a series of repressive dictators made it seem (until the revolution) that the population was quiescent. However, anger at the repression of dictator Ubico, perhaps stimulated by the idealistic language of the 1941 Atlantic Charter between the United States and Great Britain, which outlined a vision of a post–Second World War world that included human rights (which Ubico routinely trampled), boiled over in 1944. Largely spurred on by Guatemala's middle classes, the revolutionaries called for democracy and economic development that would benefit all Guatemalans.

Juan José Arévalo, the first elected leader of the new Guatemala, cautiously implemented wanted reforms. Árbenz, elected in 1950, radicalized the revolution. As a nationalist, he concluded that Guatemala would never economically develop as long as there was a miniscule internal market for goods, particularly in the countryside. The UFCO and a small number of large landholders dominated the countryside in a nation with an economy largely based on agricultural production. Árbenz decided that only a thorough land reform, distributing land from the largest landholders to the landless farm workers, would create internal demand in Guatemala and thus bring Guatemala closer to being a modern capitalist nation. Expropriating some of UFCO lands, with compensation, was part and parcel of Árbenz's vision. Also, building a highway to compete with the UFCO-owned railroads would lower transportation costs, and nationalizing the US-owned electric plant would give Guatemala control over the key commodity of electricity.

Unfortunately for Árbenz, UFCO was very well connected in Washington, DC. Moreover, the Cold War ensured that Árbenz's opponents would call him a communist. As such, because many US officials saw nationalism as simply a staging ground for communism, they feared that if Árbenz successfully implemented his land reform and continued to serve as President of Guatemala, it would facilitate the spread of communism in the region (although communist parties in the Latin American nations were very weak).

Once defined as a communist–anticommunist struggle, the conflict took a new turn when Dwight D. Eisenhower's White House decided to use the US Central Intelligence Agency (CIA) to assist anti-Árbenz military men in an attempt to oust Árbenz. (Árbenz himself was a military man, but the Guatemalan military was divided over his leftist reforms—many feared his left-wing views.) Eisenhower probably decided on using the CIA in late 1952 after it became clear that the land reform would be implemented. The plan to oust Árbenz was not executed until mid-1954. Although the coup plotting at first did not go well for the CIA, once Árbenz got wind of the plan, he quickly decided to flee into exile. Árbenz probably concluded that if the CIA-backed plotting failed, eventually the United States would send in US troops. US troops had never been used in Guatemala, and no evidence has been found that the United States aimed to send in troops in the event that the CIA coup plans failed. However, going back to 1898, US troops had been sent into a number of Caribbean and Central American nations in order to support US interests. As such, Árbenz's fears were not unfounded. With Árbenz's hasty exit, the Guatemalan Revolution of 1944 rapidly collapsed. The land reform was reversed, and UFCO's lands were reinstated. Guatemalan democracy also collapsed, and lamentably, the nation was ruled over for almost forty years by a series of repressive dictatorships.[4]

In a memoir published in the early 1960s, entitled *The Shark and the Sardines* (discussed in Chapter Eleven, from left- to right-wing nationalism), Arévalo bemoaned the fact that US economic interests were largely responsible for the disintegration of the Guatemalan Revolution. Arévalo discussed the tragedy of the change in US attitudes toward the world in the twentieth century. The United States had started out, he maintained, as a beacon of postcolonial revolutionary hope for peoples everywhere that strived for political liberty and economic independence and prosperity. But, with the rise of the power of large, US-based multinational corporations (MNCs), US foreign policy shifted to maintaining and extending the power of these MNCs. This shift, in the early twentieth century, made it difficult for nationalists in Latin America to pursue their goals of increasing the economic autonomy and prosperity of their nations, if their economic nationalist goals clashed with the interests of the MNCs.[5]

Bolivia

"Latin America is a beggar sitting atop a mountain of gold." So goes the old saying about Latin America. Bolivia is perhaps the best example of this adage. For centuries, foreign and domestic capitalists exploited Bolivia's mines, with much of the benefits flowing overseas. Politically, Bolivia was one of the more stratified economies and societies in Latin America—a tiny elite controlled the bulk of Bolivian economic, social, and political life. The economic and social systems in early twentieth-century Bolivia seemed to be throwbacks to the Spanish colonial period. Bolivian nationalists were incensed at the disastrous Chaco War loss which came at the expense of many thousands of poorer Bolivians' lives and livelihoods. The disastrous decisions of the generals and political leadership caused many Bolivians to think that more than a political reshuffling was necessary. A more thorough reorganization of society was necessary—a social revolution that would transfer power from an entrenched elite to the majority. In 1934, a group of middle-level officers in the Bolivian military during the Chaco War formed Razón de Patria (For the Fatherland), an organization that aimed to promote social and political change, which would hopefully prevent another Chaco War. In economic nationalist fashion, and partly as the result of the Chaco War, Bolivia asserted control over its petroleum resources to build up the power of the state and the nation. (This was discussed in the previous chapter.)

Unionization occurred rapidly after the Second World War because workers wanted to preserve gains in wages. Groups calling for deep social change merged into the Movimiento Nacionalista Revolucionario (MNR) in 1941. The MNR was elected in 1951, but the military, fearing that the MNR was dangerously left wing, prevented it from taking office. Not surprisingly, the MNR concluded that the only way it could achieve power was through a revolution, which occurred the following year. The battles between the MNR and the Bolivian army proved to be short lived—the Bolivian populace had tired of centuries of elite rule and thought a significant change was necessary. The MNR, largely an urban-based movement, did emphasize Indian rights, and land reform, which would benefit Indians in the camp; but once the MNR was in power, because it was forced from below by subaltern groups, implemented significant changes in Bolivian society, including Agrarian Reform and the right to vote for women and Indians.

At the core of the MNR's revolutionary reform program was expropriation of the three largest mining companies, all of them foreign owned. Reasons both political and economic explain this decision. The MNR wanted to denude the three largest mining companies (which produced about 80 percent of the nation's foreign exchange) of their political and economic power. Before the expropriation of their assets, the three largest mining companies exerted a great deal of control over Bolivian politics. The revolutionaries thought, too, that if the Bolivian state owned the assets of the three economic giants, the state could produce income it could use to diversify the economy.

Interestingly, although the revolutionaries achieved significant goals in the first few years in office, because their leadership was ideologically divided, they were forced from office by a military coup. The MNR was deeply divided between moderate and left-wing factions. Washington officials, with the novel experiment of giving large amounts of economic assistance to Bolivia, exacerbated already existing, deep divisions in the shaky MNR coalition. The US government (at the behest of the MNR moderates and against the outcries of the radicals) offered significant economic aid to Bolivia in the 1950s because US officials feared that if the MNR collapsed, radicalism and communism would triumph in the heart of South America.

Once the Bolivians received US assistance, creating dependency on Washington's largesse, Washington officials informed them that they needed to put their financial house in order, which meant cutting Bolivian government subsidies. The left-wing segment of the MNR disliked this US-imposed austerity plan, deepening the divide between the moderate and the radical factions of the MNR. With the increasing division between the two factions, the MNR became weaker and weaker, facilitating a military coup in 1964. After the military took over, two years later, Argentine revolutionary Ernesto "Che" Guevara decided that he would take control of Bolivia, establishing a base to spread revolution around the continent.[6]

Cuba

Cuban left-wing nationalism is probably the best known example of such nationalism. The connection between left-wing nationalism in Guatemala and Bolivia (where Guevara died in a failed, quixotic attempt to foment revolution there) can be seen in the charismatic figure of Ernesto "Che" Guevara, an important symbol of left-wing internationalism—but who inspired leftist nationalists throughout Latin America. Guevara had been in Guatemala in 1954 when the US-backed coup toppled Árbenz, and rumors had swirled around Guatemala that the United States was behind the coup. Guevara concluded that Árbenz should have somehow obtained control of the Guatemalan military—it would have prevented Árbenz's overthrow. In addition, Guevara concluded it was important to support left-wing movements around the hemisphere and in 1966 decided he would foment such a movement in Bolivia—even if the United States attempted to counter his efforts.

Seeking refuge in Mexico, Guevara met the Cuban Fidel Castro, also in exile, and the two decided to foment revolution in Cuba. Castro, Guevara, and their followers were vastly outnumbered by Cuban dictator Fulgencio Batista's military and supporters. However, Batista was a repressive, corrupt dictator, whose support on the island was very thin. Castro benefitted from the fact there was no viable opposition to Batista except him. Castro also benefitted from a deep well of anti-US Cuban nationalism. From 1898 to 1933, the United States, without the support of the majority of Cubans, placed a protectorate on Cuba, in which the United States determined Cuba's foreign policy and also reserved the right to send in US troops if its interests or the expatriate community were threatened. Washington officials coerced the Cubans to accept the protectorate by requiring them to place the Platt Amendment (named for Senator Orville Platt of Connecticut) on the Cuban constitution. If Cuba refused to accept the Platt Amendment, official diplomatic recognition from the United States would not be forthcoming. Such recognition would give Cuba more regional standing than otherwise; as such, Cuba reluctantly accepted the Platt Amendment.

Although the protectorate was formally abrogated in 1933, overwhelming US economic influence and the military capability of the United States allowed the United States to enjoy significant power on the island. Castro and his followers were animated by the anti-US nationalism that chafed under US power.

In addition, some of the forms that US influence in Cuba took further inflamed Cuban nationalism—especially its left-wing variant. For decades, the US-based mafia had operated freely in Cuba, most notoriously owning casinos. Cuba was a sort of "playland" for US tourists, exploited for the various tourist pursuits of drinking, gambling, and prostitution. For those that could take an inexpensive boat ride to Havana from Miami, it was commonplace for US tourists to visit Havana and engage in pursuits they could "get away with" on foreign soil. As this sort of US influence increased, Cuban nationalists only got angrier. In their eyes, the Cuban nation was prostituting itself to its giant "neighbor" to the north. It was no surprise that when the Cuban Revolution triumphed, angry Cubans ripped the "one-armed bandits" (slot machines) out of the wall and angrily destroyed them in the streets.

Arguably, the vast extent of US influence in Cuba since 1898 provoked a counterreaction with Castro's January 1959 triumph. Castro's appeal among the left in Latin America, and around the world, was profound. But, in the short run, he focused on reforming Cuba—and ultimately turning it into a socialist nation. In the name of Cuban nationalism, Castro quickly moved to purge the island of US influence. Because Guevara had been in Guatemala in 1954 and seen the results of US influence, Castro quickly purged the army of Batista's officers. Since a divided Guatemalan army had laid the groundwork for CIA assistance to the anti-Árbenz military men, Castro had no desire to be a victim of US influence, channeled through the military, in Cuba.

US companies were expropriated (with no compensation). When the United States cut the sugar quota, the amount of sugar it annually bought from Cuba, to protest Cuban action, Cuban nationalism only increased. When the United States implemented a trade embargo and cut diplomatic relations, again nationalism increased. The vast amount of US influence in the nation before 1959, and Castro's extreme, revolutionary reaction to this influence, only set the stage for a series of tit-for-tat actions that resulted in near-total Cuban isolation from the United States. Even without the rise of Castro's movement, because of the vast amount of influence the United States enjoyed in pre-1959 Cuba, Cuban anti-US nationalism would have been strong. With Castro, anti-US, left-wing nationalism proved overwhelmingly powerful.[7]

From British Guiana to Guyana

Left-wing nationalism simultaneously surged in tiny British Guyana, situated on the South American continent but culturally Caribbean. As it was a British colony until 1966 when it gained its independence, the official language was English. The racial composition of British Guyana mirrored that of many Caribbean nations: Afro-Caribbean, Indian (from South Asia), and indigenous people. British Guyana had wanted independence from Great Britain long before it achieved it in 1966. The British themselves had wanted to "cut British Guyana loose" long before then as well. But the rise of left-wing nationalist Cheddi Jagan (whose ancestors originally came from

India) helped to ensure that the nation's independence would be delayed until Jagan's political support had been nearly eliminated—in part due to US foreign policy in the nation.

In the preindependence period, the way promising young leaders, who espoused nationalist ideas, gained prominence and power was through the labor movement. Jagan was a case in point. While excelling at labor organizing, he also worked with other nationalists, for example, Forbes Burnham, his future antagonist, to form the Peoples Progressive Party (PPP) in 1950. Jagan's goal was to promote economic development and national unity, thus preparing Guyana for future nationhood—with the PPP in control. In turn, he hoped to be the president of the new nation of Guyana.

Jagan's dreams of the presidency, however, were not to be realized until decades later. In the early 1960s, British Guiana was caught like many developing world nations in the throes of the Cold War, derailing Jagan. Once Jagan made it clear that he admired Fidel Castro's experiment in Cuba and refused to publicly state he was anticommunist, Washington, DC, began to fear that British Guyana, if headed up by Jagan, would be a revolutionary menace, "another Cuba" in the Western Hemisphere. (Adding fuel to the fire of this concern, Jagan's wife, Janet Jagan, who had been a member of the US Communist Party, traveled to Cuba.) One of the main pillars of US foreign policy toward Latin America after 1959 was to prevent, at all costs, another Castro from popping up in Latin America—in particular in the Caribbean and Central American area. Washington leaders made it clear to their British counterparts that a Jagan-led Guyana was unacceptable. As such, Washington pressured Britain to delay Guyana's independence. Britain concurred. This delay in Guyana's independence allowed the CIA to fund anti-Jagan groups, including anti-Jagan labor organizations. Further, once Burham broke from the PPP and formed his own party, the United States gave covert support for his presidential bid in 1964, which he won. Burnham, ironically, and tragically for the United States, moved quickly to the political left, espousing economic nationalism. He nationalized the companies that controlled the major resource of Guyana, bauxite (the raw material for aluminum). Moreover, he reached out to the Soviet Union and the People's Republic of China. Jagan, the supreme Guyanese nationalist in many respects, was locked out of power. However, in 1992 in a remarkable political comeback, Jagan, near the end of his life, won election to the presidency of Guyana.[8]

Brazil

Next to tiny Guyana lay the giant Brazil. Due to Brazil's unique history, in which it gained its independence not through a revolutionary war in the nineteenth century but because of the abdication of a ruling Portuguese monarchy, Brazil in some respects is a separate case. But it was similar to many other Latin American nations in the twentieth century that were led by urban populists. Indeed, Brazilian president Getúlio Vargas, who served from 1930 to 1945 and from 1950 to 1954 and whose rule abruptly came to an end in 1954 with his suicide, was in many respects a classic Latin American populist.

However, Latin American populism began to run out of steam in the early 1960s. Inflation ate away urban workers' disposable income. Looking for someone to blame, left-wing nationalists made it clear that if they were in power, they would put controls on the activities of foreign companies in Brazil to ensure that their activities would promote Brazilian economic activity beneficial to all classes of Brazilians and thus benefit the Brazilian nation as a whole. With the unexpected resignation of Jânio Quadros in 1961, João Goulart assumed the presidency and intended to implement significant reforms, including land reform and pro-labor policies. Again, fearing that left-wing nationalism would automatically lead to a Castroite, communist revolutionary government in Brasilia, the United States made it clear to dissident Brazilian generals that if they rose up and threw out Goulart, they would get US support. Because Goulart's policies threatened the interests of Brazil's elite, and a good chunk of the Brazilian military shared the interests of the elite, not surprisingly, a group of anti-Goulart generals staged a successful coup, casting out Goulart's style of left-wing nationalism for decades.[9]

Panama

The case of Panama nicely shows the intersection of Latin American nationalism and globalization. Interestingly, Panama (part of Colombia until 1903) had wanted independence for quite a while before the United States helped it achieve this goal. But the price was steep. Panama had to cede control over a strip of territory in the middle of its country, the site of the future Panama Canal. US officials had wanted to dig an isthmian canal since the late nineteenth century. Indeed, US officials had tried to buy a strip of Panamanian territory from Colombia, but Colombia refused to sell. When an insurrection in Panama broke out in 1903, US officials sent US Navy ships to the Atlantic coast of Panama, preventing the Colombians from putting down the insurrection. As a result, Panama gained its independence and in turn ceded a strip of territory down the middle of the new country to the United States. The canal was completed in 1914, and though it produced significant benefit for Panama, the canal also provoked controversy in the small Central American nation.

Panamanians (most of whom were nonwhite) chafed at the racism of US personnel in the Canal Zone and wanted the "Zonians" (US citizens who lived in the Canal Zone) to fly both the US and Panamanian flags. Riots over the flying of both flags in the Zone erupted in 1964, showing the anti-US side of Panamanian nationalism. US officials quickly decided that it would be best to start a process by which the Canal would be returned to Panama. Significantly, the return of the Canal to Panama would achieve a number of results. First, it would satisfy Panamanian nationalist demands for control over its territory. Second, it would significantly improve not only US-Panamanian relations but US-Latin American relations as well. Because powerful, conservative interest groups in the United States and a number of Republican (conservative) leaders thought that the recession of the Canal to the Panamanians would represent a display of weakness that would hurt the standing of the United States in the hemisphere and the world, the agreement to transfer the Canal to Panama did not occur until 1978, when President James Earl ("Jimmy") Carter invested significant effort to get a treaty passed to ensure the Canal's transfer to Panama in the year 2000.[10]

Chile

The case of Chile is remarkably similar to that of Brazil. With populist ISI policies seemingly not producing as much benefit for the working- and middle-class majorities by the 1960s, populist leaders, such as Eduardo Frei and Salvador Allende, called for essentially a radicalization of populist policies, including land reform for the landless peasantry as well as nationalizing the all-important copper mines responsible for about one-half of Chile's foreign exchange. Frei, who was President from 1964 to 1970, continued the already existing ISI policies, discussed in Chapter Six, but did not get to the nationalization of the copper mines. To make the agrarian economy more egalitarian, he implemented land reform. Allende, who was to the left of Frei, headed up the Unidad Popular, a collection of left-wing political parties, including the Chilean Communist Party. Allende had been active in Chilean politics since the 1930s and was one of the "charter members" of the Chilean Sociality Party. He ran for president four times, only succeeding on the fourth try at the age of 65. Not only did Allende nationalize the copper mines, his election signaled to workers that they could increase their power vis-à-vis the management in the factories—in some cases even taking over entire factories, much to Allende's chagrin. He feared that the Chilean society was spinning out of control, and although he wanted to move Chile politically to the left, he feared that with workers taking things into their own hands, it could get difficult for him.

Economically, the ISI populist model, when radicalized, was not producing economic gain, and social strife sharply increased. Prodded by covert CIA funding, Allende's political opponents had more resources to better organize themselves as well as more resources to continually increase their attacks on the Allende government. The Chilean military, taking advantage of the civil strife, staged a successful coup on September 11, 1973, attacking La Moneda (the Presidential residence) while Allende was inside. Allende committed suicide, thinking it would be humiliating to flee into exile and demoralizing to his supporters. General Augusto Pinochet, who took power upon Allende's death, forced a number of Allende's supporters into exile while torturing and killing those who did not flee. The Pinochet regime was one of the most repressive in recent Latin American history. Chile remained under his military authoritarian rule until 1989.[11]

Peru

In neighboring Peru (Peru and Chile had historically been antagonists), left-wing nationalism had an interesting and rare origin. A leftist-nationalist revolution was implemented by means of a military coup, from the top down. General Juan Velasco took power in a 1968 coup and proceeded to implement a number of the goals of the Peruvian nationalist left going back to the 1930s. Previously, the nationalist left had been based in the Alianza Popular Revolucionario Americano (APRA, American Popular Revolutionary Movement) founded in 1924 that was, despite its name, a Peruvian political party. However, its charismatic leader, Haya de la Torre, never managed to win the presidency. By the late 1960s, the desire on the part of many Peruvians to deepen the populist ISI model, in particular to expropriate US industry, in particular oil wells, spurred Velasco to action. He nationalized the US oil company holdings in 1970. Remarkably, he even bought a great deal of military weaponry from the Soviet Union—in large part because he feared a buildup of the Chilean military on his southern flank, and he wanted to be prepared. Remarkably, the United States did not seem to be too concerned with the Soviet weaponry flowing into South America—probably because they viewed Velasco, a military man, as someone who would, as opposed to Allende, keep the situation ultimately under control. Also, Velasco stated to US officials that he was pro–United States.[12]

Nicaragua

In the twentieth century, Nicaraguan nationalism proved to be the strongest form of nationalism among all of the Central American nationalisms in part because Nicaragua was bedeviled by some of the most repressive and kleptocratic leadership in all of Latin America. In addition, Nicaragua suffered from the indignation of quite a number of years of US military occupation.

As such, Nicaraguan nationalism, similar to Cuban nationalism, has a strong anti-American element to it. US troops occupied Nicaragua on and off from 1911 to 1933. Indeed, the anti-US sentiment generated by the US stationing of troops in Nicaragua for about two decades bedeviled US-Latin

American relations. As such, the US occupation of the Central American nation was a major cause of the Good Neighbor policy.

In Nicaragua, US troops aimed to support pro-US leaders while at the same time attempting to promote a modicum of stability so elections could be held. It was a tall order. In the 1910s and 1920s, Nicaragua was racked with civil war between the Liberal and Conservative forces. One Nicaraguan military leader, Augusto Sandino, hated the fact that US soldiers were on Nicaraguan soil. US leaders proposed that all warring parties sit down for a negotiated peace. Liberals and Conservatives agreed. Sandino of the Liberal forces broke with them and nationalistically vowed to fight US forces until they left his country. Once they left, he would negotiate. He was true to his word. He fought US troops in his country to a standstill although the US military used dive-bombing techniques to attach his forces, the first time such techniques were used against a foreign enemy.

However, in the end the United States prevailed. Sandino proved to be a victim of the US-backed Nicaraguans. US leaders decided the best way to maintain pro-US order in Nicaragua would be to train a National Guard—a supposedly apolitical military force. Such a force was particularly important to the United States since the Good Neighbor policy prohibited the United States from stationing forces in Latin American nations. The thinking went that if the United States trained the members of the Guard, the Guard would be at the same time an efficient, uncorrupt force and also pro-United States. In 1934, Sandino was abducted and assassinated almost certainly by associates of US-trained Anastasio Somoza, head of the National Guard.

Sandino's elimination paved the way for Somoza's rise to power. Skillfully, using his leadership of the National Guard to springboard him to power, he became leader of Nicaragua from 1937 to 1947 and from 1950 to 1956 when he was assassinated. His elder son, Luis, presided over Nicaragua until he died of a heart attack in 1963. His second son, Anastasio, Jr., ruled Nicaragua until the Sandinista Revolution ousted him in 1979.

The Somoza family was known for its brutal neutralization, or elimination, of political rivals as well as for its greed. Anastasio Somoza, Jr., at one point declared "Nicaragua es mi finca" ("Nicaragua is my farm"), and many thought that he was simply stating a fact. At one point, the Somoza family controlled approximately 20 percent of the arable land in Nicaragua. Through chicanery, the threat of force, and the use of force, Somoza ensured that his family got the best lands. Not surprisingly, hatred toward the Somoza crystallized into a revolutionary nationalist movement to oust him. Formed in 1961, the Frente Sandinsta Liberación Nacional (FSLN, or Sandinista front for National Revolution, also known as the Sandinistas) worked to organize resistance to the Somoza. Putting the martyr Sandino in their name showed their nationalistic stripes. Since elections, if held, were a sham, the FSLN used political violence to attempt to weaken Somoza's hold on power. As Nicaraguans increasingly grew tired of Somoza rule, and as the FSLN positioned itself politically as Nicaraguan nationalists who wanted to retake Nicaragua for the Nicaraguans, FSLN support grew. Of course, since Sandino himself fought US troops back in the late 1920s and early 1930s, the FSLN nationalism had an anti-US element to it.

A 1972 earthquake that devastated Managua, Nicaragua's capital, proved to be a turning point. As earthquake aid poured in, much of it was brazenly stolen by Somoza. Although the dictator was known for his callous disregard of his people, this theft, which helped cause the deaths of many Nicaraguans that needed the assistance, seemed beyond the pale. Although moderate Nicaraguans disagreed with the FSLN's revolutionary mission, they joined the group nonetheless. The FSLN, similar to Castro's revolutionary force in Cuba in the 1950s, skillfully positioned itself as the only viable political alternative to Somoza. In audaciously courageous acts of political terrorism, the FSLN showed its political muscle while showing that Somoza was weaker than he seemed. In one particularly important act in August 1978, FSLN guerrillas held a good portion of Nicaragua's Congressional Assembly hostage, only releasing them in exchange for some top-level FSLN political prisoners. For his part, Somoza's people assassinated one of his few remaining critics (most had been previously jailed, tortured, or killed), journalist Juaquin Chamorro, in broad daylight in cold blood. This cruel act made Somoza seem weak, thus bringing more support to the FSLN while emboldening them.

The ultimate triumph came in July 1979 when Somoza fled the country. The FSLN aimed not just for political and social reforms but had a revolutionary agenda. Their land reform was at the same time skillful and simple. They simply took over the Somoza family's land holdings, some of which became state-run farms while others were parceled to landless farmworkers. To the chagrin of the United States, the Sandinistas boldly embarked on a nonaligned foreign policy—which tilted toward the communist world. Indeed, this Nicaraguan foreign policy reflected Nicaragua's nationalistic desire to chart its own course in world affairs. This leftist-tinged nonalignment proved impossible for the United States to swallow—after all, during the Somoza era, Nicaragua was one of the most pro-US governments in the region. Indeed, although Nicaragua's leadership was an ideologically mixed group, the US Presidency of Ronald Reagan (1981–1989) viewed the Sandinistas as a left-wing communist government allied with Cuba and the Soviet Union and aimed to undermine them in a variety of ways, including semicovert support for anti-Sandinista guerrillas (many of whom were former supporters of Somoza) who called themselves *contrarevolucionarios* or *contras*. The resulting civil war not only devastated Nicaragua socially and economically but also significantly increased the anti-US component of Nicaraguan nationalism.

Although many have compared the Nicaraguan Revolution to the Cuban Revolution, one key difference marks the two different cases. In Nicaragua, the political culture called for democracy. With Castro's revolution, however, vague talk of elections was soon proven to be hollow, and Castro (and later his younger brother Raúl) ran Cuba in authoritarian fashion. Soon after taking power, the Sandinistas agreed to internationally monitored elections in 1984 and 1990. Showing political skill, the Sandinista electoral victory gave them political legitimacy around the world. In 1990, the opposition to the Sandinistas showed their political skill, unifying around one candidate, Violeta Chamorro, a well-known (and anti-Somoza) family. Largely because the civil war against the contras proved to be economically and emotionally draining, Nicaraguan voters voted the Sandinistas out of power in February 1990.[13]

Conclusion

Although the global implications of the Cuban Revolution are more clear than the other nationalist movements discussed in this chapter, it was not the only globally significant such movement. As Latin American leaders saw the United States exerting its strength in the Western Hemisphere, they attempted to build up their own countervailing power against the United States by bolstering nationalism. In the 1950s and 1960s, Latin American nationalism tended to have a left-wing strain. By the mid-1960s and 1970s, however, a more conservative nationalism was on the rise in Latin America. This conservative strain of nationalism was in response in part to what was seen as the excesses of ISI or taking ISI too far, empowering the working class and in some cases creating inflation. Also, the rise in conservative nationalism was in response to the perceived excesses of left-wing nationalism exemplified by Cuba and Nicaragua. In Chapter Eleven, conservative nationalism will be addressed.

Study Questions

1. In the post–Second World War era, why did left-wing nationalism in Latin America become more prominent?
2. Why and how did the United States respond to this upsurge in leftist nationalism in the region?
3. What impact did the negative response of the United States have on left-wing nationalism in Latin America?

For Further Reading

Baily, Samuel. *United States and the Development of South America, 1945–1975.* New York: New Viewpoints, 1976.

Blasier, Cole. *The Hovering Giant—US Responses to Revolutionary Nationalism in Latin America, v.2 1910–1985.* Pittsburgh: University of Pittsburgh Press, 1985.

Clayton, Lawrence. *Peru and the United States—Eagle and the Condor.* Athens: University of Georgia Press, 1999.

Coatsworth, John H. *Central America and the United States: The Clients and the Colossus.* New York: Twayne, 1997.

Conniff, Michael. *Panama and the United States—The Forced Alliance,* 3rd ed. Athens: University of Georgia Press, 2012.

Dosal, Paul. *Doing Business with the Dictators.* Lanham, MD: Rowman & Littlefield Publishers, 1995.

Miller, Phyllis R. *Brazil and the Quiet Intervention, 1964.* Austin: University of Texas Press, 1979.

Paterson, Thomas. *Contesting Castro: The United States and the Triumph of the Cuban Revolution.* Oxford: Oxford University Press, 1995.

Pike, Frederick. *The United States and the Andean Republics.* Cambridge, MA: Harvard University Press, 1978.

Rabe, Stephen. *U.S. Intervention in British Guyana—A Cold War Story.* Chapel Hill: University of North Carolina Press, 2005.

CHAPTER NINE

Modernization Theory in Latin America, 1945–1970

It has been said that Latin American thought is the history of a quest to harmonize modernization and identity.

JOSÉ ANTONIO OCAMPO AND JUAN MARTIN[1]

Introduction

As left-wing nationalism surged in the 1950s and 1960s, discussed in the last chapter, Washington leaders feared such nationalism and came up with a plan to counter it—modernization theory. The early post–Second World War period is a particularly interesting time to study the intersection of globalization and nationalism in Latin America. The United States came out of the Second World War with unprecedented power—economic and military. It aimed to create a world in which private sector foreign investment (and trade) would be able to stimulate the development of vibrant free-market economies around the world. Such vibrant economic growth would then provide the backdrop for the development of stable, pro–United States, and hopefully, democratic nations.

As such, this chapter is going to focus on one period of what we might call "intense" globalization in the late 1940s and 1950s, the early Cold War. This period marks the ascendency of the United States in world affairs. This chapter will examine how the United States (and its Cold War allies) tried to channel nationalism and globalization in a way that would produce pro-US, stable governments in Third World countries. Keep in mind that the Third World itself was an idea constructed by the industrialized world. As the

European empires in Asia and Africa decolonized much more quickly—and dramatically—than most observers thought, the Western world needed a concept that represents a broad generalization of an area with an incredibly diverse mixture of peoples/nationalities/ethnicities. Latin America of course is only one part of this nonindustrialized world.

It is important to point out that two-thirds of the world's population lived in the developing (Third) world in the early Cold War era, and the portion is larger now. Most of these people are economically disadvantaged and looking for improved social/economic conditions as well. As such, the stakes were high. During the early Cold War, scholars and journalists talked about the "revolution of rising expectations." That is, if these expectations were not met, there will be problems. The twin dilemmas for the leader of the noncommunist world, the United States, were to ensure that the Third World modernized economically and politically in a noncommunist, and pro-US, way. In addition, it was imperative for Washington officials that the economies of the nonindustrialized world be integrated into the growing world market as a whole. Since some key, strategic primary sources (valuable minerals) were located in the nonindustrialized world in large amounts, US foreign policy makers wanted to ensure that US businessmen had access to such materials, in particular in defense-related industries. In addition, US leaders thought that if Third World countries restricted private sector foreign economic activity, it would reduce the potential for economic growth of those countries. The policy of self-sufficiency, or autarky, among Third World countries was anathema to Washington leaders.

The immediate post–Second World War period was a particularly fascinating time of transition in Latin America. During the 1930s Great Depression, economic difficulties had led to political strife in the region, and authoritarian governments emerged. By the early post–Second World War period, intellectuals, labor leaders, and some reformist noncommissioned military officers were spurred on by a sense of nationalism and wanted a return to representative government or democracy. The seed of left-wing nationalism in Latin America was planted. As such, in the years immediately following the Second World War, military governments gave way to more representative forms of government.

The United States sets up international financial institutions

US leaders, for their part, wanted to ensure that Latin America developed along pro-US and procapitalist lines. Because the United States enjoyed incredible military and economic power relative to other nations after the Second World War, controlling about half of the world's trade and having a powerful military that was not decimated in the war like those of the other "great powers," the United States had a chance to use its overweening power to set up global institutions. These institutions would not be directly controlled by the United States. But the United States would have a controlling interest in them (at least until the 1970s, when power within these institutions became more diffuse). Good examples include the General Agreement on Tariff and Trade (GATT), the International Monetary Fund (IMF), and the World Bank (the International Bank for Reconstruction and Development). In a sense, the creation of these agencies, largely at the behest of the United States, but with consensus among many nations' leaders, represented an extension of the New Deal to the global arena. That is, New Deal policies and reforms were put in place to try to prevent future economic dislocations like the 1930s Great Depression.[2] The post–Second World War institutions set up by the United States, which collectively are termed "International Financial Institutions" (IFIs), are meant to ensure that economic dislocations in the world economy do not become so extreme as to cause another great depression.

Even as US views predominated in setting up the IFIs, it is important to realize that the Latin American nations played an important role in setting up these IFIs, which played a key role in economic globalization in the post–Second World War era. The IFIs were created at a now famous conference at Bretton Woods, New Hampshire, in 1944. At Bretton Woods, the world's finance ministers and other economic officials gathered to chart a new course for the post–Second World War era. In addition to the creation of the abovementioned IFIs, Bretton Woods came up with a currency exchange system that pegged the world's currencies to a gold-backed US dollar.

The standard interpretation of Bretton Woods is that US and British officials shaped the IFIs to their economic interests.[3] However, it is important to keep in mind that other nations' finance ministers and officials, including India, China, and the Latin American nations, played a role in the outcome of Bretton Woods as well. The Latin American delegations called for the IFIs to focus more attention on economic development of the nonindustrialized world. Although their message at times fell on deaf ears, these nations of the global South did have an impact.[4]

The GATT ensured that countries would come to agreements to reduce tariffs worldwide. GATT was in many ways the continuation of a previous policy. The Reciprocal Trade Agreements (RTAs) during the 1930s, which was Washington leaders' attempt to use an economically globalizing world to help the United States dig itself out of the economic depression, were the blueprint for GATT. The RTAs gave the US Executive Department (the US Presidency) the power to negotiate steep reductions in tariffs without bringing Congress into the discussion until the very end of the process—in which Congress would then approve or disapprove the entire agreement on an up-or-down vote. (Today, this policy technique is called "fasttracking.") Just as the RTAs brought down tariffs and facilitated increased trade between the United States and its individual trading partners, the GATT would do the same worldwide.

The IMF would provide development loans at reduced interest rates to countries facing temporary balance of payments problems. As such, nations in need of a quick infusion of funds could "get on their feet" faster, avoiding being mired in economic doldrums which could lead to political instability and hurt its trade with other nations. In addition, IMF officials would require, as stipulated in their agreements with the recipient nations, that the host nation put in place administrative and governmental reforms to ensure that economic policies did not lead to future economic imbalances (e.g., high inflation, low employment). In a sense, the IMF was the globalization of the Export-Import Bank, formed in 1934, that loaned money to US businessmen who had identified specific opportunities for overseas trade. Without these low-interest loans, business opportunities would go untapped, which would hurt both the US economy and the economy of the "host nation." The World Bank provided low-interest loans to nations that needed specific economic development projects (e.g., infrastructure) that would remove "bottlenecks" in the economy, and, at least theoretically, unleash future economic growth and development. For its part, the World Bank was in a sense globalization of the New Deal era Reconstruction Finance Corporation, which loaned money to US companies that had fallen on hard times. To prevent a wave of bankruptcies, the Reconstruction Finance Corporation loaned money to these failing businesses at generous rates of interest to get them "on their feet again" and, at least in theory, thus prevent a wave of bankruptcies.

Modernization theory

In both the United States and Latin America, different theories of economic growth emerged in the 1950s and 1960s. The rise of the Third World was key for understanding why these theories of economic development emerged.

One of the early, main theories of economic development, popular in the noncommunist world, was modernization theory. The purpose of modernization theory was to create stable, capitalist, pro-Western anticommunist nations. At its most ambitious, modernization theorists assumed that with economic growth eventually a middle class would emerge. This middle class would provide both social and political stability and would lay the foundation for stable, democratic institutions in the future. Modernization theory assumed an economically integrated world in which trade and investment across international borders would strengthen economies everywhere.

Modernization theory presupposed a viable state; as such, it was dependent on nation-states for it to function. In developing economies, there were a wide array of problems confronting the economic modernizer, whether they were from that nation or from abroad. In some cases, bottlenecks prevented certain important products from being produced. Relatedly, there might be a severe lack of infrastructure that would prevent businessmen from having access to raw materials necessary for the production of their goods or from traders being able to trade surpluses of a good in one part of the country to where it was relatively rare in another part of the country. In addition, functional government institutions, such as security agencies and education, as well as an efficient, noncorrupt bureaucracy, might be lacking.

Another set of problems lay in the area of economic policy. If underdeveloped nations did not have the ability to produce and implement sound economic policies, that would inhibit development as well. What is remarkable about modernization theory is that it addresses all of these issues—at least in theory.

It is important to understand that economic modernization was a global phenomenon after the Second World War. The United States and the Soviet Union of course had very different views of the "proper" form of economic development. In neither case was there an agreed-upon, monolithic economic development theory. In the noncommunist West, modernization theory had long roots that stretched back to the various European imperial projects of the nineteenth century that aimed to bring progress to nonwhite nations. Although the United States did not build a large territorial empire (known as "formal empire") like the Europeans, it had a sense of "Manifest Destiny," that is, the United States had a divinely inspired (or even required) duty to spread prosperity across North America. It was thought that nonwhite groups (in particular, Native Americans and Mexicans) were to be forcibly absorbed into a larger and larger United States and both the United States and these groups would benefit from such expansion. On both sides of the Atlantic, peoples of European/white background thought it imperative that nonwhite peoples accept (by force if they resisted) European culture. This concept was termed "white man's burden" by one of the more influential writers of his day, Rudyard Kipling, because he tapped into an already existing sense of mission on the part of the European peoples in North America and in many parts of Europe. Spreading both European-style economic development and Christianity was important to the late nineteenth-century "Atlantic World" (the community of nations on both sides of the Atlantic).

One idea that sums up quite well the attempts on the part of the European nations and the United States to spread their culture and economic system to the Third World was formulated by historian Emily Rosenberg. In her influential book *Spreading the American Dream* of 1982, she coined the phrase "liberal developmentalism." With increasing trade and investment between the wealthy nations and those less well off, a rising tide will lift all boats—at least in theory. Since the industrialized world had wealth accumulation by means of capitalist market forces, automatically there will be democratic stability. Studies have proven otherwise, but this idea remains a powerful idea in the worldview of most in the United States. In many respects, modernization theory flows from "liberal developmentalism."

From the Marshall Plan to Alliance for Progress

The apogee of modernization theory as applied to Latin America was with the 1961–1969 Alliance for Progress (Alliance). Although US economic assistance to Latin America stretched back to the turn of the twentieth century with US assistance to Cuba right after the Spanish-American War of 1898, it was not until the Point-4 Program in the United States in the late 1940s and early 1950s that the US government began in earnest to fund economic development projects in the region. Such efforts were often politically motivated and done in case by case or piecemeal fashion. The Alliance, for its part, was more ambitious, calling for economic, social, and institutional reform. It also aimed to strengthen Latin America's weak middle class, because Washington officials assumed that a middle class would be a sort of political "ballast" which would provide for political stability over the long run.

The Alliance proved a key turning point not only in US-Latin American relations but also in Latin American history. One key motivation on the part of Washington leaders for the Alliance was fear that a Castro-style revolution would spread quickly around Latin America. Interestingly, and importantly, the Alliance at first reinforced left-wing nationalism (discussed in the previous chapter). The Alliance was a joint effort on the part of the United States and Latin America to spur reform and economic development throughout Latin America. (The United States contributed the bulk of the funds.) The Alliance's fund was sizable. It was proposed to eventually grow to a remarkable $100 billion over the course of the decade. At first, the rhetoric of US Alliance officials emphasized reforms, including land reform. In fact, in some countries, such as Guatemala, US-inspired community development programs (implemented by US Peace Corps volunteers) resulted in giving some radicals a voice and even coming to prominence in these communities. Later, some of these radicals formed or joined revolutionary groups, mainly in outlying areas of the jungle region of Guatemala. Ironically, what US policy helped to create, later US military assistance was given to Guatemala to repress or eliminate. Thus, by the late 1960s and 1970s, US military assistance, along with new techniques in counterinsurgency (countering left-wing insurgent groups), was dispensed to contain this new threat.

The Alliance was modeled to a degree on the US economic assistance program for Western Europe in the aftermath of the Second World War: the Marshall Plan. Indeed, the Marshall Plan was the largest economic aid program in US history up to 1948 when it began. Also, some of the same officials who formulated the Marshall Plan worked on the Alliance.

The historical connection between the two programs is significant. Because the Marshall Plan was widely seen as successful, not surprisingly a number of Third World areas wanted Marshall Plans for themselves. However, most observers conclude that while the Marshall Plan was a success (some even tout it as the most successful US foreign policy in history), the Alliance was not.

In both the Marshall Plan and the Alliance, the United States wanted the regions to integrate economically. With both plans, the end goal was not just political stability and pro-US anticommunism but also improved economies in their respective regions so that they would be more competitive in world markets. Indeed, economic integration would help to create more wealth. In both aid plans, US officials wanted the leaders of the host nations to come up with plans to promote the economic integration of the region. Also, in both aid programs, US security concerns were paramount. US and Western European officials feared that if economic growth in Western Europe continued to contract, social and political conflict would sharpen, and communists would make political gains.

Similarly, communism, as US and Western leaders assumed, could potentially grow quickly in impoverished areas by promising "food in the belly" quickly. That is, if communists promised immediate jobs and economic well-being, Third World peoples would "jump" at the attempt to join the communist party. More apocalyptic observers thought that if communism made significant gains, the Soviet Union would be able to absorb Europe into its sphere of influence. The planners of both the Marshall Plan and the Alliance saw economic integration as promoting or fostering some degree of political integration as well. That is, if nations in a particular region traded and invested in each other, a degree of codependency, or interdependence, would develop as well, which, it was thought, would blunt the more extreme tendencies of both left- and right-wing nationalists to "go it alone" economically and politically. That is, by fostering regional trading organizations, US leaders assumed that there would be less European support for autarkic right-wing movements (like the fascists of the Second World War) and autarkic left-wing movements (like Castro's Cuba, which wanted to end all economic interaction with the United States for fear that such trade/investment would deepen already existing economic dependency on the "colossus to the north").

Although in the 1950s there were a number of aid programs proposed (by both North American and Latin America leaders), the timing of the Alliance shows clearly that US security concerns were front and center. With Castro consolidating his revolution, and his popularity among the left in the region very high, US leaders feared that the example of his revolution (and left-wing nationalism more generally) would spread around the region. As such, US leaders saw a combination of economic development coupled with generous doses of economic assistance as a sort of antidote to the spreading left-wing ideologies, key among them left-wing nationalism and communism.

Indeed, security concerns can be seen in both the Marshall Plan and the Alliance for Progress. Only one year after the Alliance, US, Canadian, and Western European officials forged an alliance—the North Atlantic Treaty Organization (NATO). NATO represented a major turn in US foreign policy. A military alliance means that for the participants, an attack on one means that all of the partner nations need to respond (militarily, if necessary) to repel the invasion. The United States had avoided military alliances since it severed its alliance with the French in 1800—the alliance that proved key in securing the independence of the thirteen original colonies from Great Britain. Washington leaders avoided alliances because they represented a commitment that they would rather avoid—a commitment that might mean that the United States would be dragged into a war against its interests. The United States joining NATO was the equivalent of publicly stating that preventing the expansion of communism into Western Europe was imperative. The United States was in effect stating that it was putting a protective shield around Western Europe. Should that shield be violated (presumably by the United States), the United States would respond militarily. To make the shield more secure, the United States stated that it would consider using nuclear weapons to defend Europe.

The Alliance had a lesser-known component—sharply increased US military assistance and covert assistance to Latin America.[5] Because with Castro's revolution in Cuba, some US officials assumed that it was "one minute to midnight" in the region. That meant that if Washington sat on its hands, very quickly many Latin American nations could "fall" to radical nationalism or communism. The militaries in Latin America were traditionally pro-United States, and in many cases (along with the Catholic Church), one of the two most powerful, conservative institutions in the region. US military assistance to Latin America began in the 1920s when US military officials were posted at some US embassies (later termed "military groups" or MILGROUPS in military abbreviation) to advise the Latin American militaries on how to be more effective in a nonpolitical way.[6] During the Second World War, this military aid increased, and after the war, the number of MILGROUPS mushroomed.[7] By the 1960s, Washington leaders were becoming more involved with training Latin American militaries. Civic action, the idea that the Latin American militaries should begin to help rural communities build infrastructure, was implemented. Not only would this endear (hopefully) the militaries to the rural citizenry, civic action would keep the military (theoretically) otherwise occupied so they would be less tempted to stage *golpe de estados* ("military coup d'etats").

US economic motives are another analogous aspect of the Marshall Plan and the Alliance. First, in both cases, US government assistance was strictly viewed as "seed money" that would promote more robust private sector, capitalist economic growth, including being more open to foreign private sector economic investment. Such investment was key, officials averred, to the continual development of the economy. Recipient nations should avoid at all costs becoming dependent on government (public sector) investment, Washington leaders averred, because such dependence would dull entrepreneurial initiative and ultimately economic productivity.

Second, after the Second World War, it was thought imperative for Europe to get "up and running" economically for a number of reasons. European demand for US products could keep the United States from falling into a postwar economic slump (a feature of many postwar situations in the United States, going back to the beginning of US history). Washington leaders discussed (mainly in internal memos) a "dollar gap" problem facing the United States after the Second World War in its relations with Europe. That is, if Europeans did not purchase US goods, the price of these goods would slump, US production would fall, and economic decline would occur in the United States. The wheels of world trade might, as they did during the Great Depression, grind to a halt. Such a scenario could reverberate outside of the Atlantic World, even hurting world trade as a whole. Increasing European demand for Latin American products would help Latin America, too, of course. With regard to the Alliance, similar to the Marshall Plan, a good portion of that money was spent purchasing US goods.

Finally, both the Marshall Plan and the Alliance for Progress are important because they facilitated the "cultural transfer" of US values to key areas of the world. Along with aid, trade, and investment come people and goods; with people and goods come values, or, more generally, new perspectives on one's "way of life" or identity. It is important to understand that globalization is not a one-way process by which economic influence translates into cultural influence in a reductive way. Instead, economic and cultural influences are often transmitted simultaneously and mutually reinforce each other. In addition, an important finding of researchers investigating the nexus between economic influence and cultural impact finds that the host nations do not blindly accept the influence transmitted to them from the more powerful nations. They accept some things; they reject others; and they creatively produce a new "hybrid" culture. Such is the nature of the development of culture going back centuries.

Kennedy and Latin America

Latin America had traditionally been an important area for US investments from oil and strategic minerals to food products. Trade between the United States and Latin America had traditionally been strong and important for the economies of both regions. As the Cold War intensified, with both sides (in risk-averse fashion) assuming the worst, and a seemingly endless arms race accelerated, US demand for strategic materials from Latin America sharpened. For example, oil from Venezuela and bauxite from Jamaica and British Guiana (after its independence, it became Guyana) were key for US strategic goals as well as a globalizing US economy ever searching for more and more inexpensive raw materials. US businessmen were searching more intensively for inexpensive raw materials as trade competition by the 1950s and 1960s sharpened with Japan and West Germany.

At first, Kennedy Administration officials argued that social and administrative reforms in Latin America were important for the success of the Alliance. That is, reforms like land reform and the more efficient administration of national governments were key to making not only the Latin American economies more efficient but also ensuring that the wealth produced by increased trade and economic activity more generally was distributed more equally.

At the same time, Kennedy and his advisors were hard-headed realists and extremely concerned with the growth of communist power in the world. At the end of the day, what mattered was that Latin America was firmly anticommunist and hopefully pro-United States. If the economic growth produced by the Alliance, then, were not distributed evenly, but Latin America was anticommunist, Washington leaders would not be concerned about the grinding poverty of the majority of the people of Latin America. Washington leaders would like to see Latin America become more democratic, but democratization was not a high priority. With regard to political instability in the Dominican Republic in the 1960s, a nation with a history of being pro-United States, Kennedy put it succinctly when talking to his advisors. Avoiding "another Castro" in the Caribbean was paramount for US leaders. With regard to the government in the Dominican Republic that emerged after the fall of pro-US dictator Rafael Trujillo, Kennedy said, "There are three possibilities in the Dominican Republic: a decent democratic government, a Trujillist authoritarian government, or a Castroite regime....but we shouldn't rule out the second until we are sure we can avoid the third."[8]

From the perspective of North America, however, Latin American development was to occur within the context of a rapidly spreading Cold War conflict between the noncommunist nations and the Soviet Union. With the intensification of the Cold War in the 1950s and with the "fall" of China to Chinese Communists in late 1949, Cold War confrontation intensified while quickly spreading to the nonindustrialized world. The decolonization of the former European powers in the developing world meant the rise of new nations, and of course, both sides in the Cold War wanted to "line up" those new nations on their side. At the very least, each side in the Cold War did not want the other to line up the new Third World nations on its side.

Despite the emphasis on reform early on in the Alliance, US officials began to back away from reforms for two main reasons. First, US officials decided that it was better to emphasize economic growth and to promote such growth as quickly as possible. It was thought that reformist projects would be an impediment to or drain resources from jump-starting economic growth. More significantly, US officials thought that reforms might lead to the nonelite majority—especially the poor—to call for deep or even cataclysmic reforms in Latin American society. The main concern was if a call for land reform reverberated around the region, revolutionaries would be inspired to rise up, ultimately threatening the power of elites in Latin America. As US officials, not surprisingly, wanted to maintain elites in power, and more generally the social hierarchy in the region, Washington greatly feared the spread of radical/revolutionaries ideas.

Thus, US policy aided and reinforced an already existing shift in Latin America from left-wing nationalism (discussed in the previous chapter) to a more right-wing form of nationalism. Starting in the mid-1960s and continuing until the 1990s, right-wing nationalism arose in Latin America. It had a number of different aspects. First, it was firmly anticommunist, rooted in what was termed "National Security Doctrine," the idea that the US and Latin American militaries needed to work together to contain or repel an extra-hemispheric threat from global communism. After the success of the Cuban Revolution, in nations that seemed to be under threat from an indigenous leftist insurgency and feared to be receiving secret assistance from world communism, a right-wing authoritarian government would "preemptively strike" to prevent left-wing forces from gaining control in a city or region.[9] Second, US officials ensured that funds from the US Agency for International Development (USAID), set up in 1961, would not sponsor reforms that could "touch off" smoldering revolutionary sentiment among the poor.

Brazil, for a number of reasons, wanted to promote economic growth in its poorest area, the Northeast. It had been in economic decline for centuries as sugar production contracted and the dynamo of Brazil's economy (at least from the late nineteenth century to the mid-twentieth century) shifted south—coffee production and export. If Brazilian leadership could somehow get the depressed Northeast on its way to self-sustaining economic growth, it would be less of a drain on the Brazilian economy. Such an accomplishment also could show Latin Americans and the world that Brazil was capable of solving even the most intractable of its economic problems. Despite its economic decline, the Northeast contained about one-third of Brazil's population in the 1950s and 1960s. To revitalize the Brazilian Northeast, the 1961–1964 government of João Goulart used an already existing development agency to stimulate economic diversification and development. The agency, Superintendência do Desenvolvimento do Nordeste (SUDENE, or Northeast Development Authority) was set up during the Juscelino Kubitschek Administration in 1959.[10] Once the reform-minded Goulart came into office in 1961, not surprisingly, he wanted to use SUDENE to jump-start economic development in the Northeast—and hopefully tap into Alliance for Progress funds in doing so. However, US officials, in particular USAID policy makers, deemed SUDENE too radical for US Alliance for Progress officials, who bypassed it, instead funneling Alliance funds to more conservative regional elites—those who had traditionally wielded power in that part of Brazil. The US-backed military coup in March 1964 in Brazil terminated Goulart's leftist government. The military leaders that took power ended the leftist experiment of bottom-up economic development in the country.

The State, the Soviet Union, and Latin American reaction to modernization theory

Modernization theorists thought it important that the Latin American states be relatively strong and efficient. This differs from neoliberalism discussed in Chapter Thirteen. In the 1970s and 1980s, a new view of economic development and the state emerged, which proved to be a throwback in many respects to the elite-led, positivist regimes of late nineteenth century Latin America, including an emphasis on export-driving growth. Although neoliberalism is similar in some ways to 1950s and 1960s modernization theory, there are key differences. During the early Cold War era, US modernizers implementing their theory in Latin America saw the state—and nation—as important for the modernization process. Modernization theorists realized that it was critically important that the state be strong enough to mediate and resolve conflicts that arose from the modernization process.

Modernization theorists, after all, realized that the process of modernization would be disruptive. Modernization theory called for traditional values of kinship network, dedication to agricultural production, and nostalgic ties to one's town and region to give way to modern values of thrift, education, and modern-day citizenry. Such a change could be very disruptive. As such, a relatively strong and competent state was key for ensuring that the transition from traditional society and values to modern society and values was not a revolutionary upheaval.

Modernization theorists enjoyed increasing access to power and control over policy toward the Third World starting in US Presidential Administrations of the 1960s. In this regard, it is important to recognize that the theory of capitalist, US-style economic development was a product of the Cold War. As the conflict between the noncommunist and communist nations rose to intense levels by the early 1960s, the prominence of modernization theorists in US presidential administrations rose apace. A good example is Walter W. Rostow's *Stages of Economic Growth—A Non-Communist Manifesto*. Making a big splash when it came on the scene in 1960, it blithely assumed that the industrialization/political modernization of the Western world, which had been occurring since the nineteenth century, could easily be transported to the Third World. Further, Rostow, a professor at the Massachusetts Institution of Technology, maintained that through enlightened policymaking on the part of top noncommunist world leadership, the process of modernization could occur more rapidly in the developing world than it did in the industrialized world. The influential book helped to propel Dr. Rostow to the highest levels of policymaking in the White House in the 1960s. Rostow even served as National Security Advisor under President Lyndon B. Johnson from 1966 to 1969. As such, Rostow was poised to make the argument about the link between modernization theory and US efforts in the Cold War clearly to powerful people.

Modernization theory was a product of the Cold War. It was a response to the globalization of the world communist movement in the 1950s and 1960s. As the Soviet Union rebuilt from the devastation of the Second World War and saw its communist ideology as attractive to Third World nationalists (in particular in Asia and Africa but also in the Middle East and Latin America), the Soviet Union's leaders saw an opportunity. Starting in the mid-1950s, the foreign policy makers of the Soviet Union offered economic inducements to the leaders of the newly liberated Third World nations. Such inducements could expand Soviet power in a large swath of the world and an increasingly important part of the world. International relations observers began to argue that the side who controlled the bulk of the Third World's people and resources would ultimately win that war.

Although the 1950s Soviet economic "offensive" (from the perspective of the noncommunist world) in the nonindustrialized world would be focused on parts of the world that were near the Soviet Union, US leaders feared increased Soviet economic and political activity in the Western Hemisphere as well. Washington's concerns in this regard remained low level until Fidel Castro's Cuba effectively became part of the Warsaw Pact in the early 1960s. US foreign policy makers became increasingly concerned about Soviet influence in Latin America after that time.[11] Communist activity in the Third World became a much more complex phenomenon when some Third World nations preferred to model themselves on the Chinese model as opposed to the Soviet model, which began to falter by the 1970s.

Conclusion

Even as modernization theory responded in part to the fear of communism on the part of officials in the noncommunist world, it was also a response to economic nationalism in the Third World, including Latin America, as discussed in Chapter Seven. Part and parcel of the rise of nationalism in Latin America after the Second World War was the desire, through economic nationalist policies, to strengthen the nation. To channel the benefits of economic growth toward the society as a whole, economic nationalists called for policies to protect large stocks of valuable, nonrenewable resources through nationalization; control over key infrastructure, especially transportation and power generation; and promotion of industrialization. Industrialization provided a means by which Latin American nations could save valuable foreign exchange. Diversification of the economy, by way of industrialization, would also serve to "cushion" a nation from the problem of one particular export for its economic livelihood—monoculture. Washington, however, viewed things differently. US leaders feared economic nationalism was the first step toward growth-inhibiting autarky, which would also deprive US businessmen of access to raw materials and markets.

In the 1960s, a more radical variant of economic nationalism appeared— dependency theory. Championed by intellectuals such as Ande Gunder Frank, Fernando Cardoso, and Enzo Faletto, dependency theory took the economic nationalist critique of free trade and investment policies a step further. Dependency theorists posited that export-oriented growth strategies in Latin America would only enrich the already wealthy elite while depleting Latin America of valuable, nonrenewable resources. Of key importance to dependency theorists was the terms of trade problem. Latin America produced primary products which declined in value over time as compared to industrialized products. That meant its terms of trade were declining, relative to the industrialized nations, over time. No matter how efficient Latin America produced and exported primary products, it would never "catch up" to the industrialized world. It would never earn enough foreign exchange to industrialize. Further, the industrialized world, because of its sheer economic power and control over world markets, will control the most dynamic parts of the economies of the developing world and will ensure that the developing world does not develop to the point where it could compete with the developed world.

In the last couple of decades, more and more people are criticizing dependency theory—including in Latin America. One critique is that if you subscribe to dependency theory—you are saying you have no control over your situation. Dependency theory shifts blame for a nation's problems to outside forces, in which case it then, logically, does not try to confront and solve its own problems. With the possible exception of the 1970s, dependency theory never made any serious inroads into the academic and policy circles of the industrialized world. US and industrialized world officials still adhere to modernization theory. And, at the end of the day, it is important to realize that modernization theory was not simply a product of the Cold War that disappeared with that war. It shaped, and continues to shape, the identities of Latin Americas—as noted in the epigraph that began this chapter.

Study Questions

1. What is modernization theory? How was it a product of the Cold War?
2. How and why was modernization theory applied to Latin America?
3. How successful were "modernizers" in applying modernization theory to Latin America? To what do you attribute their success or lack of success?
4. What criticisms could you make of modernization theory?

For Further Reading

Christenson, Joel C. 'From Gunboats to Good Neighbors: U.S. Naval Diplomacy in Peru, 1919–1942'. Ph.D diss. Department of History, West Virginia University, 2013.

Helleiner, Eric. *Forgotten Foundations of Bretton Woods—International Development and the Making of the Postwar Order*. Ithaca, NY: Cornell University Press, 2014.

Roett, Riordan. *The Politics of Foreign Aid in the Brazilian Northeast*. Nashville, TN: Vanderbilt University Press, 1972.

Sewell, Bevan. *The US and Latin America: Eisenhower, Kennedy and Economic Diplomacy in the Cold War*. London: I. B. Tauris, 2015.

Staples, Amy L. S. *The Birth of Development: How the World Bank, Food and Agriculture Organization, and World Health Organization Changed the World, 1945–1965*. Kent, OH: Kent State University Press, 2006.

Racial/Gender Aspects of Nationalism, Shift to the Political Right, War and Regionalism, and Neoliberalism

PART FIVE

Racial/Gender Aspects of Nationalism, Shift to the Political Right, War and Regionalism, and Neoliberalism

CHAPTER TEN

The Racial/Ethnic and Gender Aspects of Latin American National Identity

Legal equality is not enough for the spirit of the people, as they want absolute equality, in the public and domestic areas alike; and next they will want pardocracia, *which is their natural and unique propensity, in order to exterminate the privileged class.*

SIMÓN BOLÍVAR, LIBERATOR OF SOUTH AMERICA, 1825.[1]

Are we Europeans? So many copper-colored faces deny it. Are we indigenous? Perhaps the answer is given by the condescending smiles of our blonde ladies. Mixed? Nobody wants to be it, and there are thousands who would want to be called neither Americans nor Argentinians. Are we a nation? A nation without the accumulation of mixed materials, without the adjustment of foundations?

DOMINGO FAUSTINO SARMIENTO, ARGENTINE WRITER AND STATESMAN, 1883.[2]

Introduction

One thing that makes Latin American nationalism especially multifaceted and rich is the different types of nationalism subsumed within Latin

American nationalism. To understand these different forms of nationalism, it is important to understand Latin America's polyglot nature. The region is one of the most racially diverse in the world: it has large numbers of indigenous people, people of African descent, and Europeans. The complex mixing of these races helps us to understand not only the development of racial identity but also national identity.[3] These nonwhite Latin Americans are also part of a larger national fabric within each individual Latin American nation. A good example of the intersection of racial identity with nationalism is the rise of Indigenous nationalism in the 1940s, which was discussed in Chapter Six.

The projects of the various Latin American nationalists were a reaction to the top-down, elite (virtually all of whom were of European background), positivist, and racist nationalist movements of the nineteenth century. These elites denigrated people of color, including mixed-race people (those of partial European, Indigenous, and African heritage). The mixed-race people were given different names in different parts of Latin America. Outside of Central America, people of mixed European and Indian ancestry were termed "mestizo." In Central America, they were called ladinos. Outside of Brazil, those of mixed African and European background were called zambos; there, they were termed "pardos."

Even as the nation-building projects of the early nineteenth century were top-down elite projects, led by leaders bent on forming a European-style nation in positivistic fashion, Indians and Afro-Latin Americans had a different idea. Reacting against this racist, top-down nationalism, they formed their own nationalisms. In some areas, indigenous peoples in Latin America maintained a strong ethnoracial bond in their communities which went back to pre-Columbian times. Such collective ties carry on up to the present day. In other areas, Indians constructed a collective identity among a number of different Indian groups. Later, this collective identity was conceived as a type of national identity, parallel to the nation-state in which the Indians lived. This Indian identity was in part constructed to counter the elite-dominated nationalism of the nation where the Indians lived. Indians in the Andes have agreed upon a multicolored flag, the Wiphala, as a symbol of this Indian national identity. (See Figure 6.1, p.88.)

Another ethnic group in Latin America that has formed a national identity parallel to the national identity in which someone resides is the Afro-Latin Americas. Afro-Latin American nationalism grew out of pride in Afro-Latin Americans' African heritage. But, it also formed in large part as a response to the racial exclusion meted out by those of European background and mestizos in the nations where they lived.[4]

There is a sharp distinction between the United States and Europe (the "West") on the one hand and Latin America on the other with regard to how race is constructed or conceptualized. In the West, the conception of race is polarized or binary. That is, if someone has one drop of Latin American, African, or Indigenous blood in them, they are considered Latin, African, or

Indian. This could be termed the "one-drop rule"—one drop of nonwhite blood in one's background legally defined someone as nonwhite. In some parts of the United States, this "one-drop rule" was enshrined in law. By law, someone who was one-sixteenth African American, for example, in some parts of the United States until the end of legalized segregation in the 1960s was considered African American. The physical appearance of the person was not related to how he or she was categorized racially. Lineage determined racial classification. Unfortunately, this binary conception of race was based on an ideal that European purity was racially superior to all others or at least led to the idea that those who were not purely European were somehow impure.[5]

In Latin America, as distinct from North America, the conception of race includes multiple categories of racial makeup. That is, someone who is part European and part indigenous is considered mestizo or ladino (in Central America)—not considered either white or Indian but a different racial category. Someone who is part European and part African is considered mulatto. As opposed to the West, physical appearance dictated what race someone was categorized as.[6] What that meant in practice was that a person of mixed European and African heritage was neither black nor white but mulatto. However, in some Latin American nations, someone who was physically dark could increase his or her social status if they accumulated significant wealth. The catch phrase was "money whitens."

In the nineteenth century, whites and Europeans had a sense of racial identity in the sense that they thought it was their duty to lead a society of nonwhites and Indians and Afro-Latin Americans in a positivistic way that would bring European-style progress to Latin America. (Positivism was discussed in Chapter Five.) And, of course, they wanted to maintain their privileged position atop Latin American society. For their part, Afro-Latin Americans and Indians had a sense of racial/ethnic identity (and even an emergent sense of nationalism) in that they thought it is important to maintain elements of African or Indian culture, especially as white/European aimed to get them to give up their culture.

For their part, mestizos, or ladinos in Central America, lacked a clear sense of racial identity well into the twentieth century. Since they were not part of the European or non-European ethnic groups, in a sense they thought they were not part of any group. By the early twentieth century, however, some mestizo intellectuals were talking about a collective identity. Such mestizo intellectuals made the case that mestizaje, the process of race mixing, even had a transcendent side to it. That is to say, mestizos combined the best elements of the indigenous and European cultures into one culture. José Vasconcelos, who served as minister of education in the 1920s, during the period of the Mexican Revolution, wrote and spoke about how the process of mestizaje was a "raza cosmica" (cosmic race), combining the best elements of indigenous and European culture. (This was discussed in the section on the Mexican Revolution in Chapter Six.)

It is also important to point out that simply because there are more racial categories in Latin America, it does not mean that somehow Latin America is "less racist" than the West. In fact, in most Latin American nations, there is a racial hierarchy, with lighter-skinned people at the top of the hierarchy. In some Latin American cultures, fine distinctions are made between light brown and lighter brown-skinned people, with the lighter-skinned people at the higher end of the social hierarchy. Some nations in the past consciously embarked on a pro-European immigration policy to "whiten" the population because it was those of European background who were considered superior to all others. Thus, "whitening" the population was clearly racist and if taken to an extreme could even be termed "genocidal."

Although some scholars have attempted to make a distinction between the terms "ethnicity" and "race," I will use the terms interchangeably. Some observers have noted that race is based on physical/genetic characteristics and makeup, whereas others view ethnicity as based on customs, attitudes, and achievements. However, the two ideas are so intertwined, I would argue, as to be indistinguishable.[7]

Two case studies: Cuba and Brazil

With regard to the intersection of racial/ethnic identity and nationalism in Latin America, there are a variety of "case studies" in the region as well as ways of examining how race relations helps us to understand the growth and development of nationalism, especially in the early part of what could be termed the "long twentieth century" (which one could argue began in 1898). The argument is that an examination of this time period is especially important for understanding both race relations and nationalism in Latin America today.

To make the intersection of nationalism and race/ethnicity more intelligible, we'll examine three case studies: Cuba, Brazil, and Mexico. These three examples show how complicated—and fascinating—the intersection of race/ethnicity and nationalism is in Latin America. In a sense, they are the "exceptions that prove the rule."

Cuba

Cuba is an especially interesting case study of the intersection of race/ethnicity and nationalism. To understand the Cuban case, first we must delve into the background of the Caribbean situation. In the Caribbean, the imperial powers held on to their colonies later than in the rest of the region. As such, the "imperial overlords"—the officials appointed by the mother countries to run their colonies—remained in the Caribbean for much longer than the creoles of Mexico, Central America, and South America. With the victorious wars of independence in the early nineteenth century, most of the Iberians who enjoyed their powerful position atop of the colonial enterprises of the Iberian nations quickly left the Americas.

In the Caribbean, however, European officials who were in charge of the various colonies for the imperial nations of Europe were there in some cases well into the twentieth century. (Indeed, some are still there today.) As such, it is not surprising that those in the Caribbean of African extraction saw the exiting of European power as integral to the equitable development of their emerging nations and new nationalism. Also, it is not surprising that black Caribbean people saw the end of European empire as part and parcel of the liberation of the Afro-Caribbean people and the opportunity for the full self-actualization of blacks in the Caribbean.

Cuba's "antiracism"

Cuba is an especially interesting case of racial tolerance. Some would term it "antiracism." Others would term it "racial egalitarianism." Two things that make the intersection of nationalism and race relations different in Cuba compared to other Latin American nations is that, first, its liberation experience from Spain was different than that of other nations in the region; and, second, the amount of influence it experienced from the United States (Cuba is about ninety miles from the United States) means that its race relations had been affected more by its contact with the United States when compared to other Latin American nations.

Cuba's especially long and bloody war for independence meant that its national liberation experience was protracted, in comparison with the experience of the rest of Latin America, which achieved its independence by the early nineteenth century. Cuba was different in another way. Its war for national liberation intersected with the decline and fall of the institution of slavery, which had never been a powerful institution in the rest of Latin America (outside of Brazil). Cuba was the penultimate country to emancipate its slaves, freeing them in 1886 (just two years before Brazil did so). Proindependence forces started a low-level insurrection in 1868, promising that slaves who abandoned their masters to fight for Cuba's independence from Spain would be granted freedom should the proindependence forces triumph. As such, with slaves leaving their masters in large numbers to fight for Cuban independence, the slavery system crumbled. Slaves, although they were some of the most powerless members of society, had a big impact on Cuban history and the emergence of Cuban nationalism. Even as slavery was abolished, Afro-Cubans and those of mixed European and African ancestry continued to fight for Cuba's independence.

Cuba was robbed of its dream of full autonomy by the United States, which invaded Cuba in 1898 to stop the humanitarian disaster there and for its own self-interested reasons (see Chapter Eighteen). But Cuban nationalism was undimmed and lived on to emerge more forcefully later—in particular with the revolution against the rule of Fulgencio Batista in the 1950s, which ended in triumph for the revolutionary leader Fidel Castro. Significantly, the racial tolerance that emerged from the crucible of Cuba's extremely long and violent fight for independence would mean that Cuban nationalism would be more racially egalitarian than in other Latin American nations.

Just because Cuba was antiracist and arguably more racially tolerant than many other Latin American nations, it did not mean that Afro-Cubans enjoyed social mobility on their terms. In fact, the situation was the opposite. Should Afro-Cubans desire to maintain aspects of their native African culture, or should they resist accepting the values of the dominant culture of Cuba's elites, that is, European culture, they would not be able to "work their way up" the social hierarchy in Cuba. As such, Afro-Cubans had to assimilate into the culture of Cuba's elites in order to prosper.

Because Cuba was so geographically close to the United States, and the United States invested billions of dollars in Cuba going back to the mid-twentieth century, US influence was profound in Cuba up to the 1959 revolution. When US businessmen and tourists traveled to the island, they imposed US views of race relations—the idea that there should be racial segregation and "lumping together" of mulattos and Afro-Cubans into one group. To the dismay of the darker-hued people of Cuba, visiting (and expatriate) white Americans in Cuba viewed this nonwhite group as racially inferior.

Brazil's so-called racial democracy

Brazil's supposedly racial democracy was most persuasively articulated in the 1930s by sociologist Gilberto Freyre in his widely read classic *Casa Grande e Favela* (The mansion and the slave quarters). Quickly translated into English, it had a big impact on how scholars of Latin America viewed Brazil, in particular race relations in Brazil. Sociologist Freyre argued that the Portuguese penchant for miscegenation explained both why the population of mixed-race persons in Brazil was so large and why racial tolerance was especially widespread. The racial tolerance in Brazil, according to Freyre, found its roots in the 700-year invasion/occupation of the Iberian Peninsula by the Moors who were forcibly removed from the peninsula by the Spanish/Portuguese in the 1490s. Since the Moors were dark skinned, and some of them had sexual relations with Iberians, racial mixing had a long history in Iberia.

Even as Freyre's ideas were criticized by scholars in the years after he published his work, his ideas were influential. Enjoying ample acceptance in Brazil in the 1920s and 1930s, one finds that an important aspect of Brazilian nationalism is the acceptance of other races as well as a higher tolerance for racial mixing when compared to other nations in the region. The idea of "racial democracy" as a mainstay of Brazilian nationalism became an important feature of Brazilian life by the mid-twentieth century. That is to say, one thing that Brazilians then—and still today—maintain is that Brazil is superior to other nations because it is one of the more racially tolerant nations in Latin America. Even as scholars have debunked the idea that Brazil is more racially tolerant than its neighbors and even debunked the idea that "racial democracy" exists in the South American giant, the ideology/mythology of racial democracy remains powerful. This myth is an important part of Brazilian nationalism today.

Slavery and the nation: Key differences between North and Latin America

Understanding the legacy of slavery of Afro-Latin Americans in Latin America is a window into understanding the racial side of Latin American nationalism. For their part, Latin Americans used the end of slavery as a way of building up national unity. In the case of Haiti, a slave rebellion proved to be the basis for the creation of the nation in the early nineteenth century. By the mid-nineteenth century, Latin American nations one by one abolished slavery, thus creating a more racially open and racially egalitarian society when compared to their Western Hemisphere "neighbor," the United States. (Brazil and Cuba were the exceptions, maintaining their slave systems up until 1888.)

The economic importance of slavery is key to understanding why it was so important to the United States, Cuba, and Brazil, and why it took a bloody civil war in the United States to eradicate slavery once and for all, in 1865. In fact, before the US Civil War of 1861–1865, most whites in the slave-holding areas of the United States saw the abolition of slavery by means of slave rebellion, such as in Haiti in 1803, as a very serious threat. Slave owners in the southern United States feared the Haitian Revolution because it might have emboldened slaves to rise up in rebellion in the United States. However, economics is not the only determining factor. Slavery in Latin America was a system by which whites could control large number of Afro-Latin Americans and similarly so in the United States with regard to its African slaves. It is not surprising that slavery lasted longer in the nations that it did, because in those societies there were large numbers of slaves.

In the end, the Latin Americans' decision to abolish slavery represented a bold experiment in strengthening the nation. By peacefully abolishing slavery, political citizenship was expeditiously extended to all Latin Americans, regardless of race. With this nonracially based citizenship, the various Latin American nations were quietly strengthened. For its part, because of the economic significance of slavery in the United States in the pre–Civil War era, it took a bloody four-year civil war, from 1861 to 1865, to forge a stronger national identity and extend citizenship to all on the basis of race—to all men, that is. Women were not extended citizenship in the United States and in Latin America until well into the twentieth century.

Gender and nationalism: Por la Patria/Madria!

The battles for independence against the Spanish military in the early nineteenth century were not going well. However, in 1812, a group of women (known as the *heroinas* ["female heroes"]) valiantly, and successfully, worked together to beat the Spanish to prevent them from taking Cochabamba, Bolivia. The battle became known as the women's uprising. Giving ample opportunities for a number of proindependence people (including women) to fight the Spanish, Bolivia was the first nation to rise up against the Spanish in 1809 and the last to declare its independence in 1824. As such, in this long struggle, the heroines' efforts placed them as very important in the narrative of nation building—they were willing to make the supreme sacrifice for their (emerging) nation. Their sacrifices have been reified to the level of myth. To commemorate the sacrifice of the *heroinas*, Mother's Day in Bolivia is May 27, the anniversary of the women's uprising.[8]

The *heroinas* were valiant in their courage to stand up to the Spanish. However, they did not significantly change gender roles. Women, until the mid-twentieth century in Latin America, had difficulty achieving admittance to schools, including university education. Securing work outside the home, except as a nanny or domestic worker, proved difficult as well. The fact that women were largely circumscribed to home life until the mid-twentieth century, however, does not mean that they were not an important part of the nation-building process.

The process by which nations are built is a gendered process. It helps us to understand the relations between men and women and how they have changed over time. That is to say, as nationalism unfolds over time, it both reinforces already existing gender relations and also provides opportunity, or "social space" for citizens, in particular women, to challenge already existing gender relations.

Women in colonial Latin America and in the early national period were subjected to an oppressive system of gender relations. They were subservient to men. Women had few rights outside the home. What they could do within the household was carefully subscribed as well. As such, considering that it was men, in general powerful, white or mestizo men, who had virtually total control over how the idea of the Latin American nation was constructed when the Latin American nations emerged from the Spanish and Portuguese Empires in the early nineteenth century, the nation was seen as a "patria," or fatherland, not as a "madria."

Latin American society tells us a lot about how women's activities were strictly contained and/or regulated or controlled by men. As in many societies, the system of inheritance was one in which the oldest male child enjoyed the bulk or entirety of the inheritance. As such, it was necessary for society to ensure that women were chaste upon marriage and did not engage in extramarital sexual relations. In this (old-fashioned) social system, if there was some question as to whether a male child was the progeny of the husband, it would call into question whether the inheritance should be bequeathed to him.

The logical extension of this hyper-concern about whether a male child (in particular the oldest) was the true progeny of a husband is that female "honor" needed to be maintained. "Honor" is a vague term, and its meaning changes significantly with context. What honor meant for an unmarried female was that her chastity needed to be maintained at all costs. What honor meant for a married woman was that she needed to be physically protected by a stronger male.

The epitome of a strong male would be a caudillo (discussed in Chapter Two). He was the physical protector of the territory in addition to heading up a military which would ensure stability—on his terms. In every case, caudillos were male. As such, caudillos symbolically protected the women of the country from whatever depredations they might experience. Thus, the process of nation building was necessarily a gendered process.

So, one could see the rise of (hypermasculine) caudillos as "locking-in" the close association of masculinity and nation building in Latin America. The downside of this close association (tragic embrace) of nationalism and hypermasculinity is that when women rebelled in order to achieve their full allotment of civil, even human, rights, they were seen as rebelling against the nation and nationalism. They could be portrayed as antipatriotic or even traitors.

Conclusion: Representations of Latin America outside the region

In Latin America, the gendered metaphor of the nation is male. In general, when Latin Americans emotionally invoke the nation they are proud to live in, they (in most cases) talk about a fatherland. Sometimes, they might refer to their nation as "she" or "her," but in general, the embodiment of the nation is that of a father figure.

However, the nation is also viewed in feminine terms—nationalism can seduce, embrace, and nurture; such traits are stereotypically feminine. Some popular women, such as Eva Perón, the first wife of Argentine leader Juan Perón during his first term in office (1946–1955), embody the nation in the minds of many of the citizens, and Evita (as she was known to her followers) exhibited a nurturing, seductive quality, in particular, when she spoke to/for/ about the nation.

In addition, when people in the United States represented Latin America, in particular in political cartoons, Latin America was represented as a woman (in general, a fair-skinned woman).[9] The main reasons for this female representation of the region is that the United States, going back to the 1823 Monroe Doctrine and the 1904 Roosevelt Corollary to the Doctrine, discussed in Chapter Nineteen, viewed Latin America as something that needed to be protected. Protected against what? Mainly, the United States' fears that depredations inflicted on Latin America from European imperial nations will imperil the security and well-being of everyone in the Americas. As such, the United States feels it needs to extend a protective "shield" to the Latin Americans. This logic also underlays US fear of Soviet incursions into Latin America during the Cold War. In addition, in political cartoons, in particular in years past, Latin America was often represented as nonwhite, or mixed race, and sometimes as a short adult or a child. A representation of this type indicated that because the majority of Latin Americans were nonwhite, people in the United States saw them as inferior to the United States, a majority white nation.

Study Questions

1. How do Latin Americans categorize people by race? How does this categorization differ from how people are categorized by race in the United States and Europe?
2. How are Cuba and Brazil representative of how Latin Americans conceive of race? How are they distinctive in this regard?
3. The intersection of racial identity and nationalism was discussed in Chapter Six with regard to Indian nationalism. How does Indian nationalism differ from the types of racial, national identity discussed in this chapter?

For Further Reading

Andrews, G. Reid. *Blacks and Whites in Sao Paulo Brazil, 1888–1988*. Madison: University of Wisconsin Press, 1991.

Andrews, G. Reid. *Afro-Latin America, 1800–2000*. Oxford: Oxford University Press, 2004.

Graham, Richard. *Idea of Race in Latin America, 1870–1940*. Austin: University of Texas Press, 1990.

Johnson, John J. *Latin America in Caricature*. Austin: University of Texas Press, 1980.

CHAPTER ELEVEN

The High Tide of Latin American Nationalism in the 1960s and Nationalism Shifts to the Political Right

[Converting Latin American nationalism] into useful forces will be difficult task, requiring, among other things, great patience and more integrity than is common in governing circles in Latin America or among those who control the chief organs of public opinion.

DANIEL COSÍO VILLEGAS[1]

Introduction: Left-wing nationalism gives way to right-wing nationalism

The "high tide" of left-wing nationalism in Latin America peaked in the mid-1960s. In the late 1940s and 1950s, left-wing nationalists made their case to the Latin American people—in particular those living in the rapidly growing urban areas. These urbanites were, of course, the backbone of the populist movement of the mid-twentieth century in the region. Left-wing nationalists made the point that the Latin American people had sacrificed during the Second World War by agreeing to help out the Allied cause by selling large quantities of critically important raw materials at below-market prices. Now, it was time for the Latin American nations to focus on the development of their own economies and societies.

Interestingly, starting in the early 1960s, elites and some military leaders in some Latin American nations began to fear that the power of the populist leaders and the populist movement of the 1940s and 1950s might become too large and result in radical policies that would redistribute wealth from the wealthy to the nonelite majority. The elite, and the upper middle class, thought that during the populist era, workers' demands had grown too much. As such, military coups in countries such as Peru (1962), Guatemala (1963), Brazil (1964), Bolivia (1964), Argentina (1966), Chile (1973), and Uruguay (1973) replaced grassroots economic development to military government reforms. Not surprisingly, military-led governments thought that they were best situated to implement social and economic reforms. After all, with the military firmly in control and the ability of the nonelites to influence policy diminished, the military could control the situation if the rapidly advancing process of industrialization created social dislocation or conflict. As Latin America rapidly industrialized after the Second World War, large cities mushroomed, without enough public services and infrastructure for the working class and poor. Some military leaders made the case that top-down, military-led social and economic reform was key to the national security of the country. Better integrating the rural, poorer, isolated parts of the nation into the nation as a whole would strengthen nationalism. Development of an internal market would strengthen a nation's economy and thus its sense of nationalism.[2]

The military-led governments in the mid- to late 1960s thought that the military, combined with the federal government bureaucracy, would produce both "order and progress" (Brazil's national motto) in positivistic fashion around the region. The term academics used to describe such regimes was Bureaucratic-Authoritarianism. The term was coined by the influential and brilliant Argentine political scientist, Guillermo O'Donnell.[3] Although O'Donnell at first focused on Argentina and Brazil in the late 1960s and 1970s as examples, the framework of Bureaucratic-Authoritarianism works well for many Latin American military governments during this particular timeframe. The theory is that military authoritarian governments would reduce the power of organized labor and thus reduce wages. As such, capital accumulation would grow, jump-starting economic growth. Part and parcel of this economic model was improving and increasing the size of the government bureaucracy. Cynics would conclude that the purpose of this bureaucracy would be to entrench the dictatorship in power: a new form of continuismo. (Continuismo is a traditional problem in Latin American history, that of leaders perpetuating themselves in power.)

However, there was more to it than economics. The military leaders maintained that bureaucrats were needed to more efficiently allocate societal resources to ensure that social problems were solved or to prevent already existing problems from festering and growing into bigger ones.

The bureaucrats were termed *técnicos* ("technical experts"), often trained in the countries' top universities or in the United States. Their technical expertise would ensure, at least in theory, that the government would produce good public policy. Such an emphasis on technical ability of the leadership, or at least the advisors to the leadership, was a throwback to the positivist idea of the late nineteenth century.

For economic and security (anticommunist) reasons, left-wing nationalism was on the retreat, and right-wing nationalism correspondingly was on the rise starting in the mid-1960s and accelerating in the 1970s and 1980s. With regard to the anticommunist part of the equation—the nationalist right in Latin America was given a boost by the Cold War, in particular what came to be known as National Security Doctrine.[4] Going back to the beginning of the Cold War, but becoming more prominent as the Cold War intensified, National Security Doctrine called for the Latin American militaries to promote anticommunist order in Latin America. US military officials, themselves imbued with an anticommunist mentality, helped National Security Doctrine to develop by hosting meetings, sending advisors, and sending military aid (including weaponry) to the Latin American militaries. Part of National Security Doctrine called for "internal security." This meant that some of this US weaponry was used by the Latin American militaries against their own people. "Internal security" also had an economic component. If countries were politically stable, foreign investors would be more likely to risk investing capital in Latin America, thus increasing economic growth, which would then, in turn, theoretically, provide for future political security.

Voices of Latin American experts on nationalism

As left-wing nationalism was losing its force and right-wing nationalism was becoming more prominent, nationalism was in transition in the 1960s. Although observers did not realize it at the time, in retrospect, nationalistic sentiment proved to reach its apex in the 1960s and decline in the following decades. As such, during this time period in which nationalism was both powerful and in transition, a close examination of Latin American nationalism is instructive, particularly the views of Latin American thinkers.

Many Latin American scholars had a limited sense of Latin American nationalism as a regional phenomenon. As such, they focused on the nationalism of their particular country. In Spanish-speaking Latin America, the origins of nationalism can be traced back to their nineteenth-century Wars for Independence against Spain. In the case of Brazil, the origins of Brazilian nationalism go back to forcing the Portuguese to accept their independence. Also, many Latin American scholars focused their attention on attempts to fend off or circumscribe foreign influence from a major, outside power (the United States or a European nation). Few are the Latin American scholars who examine Latin American nationalism more regionally.

In the mid-1960s, it seemed that Latin American nationalism would fully flower. Two decades of Import Substitution Industrialization (ISI) had produced stronger economies and better public services (in particular in the growing cities). An urban middle class was growing, and with it, social stability seemed to be stronger than it had been for decades. It seemed that the upheavals of the 1930s would quickly become a forgotten memory. To many, it seemed that the Latin American nations were finally developing economically to the point that they would be minimally dependent on outside capital and markets—the dream of scholars for decades, even centuries. Moreover, after the heavy demand for Latin American resources during the Second World War and the Korean War, many Latin Americans enjoyed a situation in which they were flush with foreign exchange for the first time in decades. Given this fortuitous situation, the question became how to translate this rosy economic scenario of developed/diversified/industrialized nations into an economic system that benefitted the majority.

Unfortunately, populist experiments in Argentina, Bolivia, Chile, Guatemala, and Venezuela did not produce such a system. Inflation and inefficient government proved to be a problem as well as concern among the elite and upper middle class that the working classes were asking for too much in economic terms (as discussed above). Colombia for its part became mired in civil strife, even war, by the late 1960s. Rising frustration among the poor and middle class meant that nationalist leaders/thinkers felt they needed to come up with programs to create economic/social/political systems of representative government and economies that produced benefits for the majority in relatively equitable fashion. The economic success of Latin America in the immediate post–Second World War situation and the frustrations of a faltering populism in the mid-1960 fed a new sense of nationalism. Thus, it is not surprising that four of the more insightful Latin American scholars who wrote on nationalism produced their analyses at this particular historical moment. The views of Roberto de Oliveira Campos of Brazil, Daniel Cosío Villegas of Mexico, José Figueres of Costa Rica, and Juan José Arévalo of Guatemala will be analyzed below to help the reader better understand the multifaceted nature of Latin American nationalism at its peak.

Oliveira Campos and the complexities of Latin American nationalism

Brazilian Roberto de Oliveira Campos, in his "United States–Latin American Relations" starts out by making the important point that the

United States in issuing its famous Monroe Doctrine of 1823 was being "unilateral and *nationalistic*" (emphasis in original).[5] The Monroe Doctrine called for a halt to further European expansion in the Americas. It was not applied consistently in US foreign policy. The United States did not consult the Latin Americans before issuing it. Nonetheless, the Latin American nations accepted it, in some cases enthusiastically. Some Latin American nations thought implicit in the Monroe Doctrine was that the United States would provide security for Latin America against the threat of attack from outside powers. (US leaders did not promise or provide such security.) However, when the United States made it clear that its own nationalistic interests took precedence over the interests of Latin America, US policy fostered Latin American nationalism. The Roosevelt Corollary (to the Monroe Doctrine) of 1904 stated that the United States had the right, even the duty, to intervene militarily in Latin American to preserve order on US terms.

Early twentieth-century US military and political intervention and economic influence, in particular in the circum-Caribbean region (the Caribbean, Mexico, and Central America), produced what de Oliveira terms "reactive tensions," which fed Latin American nationalism. The US military interventions (e.g., the Mexican-American War; Panama in 1903; Nicaragua in the 1910s and 1920s; Mexico again in 1914; and Haiti and the Dominican Republic in the 1910s and 1920s) took a political form as well. The best example of political intervention was the 1903 Platt Amendment placing a protectorate on Cuba. Further, US economic influence stoked Latin American nationalism; for example, US oil companies in eastern Mexico, the United Fruit Company in the Caribbean and Central America, and US sugar companies in Cuba.[6]

Ideological tensions between the United States and Latin America were used by some Latin Americans to foster Latin American nationalism. Latin American communists (there were a small number of them in the region) found it easier to work with and/or infiltrate Latin American nationalist groups after the 1917 Bolshevik Revolution in Russia and the 1949 Communist Chinese Revolution. With those two revolutions, which had a nationalistic element to them, the world communist movement was in a sense made more nationalistic. Another form of ideological tension was what de Oliveira terms "monopolistic nationalism" which posits that Latin Americans need to protect Latin American-based industries from foreign competition, which might endanger these industries' very existence.[7] Monopolistic nationalism is another word for economic nationalism, as discussed in Chapter Seven.

"Monopolistic nationalism" has a number of facets. First, many Latin American nationalists saw industrialization as key to building up the power of the nation. In the minds of many Latin American nationalists, development, industrialization, and nationalism are one and the same. Second, there is heavy reliance on the state as direct entrepreneur. Third, exporting raw materials is generally seen as humiliating and especially degrading as it robs the nation of a limited/nonrenewable stock of wealth. Fourth, there is distrust of foreign capital—especially if it is direct foreign investment and activities that explore/exploit national resources. Foreign ownership of public utilities is disliked. Fifth, overall planning by the state is considered necessary. Sixth, agrarian reform is considered necessary, in particular as a means of promoting redistributive social justice.

Interestingly, Oliveira notes that Latin American nationalism was on the rise (post-1945) as US and Western European nationalism was being muted. The United States and Europe saw the need to downplay their individual nationalisms to work together internationally to contain a feared expansion of communism.[8] Indeed, the North Atlantic Treaty Organization (NATO) was the first US alliance since 1800. Latin American nationalism was particularly important in the postwar era, as Latin America saw the need to maintain unity against the decentralizing tendencies inherent in a heterogeneous society, for example, racial/ethnic tension and conflict between social classes. Fascinatingly, Oliveira concludes that nationalism in postwar Latin America could prove crucial:

> It is in fact a major task of social dynamics in Latin America to utilize the mobilization potential of nationalism without falling prey to its intoxicating periods....if a prudent and sober view is taken of this phenomenon, if the legitimate historical grievances are recognized, if account is taken of emotional urges inherent in periods of quick transformation of dependent economies into proud self-reliant nations, we shall find that nationalism in Latin America, just as in Europe, where it was first born, may give ground to more balanced attitudes once the process of modernization of the societies is advanced and a great degree of social integration reached.

Further, Latin American nationalists sought an independent foreign policy from the United States, not seeing the threat of the Cold War as a significant, imminent problem. Instead, the problem for Latin Americans is poverty and dissatisfaction among the poor/working classes. Indeed, Castro's revolution in Cuba helped to promote Latin American nationalism, not just because of the David and Goliath nature of Castro's conflict with the United States, but because of a preexisting, long-standing linkage in the minds of many (nonelite) Latin Americans that redistribution justice was part of nationalistic longing.[9]

Latin American nationalism has a significant economic side to it. First, Latin Americans chafe at the United States, or International Financial Institutions, implementing stabilization plans that require austerity measures. Oliveira terms these "economic pressure to enforce canons of monetary stability and fiscal discipline." The biggest portion of the pain imposed by such measures is borne by the working class and poor (cuts in food subsidies and employment in state-run industries).[10] Further, Latin American nationalists seek to expropriate foreign ownership of valuable natural resources, often viewed as national patrimony (valuable minerals and oil). Although the United States and Latin America agree on the theoretical right of nations to expropriate foreign holdings, significant disagreement over how much compensation should be given to the victim of expropriation, and what form such compensation should take, result in US-Latin American tension, fueling Latin American nationalism.

Cosío Villegas and economic influence and development

Renowned Mexican historian Daniel Cosío Villegas, in his "Nationalism and Development," perceptively outlined some of the unique aspects of Latin American nationalism. First, Latin American nationalists often drink deeply from a utopian vision of pre-Conquest Latin America. That is, they perceive of pre-Conquest Latin America as a land where indigenous groups lived in autonomous freedom and felt themselves masters of the land they lived on while sustaining themselves and developing their own resources in the way they saw fit. As Villegas points out, since this perception is overly idealistic and not borne out by the known facts, such a vision tells us quite a bit about the aspirations of Latin American nationalists. However, a second tendency of Latin American nationalism looks overseas, not inward. Because of 300 years of Spanish/Portuguese colonization, an "indelible mark of foreign intervention, intervention from outside America ... left the seeds of an ultra—nationalism of which it feeds in carrying out its lasting historical experiments."[11] Not surprisingly, Latin American nationalists strongly rejected any idea of studying Iberia for any economic/social/political models. Thus, they concluded, to address the ills wrought by Iberian conquest, the Latin American elites turned to non-Iberian, industrialized nations— embracing ideologies from France, England, and the United States.[12]

Cosío Villegas points to two important, unique aspects of Latin American nationalism. In the early years of independence, Latin American nations looked to Europe, especially Great Britain, for loans to build infrastructure. European nations loaned money, but in many cases, loan repayment required Latin Americans to remit to the European creditors a portion of their foreign exchange earned by exporting products overseas. To ensure that the Latin American nations allocated a portion of their foreign exchange earned through exports, the European creditors stationed their officials in the customs posts of the ports of the delinquent, collecting duties themselves and deducting a portion of the duties for loan repayment.[13] In some cases, the European creditors sent troops to occupy the port cities of Latin America to ensure prompt/proper repayment of debts.

Second, Latin American nationalists seek to somehow promote the well-being, peace, and equality—that is, overall happiness—of their nation's people. Before the mid-twentieth century, many nationalists thought the means of pursuing those lofty goals was to emulate the rapidly industrializing nations. By the mid-twentieth century, many in Latin America instead realized that the well-being of the peoples of the industrialized world had fallen short of those countries' stated goals for their people. As such, Latin American nationalists were less likely to look abroad for models for development and instead look inward.[14]

Latin American nationalism, Cosío Villegas concluded, has an important economic element to it. Though Latin American citizens desired increased economic development, simultaneously they fear foreign investment in their nations. Many Latin American nationalists think that foreign investors, by placing their own profit motive first, do not significantly facilitate economic development in the host nation. Concomitant to this argument is that foreign investors damage Latin American nationalistic sentiment because wealthy foreign investors work with their wealthy counterparts in the Latin American nation. Those elite (and often politically well connected) Latin Americans begin to put the interests of the foreign investors before those of the host nation. Even foreign nations investment in infrastructure (e.g., railroads) did not significantly foster Latin American economic development, since most railroads were used to facilitate extraction of valuable minerals for the benefit of foreign investors. Further, Latin American nationalists fear that overweening economic intervention will inevitably translate into political power, even domination, by outsiders.[15] In sum, many Latin American nationalists, not illogically, concluded that foreign investment inevitably leads to "vende-patria" (literally, selling the country: selling off the nonrenewable wealth of the host nation to foreigners for their exclusive benefit at the expense of the nation and the people as a whole). Such concerns with regard to foreign economic activity in Latin America would be especially palpable in Mexico, Central America, and the Caribbean, considering the long history of economic and political influence of multinational companies.

Because of Latin America's extremely negative experience with Spanish/Portuguese conquest/colonization, and its dislike and fear of many forms of US and European economic investment/activity in the region, which many viewed as a form of neocolonialism, Latin American nationalism is understandably "deep" and "justifi[able]." Thus, it is understandable that nationalism is expressed "negatively in suspicion, contempt, or hatred for foreigners." Moreover, nationalism exhibits an "incredible extremity of emotion and irrationality."[16]

Cosío Villegas's conclusion was not optimistic. How to "convert it [Latin American nationalism] into useful forces will be a difficult task, requiring, among other things, great patience and more integrity than is common in governing circles in Latin America or among those who control the chief organs of public opinion."[17] Tall order indeed.

Figueres and the trials of economic dependency

Nationalist leader José Figueres, president of Costa Rica, 1948–1949, 1953–1958, and 1970–1974, walked a fine line vis-à-vis Costa Rica's relations with the United States. He was remarkably successful. He managed to pull off, in the confrontational early Cold War years, implementing left-wing reforms in his nation without being categorized by the United States as a dangerous communist. In short, his political skills arguably prevented him from being undermined by US covert action and deposed, as Jacobo Árbenz was in Guatemala, Cheddi Jagan was in Guyana, and Salvador Allende was in Chile.

Figueres's nationalism started with the assumption that many Latin American nations were "exchange economies," that is, their economy was based on export-oriented growth. They exported primary products, and using the foreign exchange earned, they purchased industrialized, or finished, goods on world markets. This system goes back to the late nineteenth century as discussed earlier in this book. Figueres noted that the United States and India are good examples of nations that are different from Latin America because they are "closed economies"—that is, "the foreign sector of commerce is relatively small" compared to their economies as a whole. Further making the situation difficult for Latin America was that the terms of trade for its exports were declining over time. That is, even as prices for their exports were dropping, prices of industrialized goods were rising over time. Thus, the terms of trade were stacked against the primary-product exporting Latin Americans. In turn, they are economically "drained," producing poverty and an unequal distribution of income with income generation skewing to the wealthy, worsening an already unequal society, in fact the most unequal in the world.[18]

Then, a depressing political-military cycle ensues. Left-wing nationalists come to power, promising to alleviate the poverty. Expectations are raised unreasonably high. Disappointment that flows from the gap between expectations and reality is fanned by the press which is owned by the wealthy. In many societies, a free press is understandably seen as a necessity for a healthy democracy because it provides information to citizens to make informed decisions and are "watchdogs" that inform citizens of government malfeasance or corruption. However, importantly, Figueres instead saw the press as solely representatives of the interests of the wealthy.

Concomitantly, leftist agitators (sometimes with international and/or communist support) fan the flames of discontent. The leftist agitators want subversion, thinking they can somehow come out on top in the ensuing chaos after the subversives create enough disorder to topple the government. The wealthy elite fear that the poor majority will work with the leftists. The wealthy fear subversion and even a full-blown revolution, which could remove them from their enjoyable position at the top of society. The military, often sharing the interests of the elite, stages a coup (*golpe de estado*) and sets up a government that maintains the status quo.[19]

Economic diversification and industrialization provide the answer, but these solutions require two important things lacking in Latin America. First, it requires significant amounts of capital, lacking in most parts of the region. That meant that the vast majority of the population will have to have a great deal of the second major thing—patience. With increased communications/ transportation technology, the poor majority wants access to industrialized goods now or in the near future. They are understandably tired of waiting— indeed, for literally centuries. To diversify/industrialize, they must endure both poverty and a maldistribution of income for years to come, as the capital is slowly built up through increased exports of primary products and increased sacrifice so that savings can be accumulated. And as industrialized goods become more "high tech," for example, as jet planes replace propeller planes, the bill for imported finished goods increases rapidly, exacerbating the problem.[20]

One "way out" of the problem of capital accumulation is foreign aid, but after looking at the small amounts of foreign assistance available, Figueres correctly concluded it could not make a dent in the problem. Politicians in the wealthier, aid-giving nations will always find it politically expedient to gain support at home by telling their taxpaying citizens that foreign aid will be kept to a minimum. Another way out is a repressive state, deciding to limit consumer spending in the medium term to allow for accumulation of foreign exchange or more generally the capital necessary for industrialization. Then, once the economy has been diversified/industrialized (especially with nationally owned industries), the state decides it is fine to spend money on consumer goods because such consumption will increase economic growth and thus promote further industrialization. Examples Figueres discusses are South Korea and the former Soviet Union.[21] These two examples, however, are of nations that were authoritarian. (In the case of South Korea, at times it was authoritarian.) Thus, how to industrialize a nonindustrialized nation with a democratic political culture might prove difficult.

Figueres sums up the challenge for Latin American nationalists. They must somehow create a more equitable society even as increased foreign commerce means:

a) [the] number of people [in Latin America] who use modern [finished, industrialized] goods is *reduced*; b) the standard of living of the majorities is *lowered*; c) the foreign debt is *increased* [to provide funds to plug the growing balance of payments gap as foreign exchanged earned from exports fails to pay for a growing bill to pay for imports]; d) the need of aid from outside is *enlarged*.

In sum, the gap between the wealthy and the nonelites in Latin America grows, as does the gap between the wealthy nations and the poorer nations. For Figueres, the foundation of the problem is the nature of economic globalization. In the present world economy, with the Latin American nations' export-driven economies providing inexpensive raw materials for the industrialized nations, what occurs is that "the rich nations…exchange one hour of their work for ten hours of the work of the poor."[22]

The only way to rectify the situation in the short run is for the international community to make sure that quotas/minimum prices are established for primary product exports from the poorer nations. Moreover, the international community must also finance the destruction of surpluses of primary products, and control production of such surpluses, lowering overall supply and thus forcing up prices. Also, subsidies need to be applied by the developed nations to reduce the prices of exported capital goods and needed services to the nonindustrialized world. Foreign investments in Latin American nations need to be "legitimately transferred to the patrimony of the host nations."[23] The development of a Latin American common market would facilitate these reforms. Thus, in an interdependent world that privileges the wealthy nations at the expense of the poor nations, Latin American nationalists must seek an international solution to their problems.

Juan José Arévalo and the influence of US-based multinational companies

Arévalo's view of nationalism dovetails with Figueres's views. Like Figueres, Arévalo thought the dependency of Latin America on US capital investment as inhibiting the creation of a diversified economy. The United States had started out, Arévalo maintained, as a beacon of postcolonial revolutionary hope for peoples everywhere who strived for political liberty and economic independence and prosperity. With the 1823 Monroe Doctrine, propounded by US president James Monroe, the United States seemed as if it would be the protector of Latin America, shielding it from grasping European imperialists. But, with the rise of large, US-based multinational corporations, US foreign policy shifted to maintaining and extending the power of these multinational companies. This shift, in the early twentieth century, made it difficult for nationalists in Latin America to pursue their goals of increasing the economic autonomy and prosperity of their nations.[24]

To summarize, Oliveira Campos and Cosío Villegas think it important for Latin American nationalism to be "channeled" away from more emotional forms of nationalism, which could lead to unsound policies. For their part, Arévalo and Figueres see nationalism in economic terms: how to ensure the economic independence of Latin American nations from powerful, outside forces that aim to control sectors of the Latin American economy. The analyses of the Latin American nationalists discussed above are fascinating because, despite the diversity of viewpoints of the different authors, there are two distinct themes. Those themes are sovereignty and economic development. These two themes are linked. Without a diversified economy, in which members of the nation have a controlling interest in the key sectors of the economy, political sovereignty will be a chimera. Thus, both of these themes are key to the development of a sturdier Latin American nationalism.

Case studies of right-wing nationalism: Mexico, Argentina, Chile, and Bolivia

As noted above, with the perceived failure of ISI, left-wing nationalism was somewhat discredited. Also, in some countries ISI had been *too* effective. It had emboldened the demands of the working class, causing fears of a left-wing uprising with right-wing nationalists coming to the fore in the 1960s and 1970s. Mexico, Chile, and Bolivia provide good case studies, as they represent very different types of right-wing nationalism.

Mexico

Although Mexico's ruling political party was oxymoronically called the Partido Revolucionario Institucional (PRI) or Institutionalized Revolutionary Party, by the 1940s it was hardly revolutionary. Through co-optation of the labor movement, it had held down wages, allowing for increased capital accumulation. By means of ISI and economic nationalism, Mexico had industrialized to a remarkable degree with economic growth growing at an impressive rate. However, the brief flowering of democracy was quashed by the 1940s with PRI leaders repressing all political dissent that could not be "bought off" or co-opted. The PRI was careful to remain on good terms with the Mexican military as well. After all, the military was in a sense the enforcer of last resort if serious unrest were to break out. The PRI techniques were ironically reminiscent of the prerevolutionary Porfirio Díaz regime, in fact.

Not everyone in Mexico, however, accepted the increasingly authoritarian tactics of the PRI. Student radicals thought they would take advantage of the fact that the world's attention was focused on Mexico in late 1968, as it was the first developing world nation to host the Olympic Games, and it wanted to make sure that the Games went smoothly.

For Mexico, of course, it was its moment in the sun. There was concern in ruling circles about protests drawing attention away from the carefully constructed image of the Mexican economic "miracle" and the resulting social stability. They were even willing to use violence if need be to quell dissent. For student protestors who were agitating for more political freedoms, they saw the upcoming Olympics as a chance to air their grievances on a world stage. The October 3, 1968, massacre at Tlatelolco proved shocking on many levels. Not the least, the Mexican leadership fired on the students of their own—upper middle class and elite. Hundreds were killed. There were no other protests during the Olympics. With the massacre at Tlatelolco, it was clear that Mexico has been slowly but surely moving to the right politically.

Argentina

Argentina, in many respects, with the rise of Perón and Peronism's ISI politics in which the urban working and lower middle classes firmly supported state subsidies and an economic nationalist foreign policy, swung to the right politically by the late 1960s. Elites and many members of the middle class feared that Peronism had "unleashed" powerful and growing demands from a growing urban working class (with increasing industrialization) that might bankrupt the economy. So in bureaucratic-authoritarian fashion (as noted above), the elites and upper middle class collectively breathed a sigh of relief when a military coup forced out the democratically elected government of Isabel Perón (Perón's second wife) in 1976. Not only, according to the military, would they successfully contain what was perceived as the unreasonably high demands of the urban working class but it would also efficiently run the Argentine state, restore order and promote national pride. US military assistance buttressed military regimes in Argentina and elsewhere in part because of National Security Doctrine (discussed in Chapter Nine).

Thus, with the military *golpe de estado* in 1976, the military unleashed a "dirty war" against radicals and suspected radicals, in which many thousands were disappeared, tortured, or killed. The military leadership played on the Cold War fears of the Argentine middle class and elite. Normally, in Latin America fears of left-wing subversion are much more intense than the power of the radical movement that the military was confronting. The case of Argentina in the late 1970s was no different. Since the leftist threat from within was supposedly being aided by the international communist movement, the military could position itself as a nationalistic defender of Argentina by fighting this "dirty war."

However, after less than a decade, the military began to tire of the day-to-day management of the government—dealing with mundane governance issues and the increasing complaints of the citizenry. Such complaints increased in number and intensity, and the economy of the 1970s sputtered. The military would have much preferred to stay in the barracks, go on maneuvers, and proclaim themselves the repository of glory for *la patria* (the nation). Further, the military committed numerous human rights abuses, jailing and torturing thousands, and killing thousands. Although estimates vary, during what was termed the "dirty war" approximately 30,000 were killed—even by dropping them from helicopters into the Atlantic Ocean.[25]

One important series of events—which began in 1977 and continues up to the time of writing—that stimulated the globalization of the human rights movement was the silent and persistent marching, every week, by the relatives of the killed/disappeared, on the Plaza de Mayo outside the presidential palace in Buenos Aires. With people dressed in white and often holding photos of their loved ones that the military government of Argentina "disappeared" in the 1970s, this protest started out as the mothers of the disappeared who demanded to know what happened to their loved ones.[26] The protest became known as the *Madres de la Plaza de Mayo* (Mothers of the May Plaza) and quickly garnered support around the world. At first only the mothers marched; later on, others joined them.

A dispute across part of that ocean led to the military government's undoing. Argentina's relationship with Great Britain turned tense when the military leaders in Buenos Aires thought that they could revive their flagging political fortunes by rallying the nation around a foreign threat. Argentina decided to rekindle a smoldering conflict over ownership of the Malvinas/ Falklands islands, about 480 km east of Patagonia, in southern Argentina. Although effective British control over the islands, which contained more livestock than people, stretched back to the mid-nineteenth century, Argentina still claimed the islands and decided in early 1982 to effectively erase the British presence there.

Considering the British imperial holdings had dwindled down to a handful of pinprick islands around the world, the British did not want to concede the islands to Argentina. It would have called into question their power in world affairs. They fought Argentina to maintain control of the Falklands. After a brief war, Argentina lost, and the military government soon fell. Argentina returned to democracy. During the 1980s, in part because the Latin American citizenry had tired of repressive military rule and was resisting it in many ways, much of Latin America transitioned away from authoritarianism toward representative government.

Chile

In the case of Chile, the transition to right-wing nationalism was more abrupt. When Augusto Pinochet came to power in 1973, he intended to purge Chile of any lingering aspects of the Allende project. Not only were thousands of Chileans forced into exile, but many were tortured and killed within Chile. Economically, Chile started a very influential economic experiment—neoliberalism. Pinochet, to help in implementing a rightist, nationalist neoliberalism, decided to invite some neoclassical economists from the University of Chicago (known as the Chicago Boys) to implement free-market policies in Chile. They cut government budgets and reduced the money supply. In the short run the economy contracted and, with unemployment's rise, those at the bottom of society were hurt the most.

Chilean economic policy privileged export-oriented production to earn as much foreign currency as possible. By the mid-1980s, the Chilean economy was improving, but the wealthy benefitted more than the nonelite majority. As such, Pinochet's economic decisions heralded a new economic system that would come to have a big impact on Latin America and the developing world more generally—neoliberalism, which will be discussed in future chapters.

Another side of right-wing nationalism was more ominous. Pinochet launched Operation Condor, an organization of intelligence agencies in the Southern Cone (southern part of South America) to monitor the activities of left-wing groups. One of its activities was the audacious and brutal killing of Allende's former Ambassador to the United States, Orlando Letelier, who was in Washington, DC, working at a think-tank in Dupont Circle. Operation Condor agents secretly placed a car bomb on Letelier's car, which detonated very close to Embassy Row in Washington, killing not only Letelier but also his assistant who was riding in the car with him.

As with Argentina, Chile's human rights abuses at home and abroad proved to be an international cause-celebre. Although a number of military governments inflicted human rights abuses on their citizens in the 1970s, the Southern Cone nations (Argentina and Chile in particular, but also Bolivia— see below) were the worst offenders during that particular decade. Although the United Nations International Declaration of Human Rights had been published in 1949, a deeply held, internationalist concern for human rights did not become a reality until the 1970s. Repressive authoritarian regimes in Latin America in the 1970s jailed, tortured, and killed thousands and forced many into exile. Because of the shock and outrage such actions caused, there were many calls for curbing such human rights abuses. Non-governmental organizations began to more commonly and systematically operate at an international level to promote human rights or at least curtail human rights abuses.[27]

Bolivia

Right-wing nationalism in neighboring Bolivia first took the form of dictatorship and then democracy. A 1964 coup by military leaders quashed democracy (spawned by the 1952 revolution, as discussed in Chapter Eight). In 1971, another military coup brought in right-wing nationalism. Hugo Banzer, a military leader trained in the United States, took power in a *golpe de estado*, replacing one of the most leftist regimes in recent Bolivian history (also headed up by a military dictator). Banzer's repression was the worst in decades, but when he was deposed in a coup in 1978, a yet more repressive regime took power. The extremely repressive García Meza government even hired former Nazi refugee Klaus Barbie as an advisor. In an ominous precursor to future strife, including numerous casualties, García Meza's government secretly facilitated the export of coca leaves (the raw material for cocaine) and coca paste (which when further refined becomes cocaine) and made a great deal of money under the table in such fashion, paving the way for future Bolivian government officials to secretly involve themselves in the lucrative trade. As such, the Bolivian people had many reasons to both dump García Meza and establish a democracy. A representative government was set up in 1982 for the first time in 18 years.[28]

Conclusion: The importance of the military and the persistence of left-wing nationalism

It is important to keep in mind that the Latin American militaries were instrumental in supporting right-wing nationalism. In many Latin American nations, right-wing nationalism benefitted from the seemingly intractable problems of civilian-led governments. For example, in 1964, the Movimiento Revolucionario Nacionalista (MNR) government in Bolivia was driven by factionalism, only exacerbated by Victor Paz Estensorro's controversial decision to seek a second, contiguous term in the 1964 elections. Bolivians, like many Latin Americans, are wary of leaders practicing continuismo—using their office to maintain themselves in power. Indeed, the Bolivian constitution forbade a president from serving for a second, contiguous term. (Paz Estensorro managed to get around this restriction.) As mentioned above, the military, suspicious of continuismo, ousted Paz in a coup in 1964. In 1973, Chile seemed at the verge of civil war—as such, the military justified its coup as a preemptive strike against such an outcome. And in 1976, as mentioned above, in neighboring Argentina, the military ousted the hapless and incompetent government of Isabel Perón, Perón's second wife and first female head of state in Latin American history, who, since she was vice president, took over power in 1974 upon Perón's death in office.

Thus, the military leadership that took power in a number of Latin American militaries from the mid-1960s to the late 1980s claimed that their takeovers were done out of nationalist devotion. In a situation where it appears that the situation might degenerate into chaos (Bolivia in 1964 and Argentina in 1976), or it appeared that the nation was on the verge of civil war (Chile in 1973), the military leadership could make a case that it was taking power in the name of saving the nation. It is important to remember, however, that simply because military coups in the late 1960s and early 1970s facilitated the rise of right-wing nationalism, left-wing nationalists did not simply disappear. In particular for workers and students, and others of a left-wing political bent, it proved to still resonate in Latin American society and would become more prominent by the late 1990s and early twenty-first century.

Study Questions

1. Discuss two reasons why the 1960s proved to be an important turning point in the recent history of Latin American nationalism.
2. Discuss how international economic activity influenced the thinking of Latin American nationalists discussed in this chapter.
3. Discuss two important differences between left-wing nationalism and right-wing nationalism.
4. Discuss how the United States responded to the rise of right-wing nationalism.

For Further Reading

Arévalo, Juan José. *The Shark and the Sardines*, trans. June Cobb and Dr. Raul Osgueda. New York: Lyle Stuart, 1961, 9–13.

Baily, Samuel. *Nationalism in Latin America*. New York: Knopf, 1970.

Longley, Kyle. *The Sparrow and the Hawk: Costa Rica and the United States during the rise of José Figueres*. Tuscaloosa, AL: University of Alabama Press, 1997.

Rabe, Stephen G. *The Killing Zone—The United States Wages Cold War in Latin America*. New York: Oxford, 2012.

Sheinin, David. *Argentina and the United States—An Alliance Contained*. Athens: University of Georgia Press, 2007.

CHAPTER TWELVE

War, Nationalism, and Supranationalism in Twentieth-Century Latin America

The peoples of Latin America cannot defend ... their sovereignty individually; they must unify for security against the design of Europe and in order to avoid wars breaking out between them.

DRAFT OF CHILEAN CONSTITUTION, 1810, QUOTED IN GLINKIN[1]

Unification efforts by the Latin American countries are becoming increasingly necessary as the state of the world economy worsens and as protectionist and discriminatory trade measures are taken by more and more of the great industrial powers.

PRESIDENT ERNEST GEISAL[2]

Background: War and nationalism—Latin American style

Inherently, nationalism needs an "other" to define itself—a foil to define itself in opposition to. But nationalism does not presuppose conflict or war. In Latin America, unlike in Europe or the United States, the foundation of Latin American nationalism does not rest on a bedrock of foreign wars.

In the United States, wars for expansion, such as the Mexican-American War and the Spanish-American War, stimulated US nationalism. In Europe, a glance at the monuments in public spaces reveal that the national experience of whatever country you choose shows that the country in question was founded, and developed, in war.[3] In the United States, if national power translates into nationalism, war is the engine that has produced US nationalism. The Revolutionary War (1776–1783) vastly increased the size of the United States, as did the Mexican-American War (1846–1848). Similarly, the Spanish-American War, the First World War, and the Second World War vastly increased US influence in the world. Scholar Miguel Centeno puts it best when he concludes, "It is not that Latin Americans have not tried to kill one another—they have—but they have generally not attempted to organize their societies with that goal in mind."[4] Importantly, the majority of violence historically in Latin America has been within nations, not between them. In addition, the types of wars in Latin America have differed from those in other parts of the world. Wars in Latin America tend to be limited wars but with long-term consequences, in particular the accumulation of debt.[5] Making payments on the debt, over time, weakens the state economically.

Thus, war is not the engine of nationalism in the region. Instead, in Latin America, nationalism flowed and still flows out of the various top-down integration projects of Latin American leaders in the nineteenth century as discussed in Chapter Two. The formation of the Latin American militaries proved especially important in this endeavor because the leaders of the new Latin American nations on occasion used the new militaries to force the creation of the type of nation they wanted. Sometimes this use of force involved putting down rebellions of those who challenged the top-down, nation-building project.[6]

Nonetheless, the Latin American militaries proved less consequential to the formation of national spirit when compared to their European and North American counterparts. There are a few exceptions, however, to the generalization that war did not have a major impact on the development of Latin American national sentiment. One was the Mexican-American War of 1846–1848, discussed in Chapter Four, which had a large impact on Mexican nationalism. Also, in the nineteenth century, the War of the Triple Alliance, between Paraguay, Brazil, and Argentina, from 1864 to 1870, was probably the only example of a "fight to the death" type of war in which the antagonists aimed to annihilate one another.[7] The war had a devastating effect on Paraguay, arguably preventing it from developing into an economically developed nation. Moving into the twentieth century, a border war between Bolivia and Paraguay erupted into a regional war, known as the Chaco War with extremely important consequences for the belligerents and Latin America as a whole.

Although the basis of Latin American nationalism lay within each individual nation and does not flow from conflicts with neighboring countries, Latin American nationalism in some respects has been and is strengthened by conflict with neighboring countries. Guatemala, for example, still claims Belize as a province, and this Guatemalan desire fuels Guatemalan nationalism. Both Colombia and Venezuela stimulate their nationalisms due to ongoing conflicts over borders, as do Peru and Ecuador. In Bolivia, the loss of its seacoast (which meant that Bolivia was henceforth landlocked) to Chile in the War of the Pacific (1879–1883) has fueled Bolivian nationalism to the present day. Anti-Chilean enmity has lasted in Bolivia up to the twenty-first century. When President Gonzalo Sánchez de Lozada in 2003 agreed to sell some of Bolivia's natural gas to Chile, some of the deadliest riots in recent Bolivian history erupted, killing seventy-nine people. Sánchez de Lozada fled the country.

Peru and Chile, in their dispute over the Tacna-Arica border area, is another good example of how a border dispute stimulates nationalist sentiment. The dispute over the border ultimately goes back to the 1879 War of the Pacific. The treaty ending that war failed to resolve a conflict between the two nations about Peru's southern and Chile's northern border. Although a US-sponsored arbitration agreement in 1929, the Treaty of Lima, brokered by a First World War era US military hero, General John Pershing, seemingly reduced tensions, the fact that both Peru and Chile received military assistance and training from some European nations indicated that neither nation saw the agreement as fixed. Indeed, into the 1960s and early 1970s, both nations were bent on increasing their military might, casting a wary eye on the other. Peru even obtained millions of dollars of Soviet military assistance—the largest Soviet military presence in Latin America outside of Cuba—in the early to mid-1970s. A major reason for the Peruvian desire for Soviet materiel was fear of Chilean military power.

Arguably, it is rare that border wars in the region cause "regime change." Interestingly, however, in Argentina, a war to regain lost territory resulted in significant political changes at home. For Argentinian nationalists, the return of the Malvinas (Falklands) islands, which the British took in 1833, is a matter of faith. Because an Argentine dictatorship in 1982 decided to provoke a war against the British to regain the Falklands— and, ironically, to rally the Argentine people behind a repressive regime that was rapidly losing public support—that dictatorship lost power. Argentina transitioned to democracy soon after their defeat at the hands of the British.

As Latin American nations in recent years have begun to explicitly state that they are multiethnic nations (*plurinacional* in Spanish), the nineteenth-century, top-down, Liberal oligarchic ideal of nationalism has been replaced by the idea that Latin American nations are comprised of a number of nations—based on race and ethnicity. The rise of the "new" Indian nationalistic movements from the 1940s and 1970s forced the top-down nationalizers to acknowledge that each individual Latin American nation is a collection of nations. So, as the ideal of a single nationalism has given way to the idea of many nationalisms within a generalized, single nation, the "glue" holding nations together has weakened. (The *plurinacional* nature of Latin American nations was discussed in Chapters Six and Ten.) As such, as the bonds of nationhood become weaker, the leadership of the various Latin American nations "reaches out" to other Latin American nations to bulwark support at home. Thus, not surprisingly, a nation's relationship with its neighbors becomes much more important. For example, Bolivia (arguably one of the most plurinational nations in the hemisphere) in recent years has increased pressure on Chile to cede access to the sea to Bolivia.

Apex of their power: The Cold War Latin American armies and national security doctrine

Arguably, the global struggle for dominance between the anticommunist Western nations (and Japan) on the one hand and the communist world on the other caused the power of Latin American militaries to increase to its highest point in history. Although Latin America was not on the "front lines" of the Cold War, US and some Latin American leaders feared the incursion of Soviet-style communism from Eurasia. In an interesting historical parallel, it seemed that the United States, by fighting the Cold War in the Americas, was returning to its Monroe Doctrine policy, which was essentially a containment policy of European imperial expansion. Now, the containment policy was containment of communism.

Both the United States and Latin America (with the exception of Cuba after 1961) shared the idea that a National Security Doctrine (discussed in Chapter Nine) needed to permeate the armed forces of the Western Hemisphere. That is, international, Soviet-backed communism, in the apt words of scholar Brian Loveman, "denied the historical and sovereign 'essence' of Latin American nations: it was godless, morally abominable, nefarious, resolute, and imperialistic."[8]

Thus, animated by intense anticommunism, US assistance flowed to the Latin American militaries like never before, in particular in the 1960s and 1970s, when US leaders feared Castro would spread his influence around the Americas. Thus, in some Latin American nations, the military attacked what it termed "subversives" with particular zeal. Although the military went too far, in particular in the cases of Argentina, Chile, and El Salvador, the militaries of these nations, criticized by those who claimed they were too excessive in their zeal to root out so-called subversives, maintained that they did the only thing that they could do under the circumstances: defend la patria (the fatherland or homeland).[9] The fact that the militaries of these three nations continued to defend their decision to jail/torture/kill thousands of innocent people even after the communist threat had largely subsided by 1990 is telling. The military's struggle against "subversives" was about more than defeating communist ideology. As Loveman noted, the military perceived they were fighting an immoral, implacable enemy which threatened the nation.

Between nationalism and globalization: Supranational regional organizations in Latin America

Globalization is a phenomenon that increases and decreases in intensity depending on world economic and political trends. However, regional organizations provide a constant source of inspiration for those in a particular region who see benefits in international integration, mainly economic integration. Regional organizations are seen by, and often act as, buffers against the aspects of globalization that would produce negative results for Latin America, in particular, declining prices for their overseas exports.

Latin American regional or supranational organizations made up of various Latin American nations have a cultural foundation—that of Hispanidad or Iberian-ness. After all, "Latin" America was so named because it was perceived to have a distinctly Mediterranean-Iberian culture as opposed to Anglo-North American culture. Hallmarks of Hispanidad include the idea that Latin America's Catholic culture makes it distinct from the more Protestant North America.[10] In addition, Latin American culture, according to many scholars, is more "group oriented" or corporatist, than the more individualistic North American culture.[11] Such cultural ties facilitate countries in Latin America overcoming parochial national interests, which allow for the formation of regional groupings.[12]

Supranational organizations in the post–Second World War era

Regional organizations in Latin America have a long history. One of the earliest was the Pan-American Union founded in 1890. Ultimately, this agreement became the Organization of American States in 1948. There are different types of regional organizations, ranging from more specialized, smaller schemes to agreements that include all of Latin America.

In parts of Latin America which are ethnically diverse and geographically dispersed, such as the Caribbean, subregional organizations have proven difficult to maintain. For example, a West Indian Federation (WIF), which had roots that went back to the 1930s and aimed to foster Caribbean solidarity, briefly flowered after the Second World War. It is not surprising that such experiments were popular in the years right after the Second World War. Many nations of the world thought that regional organizations of nations could "embed" nationalism in a larger grouping of nations, thus containing an expansionistic nation. Basically, regional organizations would theoretically prevent future conflict. The WIF, however, foundered by the early 1960s due to intra-Caribbean rivalries, which showed that the nationalism of individual countries based on long-standing ethnic and geographic divisions was more powerful that any pan-Caribbean ideal.[13]

In the post–Second World War era, it is not surprising that a number of regional organizations were set up to promote interhemispheric cooperation and unity. In 1959, the Inter-American Development Bank was established. In 1960, two trade organizations also were set up, the Central American Common Market and the Latin American Free Trade Association. Fostered in part by the cooperation spurred by the Alliance for Progress (discussed in Chapter Nine), the Cartagena Agreement (which formed first the Andean Pact, later renamed the Andean Community), the Andean Development Fund, and the Caribbean Free Trade Area were formed in 1969. (The Caribbean Free Trade Area became the Caribbean Community in 1973.) More recently, the Latin American Integration Association was formed in 1980. Two giants, one North American and one South American, were formed in the early 1990s. In 1991, many South American nations formed the Common Market of South America (known as MERCOSUR), and in 1992, the North American Free Trade Agreement (NAFTA), between the United States, Canada, and Mexico, the world's largest free-trade area, was formed. In part due to the interest in globalization right after the fall of the East Bloc and Soviet Union in 1991, Latin America and Asia in the 1990s signed around twenty new trade agreements.[14] Finally, there was the Central American Free Trade Agreement (CAFTA). In addition, some Latin American nations have formed regional agreements with nations outside of the Western Hemisphere.

Two key goals of such regional organizations are economic growth (which would facilitate economic modernization) as well as the consolidation of democracy. There is a widely held assumption that economic interchange creates a significant amount of wealth, and such wealth facilitates the rise of a stable, confident middle class that facilitates democracy. Of course, this logic can be challenged by examining Latin American history in the late 1960s and 1970s as the region grew economically but dictatorships entrenched themselves. But, nonetheless, it is a commonly held assumption that rising levels of wealth go hand in hand with democracy. And indeed, it is the case that regional organizations rose to world prominence in the 1980s and 1990s, as Latin American nations strove to both cast off authoritarianism and deepen their democracies. The two most prominent regional organizations are MERCOSUR (1991) and NAFTA (1992).

Conclusion: Latin American unity and supranational regional organizations in Latin America

In part to prevent wars from breaking out in the future, different Latin American nations have attempted to form regional, or supranational, organizations for the purposes of hemispheric cooperation and unity. "Cooperation" is of course a vague term. In general, economic cooperation was considered most important though illusive. Economic cooperation was illusive because the legacy of colonialism in Latin American often meant that the transportation infrastructure was created to connect each individual nation with a more powerful European or North American trading partner, not a neighboring Latin American nation. Further, comparative advantage can be gained as nations that do not have the stocks of resources, or climate, to produce items it wants by trading surplus goods it produces for items it wants from other Latin American nations. "Unity" includes the idea that if Latin American maintains a certain amount of political unity, it is less likely that war will erupt in the region.

In Latin America, as the reader can see from Table 12.1, intrahemispheric wars have been quite rare compared to Europe. The formation of a nationalistic identity has been more of an internal affair in Latin America compared to Europe, where nationalism is often defined in opposition to a disliked neighboring nation. Nationalism in Latin America has been more about caste and class within each particular nation and who is included in the sense of "nationhood." As scholar Miguel Centeno argues, nationalism in Latin America is about a "hierarchy of self-identity."[15] However, there have been some significant border wars in the mid- to late twentieth

Table 12.1 Twentieth-century intrahemispheric wars in Latin America

Guatemala, Central America, Honduras	1906
Nicaragua, El Salvador	1907
Bolivia, Paraguay (Chaco War)	1932–1936
Peru, Colombia	1932–1933
Peru, Ecuador	1941
El Salvador, Honduras (Soccer War)	1969
Peru, Ecuador	1981
Peru, Ecuador	1995

Source: Miguel Angel Centeno, Blood and Debt—War and the Nation-Sate in Latin America. University Park, PA: Pennsylvania State University Press, 2002, 44.

century. The Chaco War between Bolivia and Paraguay was discussed in Chapter Six. Another border war occurred between Peru and Ecuador in 1941. The conflict was caused because both nations wanted to control key, strategic areas in a disputed boundary region—in particular, they wanted to control access to rivers. The dispute flared again in 1981 and 1995 and was definitively—supposedly—resolved in 1995.

Study Questions

1. Discuss as many reasons as you can think of for forming regional organizations.
2. Discuss the impact that regional, or supranational, organizations have on Latin American nationalism.
3. Discuss how other actors outside Latin America have worked with Latin American regional organizations.

For Further Reading

Bouvier, Virginia. *The Globalization of U.S.-Latin American Relations—Democracy, Intervention, and Human Rights.* Westport, CT: Praeger, 2002.

Loveman, Brian. *For la patria—Politics and the Armed Forces in Latin America.* Wilmington, DE: Scholarly Resources, 1999.

Parker, Jason. "The Failure of the West Indian Confederation." In *Ultimate Adventures with Britain—Personalities, Politics, and Culture in Britain,* edited by William Roger Louis, 235–45. London: I. B. Tauris, 2009.

Wood, James A., ed. *Problems in Modern Latin American History: Sources and Interpretations,* 4th ed. Lanham, MD: Rowman and Littlefield, 2013.

CHAPTER THIRTEEN

Neoliberalism, Part I: Fall of the State in Latin America

Practical men who believe themselves to be quite exempt from any intellectual influence, are usually the slaves of some defunct economist. Madmen in authority, who hear voices in the air, are distilling their frenzy from some academic scribbler of a few years back.

JOHN MAYNARD KEYNES[1]

Introduction

In order to understand some of the most wrenching and momentous changes in the economic, social, and political history of Latin America in the late twentieth and early twenty-first centuries, one must understand three big changes: first, the world capitalist crisis of the 1970s; second, the increased intensity of indigenous nationalism (on the rise since the 1940s); and third, how the Latin American governments' response to the world capitalist crisis (abetted by International Financial Institutions [IFIs]) was to deregulate and reduce the power of the state, which ushered in the Age of Neoliberalism.

In the early 1970s, it appeared that a surge of nationalism in Latin America would not only challenge US influence in the region but also put brakes on the process of economic globalization. In rapid succession, there were expropriations of major multinational companies (MNCs) in Bolivia and Peru. With socialist Allende's rise to the presidency of Chile, the nationalization of the copper and communications industries occurred.

In the larger economies of Argentina and Mexico, economic nationalist policies, such as a "buy Argentina" policy, as well as the Mexican government's assertion of control over some new, key industries, it appeared that economic nationalism was on the march.[2] But as the world economy soured in the 1970s, Latin American policy dramatically changed, setting the stage for the present day.

Economically, Latin America, like much of the world, was doing poorly in the 1970s. As stated previously, the nationalist-populist Import Substitution Industrialization (ISI) model of political economy was running out of steam, even in the 1960s. Critics on the right feared the rising power of newly empowered workers and farms and were relieved when right-wing authoritarian coups displaced the populist, ISI governments that dated back to the 1930s. These Conservatives feared that the growing demands of the nonelite groups would outstrip the ability of the Latin American economies to accommodate such demands. For their part, critics on the left viewed the forced end of the populist-ISI experiments as the result of a pact between elites and the military to depose populist governments that were popular with the nonelite majority, since these populists were providing for an increased economic well-being for the workers/famers. In any event, right-wing authoritarian generals put a quick stop to the government of the left-wing populist João Goulart in Brazil in 1964, and similarly did so to the government of Arturo Frondizi in Argentina in 1972. The Allende experiment in left-wing populism fell to the military in 1973. By the time we get to the 1970s, there is a wholesale dismantling of the ISI model.

Context is important here. After a worldwide, post–Second World War economic boom, world economies were slowly grinding to a halt. One reason for the economic doldrums of the 1970s was the 1973 Arab Oil Embargo, which whiplashed oil-dependent economies around the world. As inflation mounted and employment stagnated, economists around the world sought new ways of understanding what was going on economically and developed new economic models which would help them in this regard.

The decline of ISI—and the state— in Latin America

A persuasive replacement for ISI was neoclassical economics, or what is known in political-economy terms as neoliberalism. Although its roots extend back to the 1940s as a reaction against Keynesian economics, the idea of government spending during economic downturns to prevent economies from stagnating or collapsing into depression in some ways extended back to the late eighteenth-century Enlightenment era and the founding of the science of economics (the free-market version) itself.

Neoliberalism, in short, called for a dismantling of the nationalist-populist ISI model and called for the state to remove itself from the workings of the free-market economy as much as possible. Two points are key here. Some observers have noted that the state was never very strong in Latin America.[3] Second, the state was not supposed to simply disappear—it played an important role in the neoliberal schema. The proper role of the state, according to neoliberalism, was to efficiently and in a noncorrupt manner provide needed government services to the people to allow the economy and society to function. Moreover, the state needed to prepare people in Latin America, through improved education, to better compete in a globalizing world marketplace. Finally, the state needed to ensure that government policies provided for a propitious environment for foreign economic activity. Neoliberalism, of course, called for an end to nationalist-populist ISI political economy and economic nationalism. As such, it proposed a different sort of Latin American nationalism, in which the Latin American nations needed to position themselves, as much as possible and as quickly as possible, to take advantage of a rapidly globalizing world.

Thus, as a response to the world capitalist crisis of the 1970s, Latin America dismantled ISI and implemented neoliberalism. The decision was made by Latin American elites, but Latin American "nonelites" were not locked out of the decision-making process. The bottom line is that by the 1970s ISI began to lose steam—it did not produce the same level of economic benefit for the nonelite majority as it did from the 1930s to the 1960s. As such, many working-class Latin Americans supported the decision to dismantle ISI. But, it is important to point out—the process by which ISI was dismantled—perhaps a better word is unraveled?—that the unraveling of ISI took years, even decades. The ramifications of this decision are extremely profound.

First, Latin American governments went for the "low-hanging fruit" of dismantling the state-run industries that went back to the 1930s and were set up to protect the "natural patrimony" (usually subsoil minerals) for future generations. Because these industries were inefficient and employed many more workers than were economically efficient, for political reasons, Latin American governments could make the case that they needed to be privatized to save government funds, as well as more productively produce raw materials.

Second, Latin American governments remade their labor laws to promote economic efficiency and capitalist accumulation (growth of economic wealth) as opposed to protecting workers' benefits. Latin American governments decided to increase capitalist accumulation at the expense of the working class. This was not a new idea. Indeed, in the 1960s, the series of military coups in Latin America, which shoved aside the (democratically elected) ISI-populist governments, were staged because elites and segments of the middle class feared the rise of working-class political power that ISI represented.

These elites and their conservative allies wanted to ensure that working-class power—and economic gains—did not grow any more than they already had. By the 1990s, in part due to increasing inequality between the elites and nonelites, workers would again see their power and economic well-being decline, as they had in the wake of the 1960s (and early 1970s) coups. As such, the dismantling of ISI and the rise of neoliberalism contributed to one of the more pressing problems in the world today—rising inequality.[4] Chile, with the "Chicago Boys" of the 1970s under Pinochet (whose coup against Allende was strongly supported by the United States), was the first to make labor laws more "flexible" (read: lower wages and fewer benefits for workers). Quickly implementing free-market reforms, including reducing government intervention in the economy and the repression of labor union leaders, the Chilean economy began to increase its rate of growth at the expense of the nonelite majority. Yet, wealth was created, and the neoclassical economic model gained adherents. The "dominos" then began to fall: flexible labor policies were implemented in Colombia in 1990, Peru in 1991, Argentina in 1991 and 1995, Panama in 1995, and Mexico in the early 2000s.

Interestingly, some Latin American nations even cut the budget of their militaries. This was different than the type of neoliberalism that emerged in the 1980s in the United States, for example, when neoliberal reforms were coupled with an increase in the US military budget. In some cases, the Latin American militaries, suffering from lower budgets and morale, went through a crisis of confidence. Examples of nations in which the military budget was curtailed and low morale led to factionalism and other problems are Guatemala, Venezuela, Ecuador, and Argentina. Other nations' militaries, however, did not suffer from budget cuts. Examples include Chile, Colombia, Mexico, and Peru.[5]

Neoliberalism arises: Economic and intellectual background

Now a bit of background will be provided on the rise of neoliberalism, one of the more important developments in Latin America—and world history—in recent years. Two "background" things that were going on were as follows: first, the breakdown of the Bretton Woods system that had provided a degree of economic stability to world markets from the late 1940s to the early 1970s and second, the worldwide rise of inflation in the 1970s. One cause of the "Great Inflation" of the 1970s was the worldwide rise in oil prices. The response of the US Federal Reserve to the "Great Inflation" of the 1970s was to tighten the US money supply, raise interest rates, and send the world into a severe recession in the early 1980s. Thus, the stage was set for the "neoliberal revolution" of the 1980s and 1990s.

Like the 1970s, the 1980s was a period of slow growth for Latin America. One reason for this was the tight-money, high-interest-rate policy of the US Federal Reserve (Central Bank) to quash rampant inflation in the late 1970s. As interest rates soared in the United States, investors shifted capital away from other parts of the world (including Latin America). Thus, Latin America, a part of the world prone to capital flight, experienced a significant drain of capital in the 1980s.

However, by the 1990s, economic growth increased. This was partially attributable to neoliberal policies. In addition, falling trade barriers around the world and increasing capital flows helped increase Latin American economic growth. World financial leaders took steps to lower the interest payments that Latin American nations paid on their high levels of debt. In 1985, the Baker Plan, named after Secretary of the Treasury James Baker, reduced the Latin American debt load. In addition, in 1989, the Brady Plan, named after secretary of the Treasury Nicholas Brady, also reduced Latin American debt, which also helped to spur growth. Large MNCs invested more heavily in Latin America, increasing their own profits while promoting growth in Latin America. Globalization, in short, helped to spur economic growth in Latin America. However, how much Latin America's economic growth can be attributed to globalization is debatable. But, in the minds of many, the increased economic growth that Latin America enjoyed in the 1990s was attributable to economic globalization.

Understanding the world capitalist "boom" of the 1980s and 1990s and the concomitant rise in neoliberal ideology, is key to understanding Latin American nationalism—and Latin America in general—today. To understand the 1980s and 1990s, in turn, it is necessary to go back a decade to the 1970s and arguably the most significant global capitalist crisis in recent memory. The roots of neoliberalism and the globalized economic boom of the 1980s and 1990s lay in the 1970s crisis. The global capitalist crisis of the 1970s with its stagflation and high oil prices due to OPEC's (Organization of the Petroleum Exporting Countries) increase in oil prices in the mid-1970s caused profound economic, social, and political effects in the United States—and around the world.

Many around the world in the industrialized nations had gotten used to continuing economic growth. Moreover, until the 1970s, it was conventional wisdom that if the economy overheated and prices went up, the economy would automatically respond by weakening, thus reducing prices. As such, historically, inflation had only occurred during boom times and unemployment during times of economic difficulty.

The 1970s, however, were different. First of all, with "stagflation," the economic pie was not growing. (Stagflation was the simultaneous occurrence of weak or no economic growth with inflation.) As such, scholars discussed the implications of the "zero-sum" society. In order to produce more resources for poor and needy people, one could not simply increase the size of the pie. One had to adjust the proportions such that pie was taken from the middle class and elite, and transferred to the poor. Since stagflation, and a lack of economic growth, was not the typical situation in American history, US middle class and elites were not willing to sacrifice their resources to the poor and needy—as at least some members of the middle class were willing to do in the 1960s, when President Lyndon Johnson and the (liberal) Democratic Party put in place a package of social programs collectively known as the "Great Society" programs. These programs, among other things, aimed to provide aid to poorer and working-class Americans as well as to needy students who aimed to better themselves by means of education.

The "Great Society" reflected the continuing belief, reflected in a widely held consensus in US society, that the Keynesian economic policies stretching back to the 1930s were the best way to run an economy. That is, according to prolific and influential British economist John Maynard Keynes, particularly active in the 1930s, government had the ability—and obligation—to spend money during economic downturns in order to jump-start the economy. As such, through skillful use of predictive economic models, economists could counsel government leaders as to when government spending should take place in order to stimulate the economy in "down" times, while reducing government spending when the economy was humming, in order to prevent the economy from overheating, thus causing inflation. Thus, Keynes concluded, only through skillful government intervention could the business cycle (made up of peaks and troughs of economic activity) be flattened out, and steady, consistent economic growth occur.

During times of economic difficulty, Keynesians maintained that the government had to engage in deficit spending to prevent the economy from getting worse and worse. (Deficit spending was the result of a combination of increased government spending while maintaining current tax levels—or even decreasing taxes.) That is, Keynesians did not view the economy as being a self-regulating equilibrium. On the contrary, the economy was prone to peaks and nadirs, and it was the responsibility of the government to make sure that the economy did not overheat in good times and spiral ever downward in bad times. Advocating deficit spending flew in the face of pre-1930s, pre-Keynesian "orthodoxy," which argued that if the government ran large budget deficits, it would have to sell a large number of US Treasury bonds to fund government operations. Two (interlocking) problems would ensue. First, interest rates would increase as the supply of credit was "sopped up" by the government. Second, if investors purchased these bonds instead of investing in the nongovernment part of the US economy, it would in effect "siphon off" investment from the nongovernment economy, thus reducing the amount of available investment for this part of the economy, which would reduce overall economic growth. However, Keynesians countered by stating that deficit spending during economic downturns would not cause significant economic problems for the simple reason that the government would run surpluses during flush economic times and use these surpluses to reduce government debt to a sustainable level.

Even before the 1970s, a group of economists challenged the received Keynesian wisdom, which had been popular for a generation or more. They became known as "monetarists." Monetarism's intellectual roots stretch back to what is known as the "Austrian school," because a number of the prolific, widely read authors of this group were Austrian, in particular Ludwig von Mises and Friedrich Hayek.[6] These economists (in neoclassical or free-market fashion) saw government spending programs as problematic because the higher taxes required to fund them would dampen economic growth. Further, they saw government programs to put people to work as creating a type of dependency among people on government for their livelihood, which would reduce the entrepreneurial spirit of these people. If large numbers of employees worked for the government, a mentality would emerge in which workers would simply think all they had to do to prosper was to do their (government) job and not think creatively about how to start their own businesses, thus (supposedly) increasing their productivity. In addition, if there were large numbers of government programs putting people to work, the power of the government would significantly increase and the liberty/freedom of the people would correspondingly decrease.

More importantly, monetarists saw the economic system as automatically moving toward equilibrium. That is, if the government did as little as possible to intervene in the economy, and, especially, if it maintained a constant rate of growth of the money supply, businesses and consumers would invest/buy in the nongovernment part of the economy, and economic growth would increase over time. Further, if economic actors had confidence that the rate of growth of the money supply was constant, these economic actors would not over-buy or under-buy, or over-invest or under-invest. Thus, the business cycle, in which the economy would reach high peaks and then sink to disastrous lows, would be eliminated.

Because, as noted above, the world capitalist crisis meant real economic growth slowed to zero—or even became negative in real terms—people around the world lost faith in Keynesianism. Thus, the foundation was set for a major policy change to monetarism, and more broadly, neoliberalism. Neoliberalism was a political-economic policy which stated that the government that governs best governs least. It argued that if governments put in place government programs to provide government jobs to citizens or if it provided free money in the form of welfare payments to needy people, it would dull their entrepreneurial spirit. On the contrary, individuals would benefit if they pulled themselves up by their bootstraps through personal sacrifice and calculated risk-taking in an entrepreneurial way. Government could aid in this process by cutting regulation on business, as well as lowering taxes, putting more money in the pockets of (hopefully entrepreneurial) citizens. Such *laissez-faire* policies (French for "let alone") harkened back to the late nineteenth century when businessmen in the United States and other nations successfully convinced government officials that the government that governs best is the government that governs least. (However, it is important to note that the US government was activist in ways that benefitted business. In particular, the US government did a lot of things to aid the rise of large companies in the late nineteenth century, such as pro-business labor laws and giving large amounts of free land to the railroad-building companies.)

Where the rubber hits the road: Responses in the industrialized world to the world capitalist crisis in the 1970s

The responses to this world capitalist crisis of the 1970s, which extended into the early 1980s, were, of course, different in different countries around the world. Some smaller countries aimed to deal with stagflation by means of a creation of a national consensus to ensure shared sacrifice among various social groups—attempting to ensure that those with minimal ability to weather economic storms (the working class) were not as hard hit as wealthier citizens.[7] Forming such a consensus would be very difficult in a large nation such as the United States. As such, US policy elites decided to "bludgeon" inflation into "submission," and then assumed that once inflation was low, all the other economic problems would be worked out, at least in the medium to long run. For economists who classified themselves as "monetarist," such as Paul Volcker, the head of the US Federal Reserve (Central Bank), maintaining a low rate of inflation over time would solve nearly all economic problems. Once businesses/consumers assumed that inflation would remain relatively low over time, they would invest in productive enterprises such as the manufacturing and service sectors of the economy and not invest in "inflation hedges" such as gold and luxury items (e.g., valuable art). Once individuals realized that inflation would remain low over the long haul, they would be more likely to invest in equities, which do better in noninflationary economic environments. Such investment would provide large pools of capital for entrepreneurs to start new businesses, as well as provide a good rate of return for those who purchased the equities.

As such, US policy elites led by Volcker responded to the global capitalist crisis by deciding to wring inflation out of the US economy by tightening the money supply, raising the value of the dollar, and sending interest rates through the roof. Simply put, the Fed would reduce the number of dollars circulating in the US economy by selling increasing amounts of US Treasury bonds, thus sucking dollars out of the economy. With fewer dollars circulating, interest rates would of course increase. As interest rates increased, the cost of credit increased and businesses could not afford to borrow money to expand production. Also, increased interest rates made consumer credit more expensive, so consumers purchased less, which caused the economy to decline. Higher interest rates also sucked capital out of other parts of the world—such as Latin America—as investors naturally sought higher rates of return on their investments. Latin America's economy, already reeling from the 1970s economic downturn, got worse.

Volcker made the momentous decision to sharply raise interest rates in late 1978. (Of course, those outside of the United States had no input with regard to this decision, yet it had important ramifications worldwide including in Latin America—as will be discussed below.) Unemployment in the United States rapidly increased. The political cost for President Jimmy Carter and the Democratic Party was high. Both would lose heavily at the polls in 1980. Yet, publicly, Carter did not criticize Volcker or the Fed. With the (relatively) high value of the US dollar, imports became relatively less expensive and exports more expensive. US companies had already begun to shift their operations overseas in search of lower labor costs, in particular to countries that were close to the United States, such as Mexico. Not only did US jobs shift overseas, high-wage manufacturing jobs were also transferred overseas, "hollowing out" the US middle class. Working-class Americans could no longer easily find work with salaries and benefits high enough to comfortably raise their families. The number of hours worked by all Americans (especially working-class Americans) increased. Politically, the effects of such outsourcing, which could be more generally termed "deindustrialization," were significant. Deindustrialization reduced the power of labor unions, which is one of (liberal) the Democratic Party's key constituencies. More than simply providing probably the biggest voting bloc in the Democratic Party, unions were very important for Democrats because they had financial and organizational resources for "getting the vote out" in US elections. It is no surprise that voter turnout fell starting in the 1970s, as the power of unions fell.

When Ronald Reagan took office in 1981, some saw it as the unalloyed victory of monetarism over Keynesianism. Indeed, Reagan did maintain Volcker's monetarist policies, and Volcker served through 1987, almost to the end of Reagan's tenure as president. Reagan's policies, however, were a mixture of monetarism and Keynesianism. The Reagan Administration maintained tight monetary reigns but engaged in an expansive fiscal policy of tax cuts (mainly for the wealthy) and military spending, sending US government budget deficits sharply higher. They would remain relatively high until the late 1990s. As the US economy and the world economy brightened in the late 1980s, many saw this improved economic picture as vindication for Reagan's conservative, monetarist policies. But, as noted above, Reagan's policies were a combination of monetarism and Keynesianism. Reagan's use of deficit spending to pump-prime the US and world economies would become the standard operating procedure for Republican presidencies up to the present day. The growing gap between the elites and the rest of the population would continue to be a problem for the United States, and much of the world, up to the present day.

Conclusion

The rise of neoliberal ideology was due in large part to the perceived failure of Keynesianism in the 1970s. As the world's capitalist nations were searching for a post-Keynesian solution, monetarists had a ready answer and had the ear of powerful politicians. As such, neoliberalism was implemented and had a tremendous impact on the developed world. As middle-class jobs in manufacturing shifted overseas, the gap between the wealthy and the nonelites began to widen. The same thing happened in the developing world, including Latin America. With the implementation of neoliberalism in Latin America, the power of the state began to wane. Into this "political vacuum" stepped two groups. One group saw the decline of the state as an opportunity for more autonomy. Another viewed the decline of the state as a problem, as previously the state had provided benefits and security. These differing responses to the decline of the state will be discussed in Chapter Fourteen. To best understand the "why" and the "how" of the origins of neoliberalism in Latin America, Chapter Fifteen will focus on two of the early neoliberal experiments in the region, Bolivia and Chile.

Study Questions

1. What important global currents led to the implementation of laissez-faire policies in the 1970s and 1980s?
2. Discuss how the Latin American nations responded to the world economic crisis of the 1970s.
3. Discuss why the Latin American nations decided to dismantle many aspects of the Import Substitution Industrialization (ISI) model of political economy in the 1970s.
4. How did the policies of the United States impact Latin America in the 1970s and 1980s?

For Further Reading

Ferguson, Niall, Charles S. Maier, Erez Manela, and Daniel J. Sargent, eds. *The Shock of the Global—The 1970s in Perspective*. Cambridge, MA: Harvard University Press, 2010.
Hayek, Frederick A. *Road to Serfdom*. Chicago: University of Chicago Press, 1944.
Yergin, Daniel and Joseph Stanislaw. *The Commanding Heights: The Battle between Government and the Marketplace That Is Remaking the Modern World*. New York: Simon and Schuster, 1988.

CHAPTER FOURTEEN

Neoliberalism, Part II: The Rise of Indigenous Nationalism in Latin America and the Anti-Neoliberal Protests

La agua es nuestra! Carajo! [The water is ours, damn it!]

POPULAR QUOTE WRITTEN ON WALLS BY GRAFFITTI ARTISTS DURING THE
"WATER WAR" IN COCHABAMBA, BOLIVIA, IN 2000

The rise of indigenous nationalism

Neoliberalism calls for a reduced role of the state in the nation's affairs. Not surprisingly, with a less powerful state, indigenous peoples have become more active in society and politics. One thing that flows out of neoliberalism (perhaps not intended by acolytes of neoliberalism) is pluralism, or more specifically a plurinational state, which replaced a socially integrated state backed up by a strong leader and the influence of the nation (i.e., twentieth-century populism, discussed in Chapter Six). Going back to the Liberal oligarchies of the nineteenth century, national integration was key—how to physically and socially integrate the nation in a manner controlled by elites. This was a powerful idea that was carried through to the mid-twentieth century by a number of left- and right-wing nationalists. However, by the late twentieth century, the idea of an integrated, top-down unified nation gave way to a plurinational state—the state as conceived as a group of different ethnic groups. In this new, plurinational state, individual ethnic groups could speak their own language, practice their own traditions, and maintain their own lifestyles. The nation would not force top-down social integration.

Globalization accelerated the shift from a top-down state to a plurinational state. Starting in the 1970s, individual Indian groups in individual nations began to organize to prevent anti-Indian discrimination as well as to preserve Indian culture. Starting in the 1990s, in part due to the globalization of instant communication (fax machines and later the internet), nation-based Indian rights organizations could more easily organize internationally.[1] The ramifications of this shift, for the idea and ideal of nationalism, are profound. Previous to the late twentieth century, nationalism for many nations rested on the idea that physical and social integration was key to maintaining the integrity of the nation. However, with the idea of a plurinational state (made up of different ethnic groups) comes an effort to forge common ground and thus solidarity among its constituent parts.

Since plurinational states are weaker than states organized in a rigid, top-down fashion, the leadership of the plurinational states seeks to increase the strength of the state. Not surprisingly, the leadership of these plurinational nations decide to emphasize potential foreign threats more. Pointing to an outside threat gives the leaders an excuse to demand increased unity at home—for the security of the country. Taking the argument a step further, the relatively weaker plurinational state attempts to further its national security by creating supranational, regional organizations. For example, some nations in the Americas banded together to form an organization, headed up by Hugo Chávez and termed a "Bolivarian union," which tried to collectively increase their power vis-à-vis the United States.

The case of Bolivia

In the case of Bolivia, by the early twentieth century two separate trends emerged which would frame indigenous politics for years. First, Indians began to organize congresses to unify themselves and more effectively push for their rights as citizens as well as to build up the strength of their traditions (discussed in Chapter Six). Second, populist-type governments aimed to "corral" the support of Indian groups and use force against them if they resisted. To entice them into agreeing with the government agenda, after 1952 Bolivian Indians had the right to vote and participated in government-sponsored labor and campesino organizations. However, this participation in government-sponsored organizations meant Indians needed to "tow the government line" with regard to their demands. Because in effect the Bolivian government co-opted the power of Indian groups, their influence in society seemed muted.

By the 1980s, however, there was a new impulse among Indians to organize politically and socially.[2] As the power of the state was sharply restricted by the neoliberal reforms of the 1980s, requiring the state to cut back its size and budget, not surprisingly Indians realized that they could more effectively resist state power if they organized. Newly emboldened Indian movements revived the organizational impulse of the 1940s. In addition, once, by the 1990s, the Bolivian state and nation embraced the idea of a pluriethnic nation, Indians perceived that their demands for dignity and better economic well-being would no longer fall on deaf ears. Even though Indian movements in the nation could trace their roots back to the 1940s, and became increasingly popular by the 1970s, it was in the 1990s and early 2000s that their organizations became more powerful. For many indigenous peoples in Bolivia, by 2005 it seemed finally Indian rights would be firmly established by the Bolivian state. In that year, Bolivians elected their first Indian leader to openly acknowledge his indigenous roots, Evo Morales.

Urban protests challenge neoliberalism

The increasingly prominent indigenous movements in Latin America were for the large part anti-neoliberal. Indigenous peoples viewed neoliberalism as an economic system that benefitted the wealthy in their nations, as well as wealthy foreigners.

The increasing power of Indian movements in Latin America contributed to the increasing power of the antiglobalization movement in the region. The high tide of neoliberalism was in the 1990s. Neoliberalism produced a great deal of economic growth and wealth. However, as the economic benefits of neoliberalism flowed to the wealthy, it exacerbated the already widening gap between the wealthy and poor. Not surprisingly, the nonelite majority called for a return to leftist policies that would benefit the majority. Urban protests against neoliberalism included both Indians and mestizos, reflective of the emergent idea of a plurinational state, increasingly popular in post-populist Latin America.

The first major response to neoliberalism came in 1989 in Venezuela. A major protest in early 1989 occurred in Caracas, Venezuela, in response to neoliberal-inspired cuts in subsidies for food and gasoline. It is interesting to note that this protest occurred in one of Latin America's wealthier nations. Often, protests occur not among the most destitute and downtrodden but among those that have grown used to certain government benefits. When such benefits are swiftly removed, the former beneficiaries feel wronged.

A bit more than ten years later, the city of Cochabamba, Bolivia, put itself on the map with the so-called Water War in 2000. Neoliberal ideology, in particular so called "free trade," laid the groundwork for an anti-neoliberal backlash. Although many in the Western, industrialized world see free trade as self-evidently beneficial to all who participate in it, the reality shows that trade agreements between larger nations and smaller nations often compel the smaller nation to accept terms which can threaten their control over basic services—such as water. In the late 1990s, the United States and Bolivia agreed to lower trade barriers between their nations. Access to the biggest market in the world obviously motivated Bolivia to sign the deal. But, in exchange, Bolivia had to allow large multinational corporations the option to purchase the right to control and run the water systems for entire cities.[3] When the Bechtel Corporation purchased the water system for Cochabamba, Bolivia in the late 1990s, they sharply increased prices. The people of Cochabamba protested and thus began the Water War of early 2000 in which a number of protestors were injured and four killed.[4] The result was that the water system reverted to public control, even as the government of Cochabamba had to pay a fine to Bechtel.

New social movements: A new leftist nationalism?

Starting in the 1990s, some observers noticed a "new politics" of social movements in Latin America. Although the roots of this "new politics" extend back to the mid-twentieth century, in the 1980s and 1990s many Latin Americans used the neoliberal "revolution" as a rallying point. These social movements have upended politics in some countries. (Bolivia, Ecuador, and Venezuela are good examples.) One important feature of these social movements was a firm commitment to democracy—largely because dictatorships had ravaged Latin America from the mid-1960s through the 1980s. A second important feature of this "new politics" was the coming together of previously antagonistic groups, such as Marxist revolutionaries and Catholic liberation theologians. The end of the Cold War facilitated this convergence. A third key aspect of this new politics is the urban poor emerged as key political actors. "Slum dwellers" uprisings went back to the late 1940s, if not earlier. But, as urbanization rapidly occurred from the 1950s onward, with massive numbers of people living in subhuman conditions (the favelas of Brazil are an often-cited example), the poor in cities have grouped together to press for better living conditions and basic human rights. A fourth key aspect of this new politics is increased labor militancy. These unionists pressed not only for higher wages and better working conditions but for increased influence over decision making in the workplace. A fifth key aspect of this new politics is that women were playing key leadership roles in the various social movements. A sixth important aspect is that Indians pressed not only for equal rights but environmental protection and the right to have their native languages taught in the public schools. A seventh key aspect of the new politics is broad-based peasant movements in many Latin American countries. An eight key aspect was the increased prominence of young people. The ninth key aspect of this new politics is the emergence of a populist/reformist/nationalist segment of the military. The rise of Hugo Chávez in Venezuela, a military man who attempted a coup in 1992 that was turned back, is a good example. Chávez was democratically elected in 1998.[5] In sum, one thread that runs through this "new politics" is that many nonelite Latin Americans on the left end of the political spectrum conclude that it is the duty of the individual Latin American nations to ensure that its poorest members do not continue to remain mired in poverty.

The lurch to the left politically in Latin America, particularly South America, from the 1990s to the present represents a new tide of nationalism. This new sense of nationalism cannot be understood without examining it in the context of globalization. Globalization allowed for increasing amounts of foreign capital to enter the region. Neoliberalism called for trade barriers and capital controls to come down, facilitating this influx. The left-wing surge is called by some observers a "pink tide." It is "pink" and not "red" because the leftists in control of many of Latin America's governments were not hard-line ideologues but instead flexible pragmatists. They blended pro-poor domestic policies with the fiscal austerity demanded by the International Financial Institutions (IFIs). By maintaining fiscal austerity and (somewhat) balanced budgets, these nations could raise capital in international financial markets where such financial rigor was a necessity. In addition, the different types of governmental policies in the "pink tide" are remarkable. Brazil, Argentina, and Chile, for example, maintain many neoliberal policies. The more radical Venezuela, Bolivia, and Ecuador have mostly discarded neoliberalism, opting for more populist/statist policies— economic nationalism on the rise.[6] However, in the second decade of the twenty-first century, Brazil has experienced political problems; and Venezuela has experienced both political and economic problems, calling into question whether this economic-nationalist reaction to neoliberalism will continue.

Although neoliberalism increases economic inequality and makes it difficult for those at the bottom of society in terms of income to find any time at all in their busy lives to participate as a citizen in a democracy, neoliberalism has an "upside" for some. By calling for the role/power of the state to be minimized, more political "space" is created for citizens to exert their rights and responsibilities as citizens.[7] Indeed, one interesting example is in Mexico. After the 2000 democratic transition, the power of the Mexican state was diminished, allowing for the Zapatista rebels to run schools and other social services in their native Chiapas. Ironically, there is a convergence of interests with some neoliberal leaders on the issue of providing services to the poor in Mexico's poorest state. Both the neoliberal leaders, who would rather save government funds than spend it on Indians in Chiapas, and the Indian rebels, who do not want to have any connection with the Mexican government for fear it would compromise their independence, can agree that the Indians in Chiapas do not want public sector resources coming from the Mexican national state.

Study Questions

1. How did the indigenous peoples of Latin America respond to neoliberalism?
2. How did neoliberalism affect the lives of the nonelite indigenous peoples of Latin America?
3. On balance, was neoliberalism a good thing or a bad thing, for the indigenous peoples of Latin America?
4. Why did protestors rise up against the neoliberal reforms?

For Further Reading

Gotkowitz, Laura. *A Revolution for Our Rights: Indigenous Struggles for Land and Justice in Bolivia, 1880–1952.* Durham, NC: Duke University Press, 2007.

Gott, Richard. *Hugo Chavez: The Bolivarian Revolution in Venezuela.* London: Verso, 2005.

Healy, Kevin. *Llamas, Weavings, and Organic Chocolate : Multicultural Grassroots Development in the Andes and Amazon of Bolivia.* Notre Dame, IN: Notre Dame University Press, 2001.

CHAPTER FIFTEEN

Neoliberalism, Part III: Neoliberalism at High Tide

In the cabaret of globalization, the state shows itself as a table dancer that strips off everything until it is left with only the minimum indispensable garments: the repressive force.

SUBCOMANDANTE MARCOS, ONE OF THE LEADERS OF THE
ZAPATISTA REBELLION IN CHIAPAS, MEXICO[1]

The decline and fall of Import Substitution Industrialization

Worldwide intellectual trends, as well as economic problems in Latin America and the rising power of indigenous movements, set the stage for one of the most important turning points in recent Latin American history: the rise of neoliberalism in the region (discussed in Chapter Thirteen). How Latin America dismantled Import Substitution Industrialization (ISI) is one of the more important transitions in recent Latin American history. Because it occurred in the (relatively) recent past, it is difficult to put it into perspective. Also it is important to note that the "neoliberal turn" was something that had many causes, took quite a while, and was the result of decisions made by Latin American nations, who were influenced by International Financial Institutions (IFIs).

The crisis of ISI was a long, slow-burning crisis. It became clear by the mid-1960s that ISI had fueled the expectations of the Latin American urban working class, and middle-class Latin Americans and elites feared that the (growing) working class, which of course was the majority, would use ISI to further increase their political gains they had notched up with the creation of ISI. To put the brakes on the rising political power of the working class under ISI, the middle class and elites supported military coups to contain the growing influence of the working class. Scholars have termed this phenomenon "bureaucratic-authoritarianism." The generals thought they could "put the financial house in order" through skillful implementation of "rational" (from the point of view of elites) economic policy by means of talented officials (that's the bureaucratic part) (discussed in Chapter Eleven). Then, if political opponents of the regimes teamed up with laborites to protest the restrictions on labor activity, the generals would use repression (funded at times by US military assistance) to keep labor "in line."

A big blow to ISI came in the early 1970s with the Organization of the Petroleum Exporting Countries (OPEC) oil price hike, followed by the 1978–1979 price hike due to the Iranian Revolution. For non-oil-producing Latin American nations in which oil was denominated in US dollars, which became very expensive in the late 1970s due to Federal Reserve policy, the price of imported oil skyrocketed relative to the price of their exports. Latin America's exports in the 1970s had already suffered two big body blows. First, demand was slack because of the weak economies in the industrialized world, and as such prices declined. Second, some First World producers had become incredibly efficient (i.e., the United States and Canada) at producing foodstuffs, sharpening competition in world markets for foodstuffs and further depressing prices. Since the independence of the Latin American nations in the early nineteenth century, Latin America had suffered from the problem of declining terms of trade—the price of agricultural and primary product exports fell relative to the price of industrialized goods which the Latin American nations imported from abroad. As a result, Latin America's balance of payments deficits widened. Up through the early twentieth century, many Latin American nations enjoyed a positive balance of payments with the industrialized powers. But, as the terms of trade between primary products and industrialized goods fell and competition vis-à-vis other regions exporting primary products intensified (Asia and Africa), simultaneously Latin America's appetite for industrialized products grew and competition from Latin America's balance of payments went into the red by the mid- to late twentieth century.

To plug the gap in the balance of payments, Latin American nations borrowed. For oil-producing Latin American nations, their coffers of foreign exchange swelled. As such, investors, including the flush Middle Eastern oil-producing nations, saw the oil-producing Latin American nations as a good place to invest. A big chunk of this investment came in the form of loans from banks where the Middle Eastern countries had deposited millions of their earnings. As such, part of the "recycling of petro-dollars" as it was termed meant that banks saw oil-producing Latin American nations as a good investment. So when these nations wanted to borrow money, the banks gladly obliged. Therefore, for different reasons, both non-oil-producing and oil-producing Latin American nations borrowed lots of (dollar-denominated) loans.[2]

The ramifications of this run-up in debt were profound. For those who subscribed to the dependency framework for explaining Latin America's relationship with the industrialized world, they saw the large flow of money out of Latin America to make payments on the debt as the industrialized world siphoning off resources from Latin America. It is important to point out that the run-up in debt occurred just before the Fed's decision in 1978–1979 to drastically reduce the US money supply, sending US interest rates up, as well as of course increasing interest rates on dollar-denominated financial assets (including loans in dollars to the Latin American nations, discussed in Chapter Thirteen). With higher interest rates, making timely payments on the debt became more difficult.

We're all in the market now: Neoliberalism arises

With the sharp contraction of the world economy in the late 1970s and early 1980s, which came after the slow growth of the 1970s, it became clear that many Latin American nations could not earn enough foreign exchange to continue to make timely payments on their voluminous debt. As such, it was clear that some nations would default, which sent shock waves through the world economy. Thus, the "world debt crisis" of the 1980s was born with tremendously important effects on Latin America. First, the authoritarian governments of the 1980s in the region, which had become more repressive by the late 1970s, were discredited. The generals in many Latin American nations had taken power because they thought (along the lines of bureaucratic authoritarianism, discussed previously) they could run the economy and government better than their (democratically elected) populist predecessors—who brought in ISI. Now, however, the tables were turned. It was the generals who were being discredited. Fortunately, as it became clear that the military dictatorships could not deal with the mountain of economic problems—exacerbated by the debt crisis—there were movements to push the generals out and reinstate democracy. US foreign policy is important in understanding redemocratization as well. To his credit, President Jimmy Carter, much more concerned with human rights than his two immediate (conservative and Republican) predecessors, wanted to punish authoritarian regimes in Latin America that systematically abused human rights through political repression, including torture and death. Carter cut off part or all US assistance to such regimes, informing them that aid would not be restored until they stopped abusing human rights. Chile and Argentina were probably the worst human rights offenders, but other nations systematically abused their citizens' human rights as well.

Many around the world realized that a Latin American default on their large stock of debt would be disastrous not only for Latin America but also for the world financial system and thus the world economy. Various plans (such as the Baker and Brady Plans of the mid- to late 1980s) were implemented. In these plans, top US policy makers worked with the large banks, wealthy owners of large numbers of Latin American bonds, and the Latin American nations to write down a portion of the debt to stave off a default of heavily indebted Latin American nations, which could touch off a worldwide global panic. Unfortunately, because interest rates stayed high, few Latin American nations could dig themselves out of debt and thus remained dependent on private sector foreign financing.[3]

However, another dynamic was at work which shows that understanding globalization—in particular economic globalization—is key to understanding the demise of ISI, the rise of neoliberalism, and the resulting delegitimization of the Latin American state, which weakened Latin American nationalism. The International Monetary Fund (IMF) stepped in to "solve" the 1970s and 1980s economic crisis in Latin America—in a neoliberal way.

Since in the 1980s and 1990s many on the political left, both within and outside of Latin America, sharply criticized the IMF for instituting policies that both curbed economic growth in Latin America and imposed tremendous costs on the poor, as will be described below, it is important to point out that Latin American nations initially, back when the IMF was created, supported the institution.

The IMF was one of the IFIs created by the Bretton Woods Conference at Mount Washington Resort, Bretton Woods, New Hampshire, in 1944. (The other main IFI created at Bretton Woods was the International Bank for Reconstruction and Development [IBRD, or World Bank].) As the Second World War was drawing to a close, finance ministers of the Allied powers and nations that were supporting them thought it was important to draw up economic and financial "rules of the game" to ensure that the postwar world was prosperous. The IMF was created to loan funds to nations that were facing temporary foreign exchange crises to prevent economic problems from becoming political crises. Not surprisingly, the delegates to the Bretton Woods conference saw such initiatives as preventing a global financial crisis which beset the world in the 1930s, resulting in trade wars between nations, further reducing economic growth during the Great Depression. It is important to note that many top world leaders in the late 1940s saw the creation of the IBRD and the IMF as equally important as the creation of the United Nations at that time.[4]

Even though the prevailing narrative among scholars of Bretton Woods is that the more wealthy and powerful nations prevailed at the Conference, the Latin American nations did influence the decision-making process. Indeed, Latin American nations thought that they had, potentially, a great deal to gain from the IMF, since the Latin Americans wanted to develop economically. The IMF and the World Bank could aid in that process.[5]

But, four decades after Bretton Woods, the IMF was something that hindered, not helped, Latin American economic development. The IMF implemented "stabilization" or "structural adjustment" programs (really euphemisms for austerity) in the 1980s to ease the Latin American nations out of their debt crises, while promoting efficient—neoliberal, in the new parlance—economies and governments in the region. The IMF would loan money or facilitate new loans, so the Latin Americans could continue to make their payments on their previous obligations. But, in exchange for this infusion of new funds, the IMF exacted steep concessions. Latin America was to make efforts to promote exports, so as to bring in more foreign exchange. The Bolivian government was to cut its government budget deficit, which meant in some cases subsidies for the working class and poor would be cut.[6]

In sum, the costs of the austerity or stabilization plans fell disproportionately on the poor as the Latin American nations borrowed from the IMF only with conditionality—strings attached. They were required to cut a variety of government subsidies which had allowed the poor to barely scrape by. Now, the poor were not even doing that.[7]

Vanguard of neoliberalism in Latin America: Chile and Bolivia

Interestingly, relatively poor and landlocked Bolivia proved to be a trailblazer in this regard, way back in the 1950s. The Movimiento Revolucionario Nacionalista (MNR), which had won an election in 1951, was prevented from taking office by a coup and thus staged a successful revolution to take power the next year (discussed in Chapter Eight). The MNR implemented significant reforms, among them extending suffrage to Indians and women, a land reform—one of Latin America's most thorough—and put in place the nationalization of the three largest (with significant foreign ownership) mining companies. These companies produced about 80 percent of the nation's foreign exchange and enjoyed overweening political influence— which came to an end with the nationalization. Also, MNR leaders thought that the new state-run company formed from the nationalized companies (the Corporación Mineral de Bolivia [COMIBOL]) would produce significant profits which would be used for infrastructure and other programs to help the Bolivian public.

Unfortunately for the MNR, foreign technicians and capital left the country as tin prices collapsed in the mid- to late 1950s, and COMIBOL turned out to be a drain on the Bolivian government treasury. Falling tin prices also hurt the company. The Bolivian government printed too much money to cover its losses, and inflation shot up. Because the MNR was a divided, tenuous coalition, the economic crisis gave the smaller, more moderate segment of the party—which enjoyed the majority of the leadership positions—an opportunity. Because US leaders feared a collapse of the MNR and a political vacuum in the heart of South America, Washington extended economic assistance, which included food aid, in 1952, only a few months after the US government officially recognized the MNR. With the inflationary problems of the mid-1950s, US officials offered increased assistance, but it was "tied aid." That is, US assistance would now be predicated on the Bolivians reducing not only the size of their money supplies but the power of the Bolivian state itself, and thus reducing the state's role in the economy.

The moderate MNR members saw an opportunity and seized on it. US stipulations for reducing the role/size of the Bolivian state meant in effect that the Bolivian state had to severely cut back on COMBOL subsidies. These cutbacks, which resulted in a number of mines being closed and large numbers of workers losing their jobs, led not only to increased social conflict—some of it bloody—but it also led to the radical wing of MNR losing power. The combination of increasing social conflict and the left losing power laid the groundwork for a military coup in 1964. Because the MNR was so divided and weaker, the military logically—and correctly— concluded they could, relatively easily, stage a successful coup. Democracy came to an end, as did some of the MNR-sponsored reforms. Examples of reforms included improving the Bolivian educational system and promoting infrastructure development that ultimately, it was thought, would lead to economic diversification.

Fast forward to the 1980s, and "expand the lens" to include many parts of Latin America—including Bolivia. The debt crisis of the 1980s caused a number of Latin American nations to almost default. Mexico in the early 1980s and 1990s was a case in point. As such, the Latin American nations needed a solution, and one came in the form of the IMF "stabilization" plans, or, more accurately, austerity plans. The IMF loaned money to the Latin American nations that needed funds quickly and at below-market rates. However, the IMF stipulated that the recipient nation cut their money supply (if it was deemed too large) as well as government subsidies. The cuts in subsidies hurt the poor, and in some cases, the agricultural sector.

The effects of the IMF-imposed austerity plans were profound. The timing could not have been worse for Latin America. The high oil prices of the 1970s hit the non-oil-producing nations hard. Then, the US Federal Reserve's decision to sharply tighten the money supply to "wring" inflation out of the US economy drove up interest rates—to dizzyingly high levels. Considering the heavy debt load of the Latin American nations, the increase in the cost of debt and repaying it was profound. Economies slumped. It is important to understand that this context in viewing the IMF stabilization programs. Because these programs required cuts in Latin American government's budgets, and often these cuts disproportionately hurt the poor, the IMF stabilization programs occurred at a time when poorer Latin Americans could ill afford to make economic sacrifices. As such, many Latin Americans considered these stabilization programs as socially and politically destabilizing. In some parts of Latin America, the economic crisis of the late 1970s and early 1980s, abetted by the IMF, helped to spur an increase in the production of illegal narcotics or the production of the agricultural products that are the raw materials for the production of such narcotics. As the Latin American economies were hard hit by the outflow of funds to make repayments on their large amount of debt, poor Latin Americans were hit hardest by the economic crisis of the early 1980s. Not surprisingly, and often out of desperation, they turned to the drug trade for economic survival. The growth in the drug trade, as well as the ineffectual, US-sponsored "war on drugs," had a tremendously important legacy for both Latin America and US-Latin American relations, and Latin America's relationship with many other parts of the world. Unfortunately, this legacy is a negative one.

With regard to cuts in agricultural subsidies, the agricultural sector was hit hard. As a result, a large number of campesinos gave up on farming and moved to the cities—which were already growing quickly with former rural residents moving in. As such, the cities could not provide basic services to these poorer residents, and shantytowns mushroomed on the outskirts of many of the larger cities.

But there were other effects. Some Latin American leaders, of a moderate or conservative bent, found the stipulations of the IMF useful. It allowed them to say to their advisors, and their people, "well, I don't want to have to make these painful cuts—but the IMF made me!" Some leaders, for example, were looking for ways to sell off inefficient state-run industries anyway; the IMF stabilization plans simply gave them the leverage to do what they wanted.

Some Latin American leaders, in an attempt to build political support for their position to end the austerity programs, called attention to the fact that the austerity programs hurt the US economy. In 1989, the President of Venezuela, Carlos Andrés Pérez, in a public talk at Cornell University in Ithaca, New York, stated that the austerity programs sharply reduced Latin America's ability to purchase exports from the United States. Indeed, historically, Latin America has been a part of the world in which US exporters have enjoyed a lucrative business. Andrés Pérez stated that austerity programs from 1981 to 1983 caused the loss of 200,000 jobs in the United States and the non-generation of potentially an additional 400,000 jobs—a significant number of jobs considering the United States was experiencing its worst economic recession since the Great Depression.[8]

Bolivia's experience with the rapid implementation of neoliberalism caused one of the more important economic changes in its recent history. IMF-required cuts to Bolivia's state-run mining sector led to the rapid privatization of the mines and a large number of layoffs. These former miners moved to the western part of the Amazon basin, in particular the Chapare, to grow coca leaves that were refined into cocaine. Producing coca leaves was the most lucrative economic endeavor available to these former miners. By the late 1980s, the illegal trade in cocaine was a very important part of Bolivia's economy. The United States began to implement a "war on drugs" to suppress not only the flow of cocaine into the United States but also the production of coca leaves that were used to made cocaine. This "drug war" led to increased tension between the United States and Bolivia, as well as increased anti-US sentiment in Bolivia.

The second neoliberal precursor was Chile, which went from a socialist republic to an authoritarian, military dictatorship in 1973. The Pinochet regime, which deposed the democratically-elected socialist government of Salvador Allende in September 1973, proved to be one of the more brutal regimes in recent Latin American history. The regime tortured and killed thousands, and thousands fled into exile. In order to stimulate the economy, Pinochet hired neoclassical economists from the University of Chicago, known as the "Chicago Boys," a team of economists headed up by renowned economist Milton Friedman. Labor unions were repressed, and price controls were loosened. By the late 1970s, the Chilean economy was doing well, but the benefits of this economic bonanza mainly flowed to the wealthy in Chile. Although neoliberalism calls for minimal intrusion of the government in the economic marketplace, it is important to note that in the Chilean case, the government remained a very powerful actor in society.

Globalization and neoliberalism: The case of Argentina

If there ever was a case of displaying how globalization could impact a society and economy, it would be Argentina. The Southern Cone nation's economic (and to some extent social and political) fate has been intimately intertwined with the global economy for over two centuries, but globalization really became a major force in the nation starting in the late nineteenth century. Argentina, quickly recovering from the 1890 Baring financial crisis, greatly benefitted from exports of primary source products, especially foodstuffs, in the late nineteenth and early twentieth centuries, to the point that Argentina was one of the wealthiest countries in the world before the First World War, with an income roughly equal to that of France. With the Great War, trade and investment ties to Europe were cut, sending Argentina (and a number of parts Latin America) into an economic tailspin. Not surprisingly, then, with the downturn in trade during both the world wars and the Great Depression, Argentina opted instead for an economic nationalist policy, known in Argentina as Peronism, a variant of ISI. Indeed, Argentine's history seems to swing from intimate integration into the global economy to economic nationalism—and, with the fall of Peronism in the 1980s and 1990s, back to integration into the world economy—with its attendant risks and problems.

History is important here. Because in the late nineteenth and early twentieth centuries Argentina was deeply connected economically with the European (and to some extent US) economies, and the elite/middle class segment very much benefitted from globalization, it is not surprising that Argentina "took the plunge" into neoliberalism. Besides, many in Argentina concluded by the 1980s, with the foreign debt crisis, and the attendant skyrocketing debt repayment costs, Argentina had to make major change. The Peronist system could not produce enough resources to make even the lowered debt payments (agreements to "write off" part of the mountain of debt). The majority of Argentines concluded that, with neoliberalism, the Argentine economy could produce enough to simultaneously make payments on the debt and produce wealth for the citizenry.

Prodded by the IMF, which required Argentina to make painful cuts to government programs, including food subsidies for the economically disadvantaged, Argentina embraced neoliberalism.

The deepening of neoliberalism

The near-defaults of the 1980s and 1990s were an important precursor to the "neoliberal revolution." The neoliberal critique of the populist-ISI governments of the 1930s through 1970s was profound. For almost four decades in many Latin American nations, a powerful coalition of urban- and middle-class Latin Americans used government policies, such as high tariffs and subsidies, combined with a powerful, charismatic leader (sometimes of a military background), to basically control the political destiny of the continent. With the neoliberal revolution of the 1980s and 1990s, this was no longer the case.

Neoliberals feared the powerful, charismatic leaders of populism (e.g., Perón in Argentina and Betancourt in Venezuela). They feared these leaders would encourage the working class to expect steadily increasing wages and a better economic well-being in general. Neoliberals feared that the charismatic, powerful populist leaders had too much control over the political process and political participation. Indeed, neoliberals feared that the political power of the (elected) populist leaders would somehow grow so much that individual liberties would be diminished.

Neoliberalism (also known as the "Washington Consensus" after an important meeting of top US and Latin American leaders in Washington in 1990) had a core belief in the faith of free markets to steadily produce economic benefits over time—that is, the accumulation of wealth. Although at times the accumulation would be enjoyed much more by the wealthy than others, neoliberals had a faith that "a rising economic tide would lift all boats" in the long run. (Keynes acidly observed many years ago, however, that in the long run, we are all dead.)

The "neo" part of neoliberalism meant that even as all humans had the right to basic political and economic freedoms, some freedoms were more important than others. The "liberal" part of neoliberalism meant nineteenth-century liberalism—all humans had a right to political and economic freedoms. For neoliberals, economic freedoms were key—and more important than political freedoms. Neoliberals argued that all had the right to work where they wanted (and migrate to where they could find the best job) and the right to invest where they wanted with minimal government influence.

Neoliberalism called for the end to ISI. There were two main reasons. First, with less government intervention in the economy, individuals would have more freedom to allocate their wealth where they wanted to and more freedom regarding spending their money. Second, neoliberals feared that the authoritarian side of the populist-style governments would overly restrict political freedoms and expression, so therefore dismantling the ISI governments would mean an increase in political participation and political freedoms.

Neoliberalism was different from the modernization theory of the 1950s and 1960s in key ways. First, modernization theorists maintained that viable, well-developed government institutions were necessary to lay out and maintain the political/economic "rules of the game" to mediate, organize, and (in some ways) channel the process of wealth accumulation. Without such institutions, economic development and political stability (which could be produced, it was thought, through building/maintaining an effective civil society) would suffer, and the benefits of economic growth would accrue mainly to the wealthy. Modernization theorists understood that modernization would be a wrenching social and economic process—even a "heartless" process, as winners were rewarded and losers punished in a rapidly changing political and economic scene. Such a process would inevitably create conflict. As such, viable, stable, and dependable institutions—to mediate this conflict—were key to maintaining political stability and economic development. Neoliberalism, however, has a much different view of the state. Neoliberals had such faith in the supposedly self-equilibrating nature of economic markets that they thought that a state that governs least is the state that governs best. Even as neoliberals realized that in the short run the wealthy would enjoy a larger portion of the wealth accumulated by means of neoliberal policies, they had faith that over time all would benefit to some degree—"a rising tide would lift all boats." (They were in for a "rude awakening" in this respect, as will be discussed later.)

Neoliberals argued that their policies would in the long run produce industrialization that would be more beneficial to the Latin American economies than ISI-fostered industrialization. One criticism of ISI-type industrialization (leveled not only by neoliberals) was that it did not produce "deep" or "high-level" or "high-technology" industrialization that would help to produce more middle-class jobs as well as a more diversified economy. With the high tariffs of the ISI governments in Latin America, infant industries were protected, but such protection led only to "light" industrialization—consumer products, for example. ISI industrialization, these critics concluded, would not lead the Latin American nations into "high-technology" type economies, such as Taiwan, Korea, or Singapore. To foster such industrialization, neoliberals advocated the creation of regional trading blocs—the key example being the North American Free Trade Agreement (NAFTA) in 1992. According to neoliberals, with the fall of trade barriers and the loosening of capital controls, there was the potential (absent in the ISI-style industrialization, they said) for a much larger amount of, and a more rapid movement of, capital and people into the developing world. Over time, this process would automatically lead to more diversified, and more wealth-producing, industrial economies in Latin America.

A key principle—and the main international aspect of neoliberalism—is that for Latin America (and the entire nonindustrialized world) to prosper, it needed to effectively insert itself in a rapidly globalizing world. That meant each individual nation needed to reform its government policies in a way to allow as many of its citizens to prosper in a globalizing world. One example would be that governments needed to refrain from privileging one type of economic activity over another by cutting subsidies or capital controls. Another example would be that governments needed to promote educational programs that would allow the citizens of a nation to build their "human capital" in a way that would allow them to better position themselves—to obtain more economic benefits—from a globalizing world. Put more simply, the citizens of the various Latin American nations needed somehow to be able to economically profit from globalization—to produce what others wanted to purchase.

Interestingly, neoliberalism resembled the export-driven agricultural development of the late nineteenth century (discussed in Chapter Five). Nations that had factor endowments that allowed them to produce certain crops or primary products should maximize the production of those products, and then, by earning foreign exchange, could invest in the industrialization—and thus diversification—of their economies. Also, it is important to point out that the main problem of export-driven agriculture—monoculture, or emphasizing the production of one main export crop/product—was also a problem that neoliberals had to face. What if after a nation has spent years developing a lucrative export crop the market for such a crop quickly contracts? Such a contraction could be caused by changes in tastes/preferences in the industrialized world. (That is, people simply decided that they didn't want to buy a certain product from Latin America any more.) Also, through technological achievements, substitutes for primary source exports from Latin America could be produced in the industrialized nations themselves. A good example of such a technological achievement was the production of artificial rubber which greatly reduced demand for natural rubber.

As Latin American nations dismantled ISI, many Latin American citizens asked the question: what is the purpose of the state? As such, by the 1990s, there was a crisis of state legitimacy and political authority. With the advent of the neoliberal state in the 1990s, the state was much weaker than it was during the days of ISI. As such, there was more political "room" or "space" for political movements to assert themselves without the fear of being suppressed or attacked. Indian nationalist movements had existed in Latin America since the 1940s; but because of the power of the ISI state, they did not have much of a chance to assert themselves. With a much weaker Latin American state in the 1990s, Indian movements became more prominent and powerful in Latin America.

Resistance: Rise of the Zapatisas in Mexico, mid-1990s

A good example is the Zapatista uprising in Chiapas, Mexico, in 1994. Named after the most prominent Indian leader and hero of the Mexican Revolution (1910–1920), Emiliano Zapata, and "kicked off" on January 1, 1994, the day that the NAFTA agreement was officially implemented in Mexico, this Indian movement captured the attention of the world for a number of years in the 1990s. Interestingly, the Zapatistas capitalized on Mayan Indians' centuries-old grievances while harnessing new rapid-communication technologies (the fax machine and later the internet) to broadcast their movement to the world.

The world responded positively to the Zapatista's daring plans not only to denounce the ruling Partido Revolucionario Institucional (PRI), which had ruled Chiapas, and Mexico, since 1929, but also to control actual territory with the creation of "autonomous zones" in Chiapas where the rebels would imagine and implement a social order that would provide much-needed and systematically denied justice to the Maya in Chiapas. Although ultimately these autonomous zones were and are very small regions, in the end, the point was not to control actual territory but to inspire.

Many anti-neoliberal groups quickly rushed to support the Zapatisas because it was a tangible movement that feared that neoliberalism would ultimately be destructive with regard to the Indians' interests. Interestingly—and ironically—the neoliberal "turn" of the Mexican state in the 1990s inadvertently laid the groundwork for the Zapatista rebellion. First, policy changes with regard to land reform and opening up Mexico's economy to low-priced foodstuffs that would put Mexican farmers out of business scared many in Mexico. Second, neoliberalism called for diminishing state intervention in the economy while reducing the power of state institutions. Although neoliberals would deny that weakening state institutions would lead to the delegitimization of state authority in Mexico, arguably, that is what happened. After all, poorer and working-class Mexicans could logically conclude that if neoliberal leaders were going to dismantle aspects of the ISI state that had protected these Mexicans from the vagaries of the world economy, then what good was the state anyway? As such, this "crisis of legitimacy" benefitted the Zapatistas. The Zapatistas—over time—worked to build up their own institutions, in particular in the area of education. Thus, the Zapatisas "filled the gap" between what some Mexicans thought the state should be doing to help them and what it was actually doing. Importantly, the Zapatista rebellion played a role in the PRI being voted out in the summer of 2000. Because the Zapatistas had made it clear to Mexicans and the world that the PRI (which implemented a populist-ISI polity) had no response to the Zapatistas' demands except violent, military repression, the Zapatistas displayed the political bankruptcy of the PRI not only to Mexicans but also to the world.

Conclusion: Neoliberalism and the economic power of the developed world

One tangible fear of the Zapatistas was that NAFTA would facilitate the flooding of foodstuffs from the North American market, putting small producers in Mexico out of business, thus destroying their livelihood. There is another side to Latin America's fear of neoliberalism as it relates to multinational corporations (MNCs)—increased access to Latin America's large stock of raw materials. Indeed, Latin America is unique in that it has a wide variety of untapped resources, and it is not exploiting them as rapidly as many would like.

As the United States forms its own trade agreements with separate Latin American nations or with groups of Latin American nations, large companies (often based in the United States) will have increased access to critically important, dwindling stocks of resources that will be key for the future. Two examples are oil and water. Powerful outside entities could control these important resources for their own profit-making purposes at the expense of Latin America.[9] To careful readers, MNCs' access to Latin America's natural resources would come as no surprise. After all, by the late nineteenth century, many developed nations, in particular Europe and the United States, and the emerging MNCs based in those nations, in particular petroleum companies, had invested a great deal of money in Latin America to pump out large quantities of petroleum for world markets. Wanting to earn large amounts of foreign exchange, which would strengthen the state, many Latin American nations welcomed such investment. Thus, with the increased access to Latin America's raw materials that neoliberalism facilitated, we see historical continuity in the interlinked processes of globalization and nationalism.

Study Questions

1. How did Latin America respond to the economic crises of the 1970s?
2. How did the economic crises of the 1970s help cause the rise of neoliberal policies in the Latin America at that time?
3. How has economic globalization benefitted the majority of nonelite Latin Americans? How has such globalization hurt such Latin Americans?
4. How have Latin Americans resisted economic globalization and neoliberalism? Has their resistance been successful? Why or why not?

For Further Reading

Duque, G. Martha Alicia. "Colombia en subasta. Recursos estrategicos, bioversidad, y TLC: la nueva amenaza." In *La insertacion de America Latina en la economia internacional*, edited by Jaime Estay. Buenos Aires: Clasco, 2008.

Green, Duncan. *Silent Revolution—The Rise and Crisis of Market Economies in Latin America*, 2nd ed. New York: Monthly Review Press, 2003.

Robinson, William. *Latin America and the Global Economy—A Critical Globalization Perspective*. Baltimore, MD: Johns Hopkins University Press, 2008.

Womack, John Jr. *Rebellion in Chiapas: An Historical Reader*. New York: Norton, 1999.

PART SIX

New Directions: Popular Culture, Migration, and Inter-American Relations

CHAPTER SIXTEEN

A Brief Analysis of Latin American Cultural Nationalism

[F]ootball is more than a sport to us; it is a national passion.

LUIS IGNACIO LULA DE SILVA, OR LULA, PRESIDENT OF BRAZIL[1]

Introduction: Banal or significant?

In 1995, author Michael Billig published his influential *Banal Nationalism*, which caused many scholars to rethink nationalism—in particular the relationship between political nationalism and cultural nationalism. It was written soon after the end of the Cold War, when, with the "thawing" of the Cold War blocs, nationalism not surprisingly was on the march in many parts of the world. Nationalistic conflicts during the Cold War were in a sense "frozen" into the communist and noncommunist blocs until the Cold War quickly dissipated in the early 1990s. Then, as many observers at the time noted, nationalism in a sense "rose up" to become more prominent. Many wanted an explanation for this increase in nationalist sentiment, and Billig contributed a compelling explanation.

For his part, Billig urged readers to extend their concept of nationalism beyond simply political nationalism to include "everyday" nationalism. Everyday nationalism is of course a more positive way of putting banal nationalism. Billig urged readers to understand nationalism as a quotidian (daily) phenomenon—for example, the flag hanging unobtrusively but publicly in many public and private spaces.[2] But how can one measure the importance of this everyday nationalism? Was everyday nationalism simply something that most people accepted but was not that important

FIGURE 16.1 *Dancers dancing the Cuenca.* Source: *Columbus Memorial Library, Organization of American States, Washington, DC.*

FIGURE 16.2 *An Argentinian gaucho, an important symbol of Argentinian nationalism.* Source: *Columbus Memorial Library, Organization of American States, Washington, DC.*

to them? Or was it important for their identities? Billig concludes that if nationalism is unobtrusively but often invoked ("constant flagging"), then it must by definition be significant.[3] In this chapter, I will look at a number of nationalistic expressions that happen in everyday life in Latin America and assess how they allow citizens of Latin American nations to express their nationalistic feelings. One way of "getting at" everyday nationalism is to look at some examples (I would argue the most significant ones) of cultural nationalism. I define culture as the sum total of the beliefs and ways of living of a people as passed on from generation to generation. I define "cultural nationalism" as how everyday nationalism manifests itself culturally, in which culture is a widely shared set of important mores and societal values.

Since nationalism is based on the idea of myth—of shared values that (theoretically) everyone in the nation shares—foundational myths are extremely important for nationalism. Cultural expressions of these foundational myths, therefore, tell us a great deal about how citizens experience nationalism in a concrete way. For example, in Bolivia, the Andean new year (winter solstice in late June) is a national holiday. At Tiawanaku, outside of La Paz, Bolivia, the largest archeological site in Latin America, a celebration is held at sunrise at which local political groups and national political leaders in front of thousands of on-lookers pay homage to the importance of the Tiawanku—precursors of the Inca. The nationalistic logic is clear in the minds of many Bolivians: Tiawanku inspired the Inca, who preceded the Spanish, who preceded the present-day Bolivian state. As such, the foundation of Bolivian nationalism is the Tiawanku culture. As discussed in Chapter Six, the Indian past is of course not only important for indigenous nationalism in the region but also important for the nationalism of particular nations.

By way of introduction, it is also important to emphasize that cultural nationalism can be a form a resistance. It is not the case of course that Latin Americans simply imbibe the form of cultural nationalism that the government wants them to. For example, during the Mexican Revolution (discussed in Chapter Six), the Mexican state wanted to purge Catholic influences from society, including, importantly, the educational system. Priests were not allowed to wear their ecclesiastical garments in public nor to serve mass. The resistance to these prohibitions created a powerful social movement, Vivo Christo Rey (Long live Christ the King), which forced subsequent Mexican governments to allow for a more open expression of Catholicism.

Archeology/architecture, film, food, fashion, theatre, and of course *futbol* (soccer)

Regarding Tiawanaku, Machu Picchu serves the same purpose in Peru, the Mayan ruins play the same role in Central America, and the Mayan and Aztec ruins play that role in Mexico. The nationalistic message is important. First, the ruins are distinctive—where else but Peru can you find the so-called "Lost City of the Inca"? (This was briefly discussed in Chapter Six.) Second, the impressive ruins send a signal that the present-day Latin American nations are descendent of impressive ancient peoples and cultures. As such, the nationalistic logic runs, some day present-day Latin American nations will somehow regain that lost grandeur. Indeed, if nationalism can be defined as mapping a narrative (constructed national history or national memory) onto a territory (the sovereign space of the nation), in some respects archeology is a perfect vehicle for nationalism. By placing archeological ruins at the center of the constructed national narrative, a direct link from the indigenous past to the present can be clearly delineated. In this way, nationalists can privilege the precolonial indigenous experience over that of the colonizer. Critics, especially left-wing critics, of the Spanish and Portuguese colonizers can thus use archeology to establish the "true foundation" of the nation as the indigenous past, not the colonial past. In this way, archeology in effect "rais[es] the nation from the ruins of the past."[4] Modern-day architects in the Andes have used styles and techniques that imitate the Inca and pre-Inca archeological ruins.

The history of film provides a good example of nationalism at work. In the 1930s, filmmaker Sergei Eisenstein made a movie about the indigenous reality in Mexico, *Que Vive Mexico!* One of the underlying ideas of the film is that indigenous culture in Mexico, with one of the largest populations of Indians in Latin America, is what makes Mexico distinctive. That is, Mexican nationalism cannot be fully understood unless one understands the Mexican reality. The portrayal of the Mexican Indians is that of the "noble savage," the idea that the Indian peoples' existence is tied closely to the land and the environment and that Indians are somehow "naturally" (in a childlike fashion) good—unable to do harm, until, of course, they come in contact with Western culture.

Bolivian films of the 1960s and beyond help us to understand the transition from top-down, oligarchic Liberal nationalism of the nineteenth century (which as stated before, lingered well into the twentieth and even twenty-first centuries) to the bottom-up ethnic/racial/indigenous nationalisms of the mid-twentieth century. Filmmaker Jorge Sanjines is key in this regard. His films argue that the Indian populations in Bolivia were colonized by the Spanish invaders in the early sixteenth century, and the Indians remain colonized. The Indians were, in a sense, in separate (but vastly unequal) nations. As such, in order for Bolivian Indians to fully achieve the full citizenship rights of Bolivians, there must be a "decolonization" of the internal Indian "colonies" in Bolivia.

Another good example of cultural nationalism is food. Many in Latin America see the food of individual countries as distinctive to that particular nation, and as such, part of that nation's cultural identity. An example is that when McDonald's wanted to come to Bolivia, the Bolivian nation required them to use locally grown potatoes. After all, potatoes were first cultivated in the Andes and the Andean people are quite proud of that fact. Jeffrey

Pilcher in his influential *Que Vivan las Tamales! Food and the Making of Mexican Identity* discusses how maize, or corn, as the main ingredient of both corn tortillas and tamales is key to understanding Mexican identity. Even as the Spanish invaders in the early sixteenth century brought their foods and informed the Indians that eating wheat was civilized and eating corn was not, Mexicans stubbornly clung to their corn-based diet—as a key part of their national identity. Once the middle class in Mexico-embraced traditional, indigenous-style foods (of course modified by European and North American influences) as key to their conception of national identity, food became a key part of that identity.[5] However, it is equally important to note that the globalization of Mexican food had been a significant part of the process of cultural globalization. Pilcher's more recent book *Planet Taco: A Global History of Mexican Food* (2012) makes note of the importance of Mexican food in the process of cultural globalization.

Other examples of cultural nationalism include fashion and theatre. Scholars have examined how some Latin Americans have created a particularly Latin American style of fashion, combining indigenous and non–Latin American forms of dress into a particularly unique Latin American style of dress.[6] Theatre has provided a very important outlet for nationalistic sentiment in Latin America. In addition, a number of theatre productions highlight the cultural significance of the Indian past. However, it is important to note that the attitude of mestizos with regard to the depictions of Indians in film is that they would like to connect themselves with a glorious Indian past but not deal with the problems of racism and prejudice still experienced by Indians in Latin America today.[7] Such examples of "everyday" nationalism help us to understand how nationalism intersects with, and influences, individual identity.

Soccer is of course a national obsession in Latin America. When a country's national team is playing a rival team, it is the one event, like a national election, in which the entire country is focused on the same thing at the same time. Soccer is also a good example of how Latin America has exported its culture overseas. One reason why soccer is so popular in the United States is that the increasing number of US Latinos play the sport and have got others in the United States interested as well. In addition, some of Latin America's finest players play professional soccer in the United States and Europe.

Conclusion: Globalization as cultural onslaught?

Some Latin Americans see a homogenizing culture that comes from globalization as a threat to national/regional/local cultures in Latin America. Some Latin Americans see increased penetration of US culture into the region as a threat. But other Latin Americans make a clear distinction between US government policy (they dislike it) and US culture (which they, like many around the world, find attractive). US culture is attractive to many around the world for a number of reasons, but it's important to point out one key reason. US culture (and the culture of the Western world more generally) is focused on the humanistic development of the individual—even glorification of the individual to the expense of the community, whether local/regional/national. Perhaps, then, US culture is attractive to those in Latin America who want to cultivate a more international, cosmopolitan sense of identity or self. It's important to recognize also that Latin American culture has become popular worldwide, with the sharp increase of consumption of Latin America food around the world as a good example.

In the area of religion, globalization has provided Latin Americans with a different tendency. Even as evangelical Christianity is a relatively recent import to the region, it has become very popular very quickly. This fast spreading evangelicalism might seem surprising to some. For many Latin Americans, Catholicism has been part and parcel of their national experience from the beginning and thus see religious symbols and national symbols as part and parcel of the same process of nation building—Mexico's Virgin of Guadalupe, a national symbol of Mexico, being a commonly cited example.

However, the rise of evangelical preachers in Latin America, some from the United States, and others inspired by US evangelicals, provides a powerful alternative to Catholicism in the region. Guatemala has even had an evangelical president—the controversial Rios Montt (whose early 1980s government perpetrated numerous human rights abuses). Evangelical Protestantism's message includes a strong dose of the ideology of self-help. That is, people are responsible for their own economic well-being and need to lead austere lives so they have capital to invest in small businesses. Max Weber's famous and very influential book *The Protestantism Ethic and the Spirit of Capitalism* does have a kernel of truth to it. As such, interestingly, the rise of evangelical Protestantism dovetails with the neoliberal "revolution." Neoliberalism, of course, calls for individuals to build their human capital and take calculated economic risks so as to maximize their economic benefit from the opportunities offered by a globalizing world free-market system. Some protestant preachers go so far as to assert that doing well economically on earth facilitates entrance into Heaven in the afterlife. And, of course, if parishioners do well, and give their tithe to their Church, the coffers of the Church will be wealthier as well. As such, the connections between cultural nationalism and the momentous economic changes in Latin American between the 1970s and 1990s are important to understand.

At the end of the day, in Latin America, as in other parts of the world, cultural globalization is an important reality for understanding our everyday world. Relatively less powerful nations will have more cultural impact than less powerful ones. But that does not mean that the less powerful nations are prostrate before the powerful nations.

Study Questions

1. What is banal nationalism? What is cultural nationalism? How are they similar? How are they different?
2. Discuss the most important forms of cultural nationalism in Latin America.
3. How does globalization impact Latin American cultural nationalism? Do you see the impacts as temporary or long lasting? Why?

For Further Reading

Joseph, Gil M. and Daniel Nugent, eds. *Everyday Forms of State Formation: Revolution and the Negotiation of Rule in Modern Mexico*. Durham, NC: Duke University Press, 1994.

Kuenzli, E. Gabrielle. *Acting Inca—National Belonging in Early 20th Century Bolivia*. Pittsburgh: University of Pittsburgh Press, 2013.

Pilcher, Jeffrey M. *Planet Taco: A Global History of Mexican Food*. Oxford: Oxford University Press, 2012.

Root, Regina A. *The Latin American Fashion Reader*. New York: Berg, 2005.

CHAPTER SEVENTEEN

Migration and Identity

[The] spectacular success [of the United States] was due in large measure to the unique brand of representative democracy, the spirit of bold enterprise, the respect for individual liberty, and the rugged devotion to hard work that characterized so many of the early American settlers. But there was another aspect to that success ... the details of which most Americans knew nothing about, but which was always carried out in the in their name. It was a vicious and relentless drive for territorial expansion, conquest, and subjugation of others—Native Americans, African slaves, and Latin Americans—one that our leaders justified as Manifest Destiny for us.

JUAN GONZALES[1]

There is a resurgence of anti-migration sentiment driven by fear: fear of a loss of jobs, fear of the post 9/11 security syndrome, and then mostly the fear of a loss of identity.

WILLIAM L. SWING, DIRECTOR GENERAL OF THE INTERNATIONAL ORGANIZATION FOR MIGRATION, QUOTED IN AZAM AHMED AND SANDRA E. GARCIA[2]

Introduction—bats, balls, nationalism, and globalization

The commentary for the Toronto Blue Jays baseball game was announced in Spanish. A sport associated with the United States, which had become very popular in Canada, was announced…in Spanish? It seems that if the Blue Jays were to choose a non-English language to announce the game in, it would have been French, this being Canada. However, given the large number of players from the Dominican Republic on the Blue Jays team and the large Dominican community in Toronto, the decision made sense. Indeed, when a popular Dominican player was at bat, Dominicans in the stands stood up, cheered, sang, danced, and waved Dominican Republic flags. The Dominican community in North America was quite large in part because of a large inflow of Dominicans in the early 1960s due to the political crises in the Caribbean nation in those years.[3] As is typical of migration patterns, once a "critical mass" of migrants is established, a process of chain migration ensues in which the migrants in North America facilitate the arrival of other migrants.

In the previous chapter, on cultural nationalism, soccer was not discussed in great detail, even as it is arguably the most important sport in the region. But, baseball is catching up fast. In some countries in the region, baseball is so popular that it is arguably as popular as soccer. (Interestingly, and importantly, baseball was most popular in countries in which the United States had sent in troops in the nineteenth and early twentieth centuries: Mexico, Nicaragua, Cuba, and the Dominican Republic.) And, because often immigrants seek out events and opportunities to show their national pride and because the game was being played outside of the Dominican Republic, the Dominicans in the stands cheered especially loudly.

In the above context, globalization seems a positive force. The quality of the play of the Blue Jays greatly improved when they started hiring Dominican baseball stars. Both fans and the Dominican players benefitted. The Dominican players, of course, earned vastly higher salaries than they would have if they had not left their island nation. In this setting, globalization seems a win-win.

The significance—and controversy—of globalization

Many people view the effects of globalization as beneficial—increased economic opportunities and access to different cultures from overseas. But many perceive that globalization has negative effects and thus oppose it. These effects include increased economic dependency of their nation on often fickle world markets for their nation's exports. In addition, some fear that globalization will enrich those in their nation who are already wealthy, in that the wealthy are more poised than others to invest in industries that produce items that fetch high prices on world markets. Thus, these opponents of globalization contend that it will increase the already wide gap between the wealthy and the poor. As such, some opponents of globalization conclude that the nation-state, in an era of rapid globalization, is more important than ever for protecting the working class and poor. As commodities and information more easily spill across national borders, the prime responsibility of the nation-state is to exert control over one key "commodity": the labor market. That is, in a rapidly globalizing world, many (particularly those whose identity is closely identified with the nation they live in—they are vehement nationalists) are loathe to open their borders to people from abroad; as such, immigration policy has become of late one of the most important issues for nation-states.

One of the assumed rights of sovereign nations is that they have the right to determine who is a citizen and the terms by which noncitizens can reside in their nations. As migration increases, it advances globalization. But, as migration increases, many people fear that their home culture will be irrevocably changed; that immigrants will threaten their security by bringing in illegal drugs and participating in criminal activity; and that increasing flows of migrants will depress wages. This chapter will focus on US immigration policy, which has had a big impact on recent Latin American history as well as globalization more generally. Oftentimes, when people think about globalization, they focus on flows of information, money, goods, and ideas. But the process of globalization has also sped up the movement of people across national borders.

Many Latin American nations benefit tremendously from the remittances (savings of immigrants sent back home) earned by their nationals living in the United States. Thus, immigration increases the economic strength of many Latin American nations. For its part, the United States has benefitted from the labor and know-how of immigrants from overseas. Further, the immigration of people from Latin America to the United States has greatly changed US culture, particularly so in recent years. Because of the sheer size and economic power of the United States, changes in its immigration policy affect the process of globalization in the Western Hemisphere.

Shared histories of people arriving from distant shores

Before delving into Latin American migration to the United States and US immigration policy, it is important to note that Latin America, like the United States, is a region largely populated by migrants from overseas.

Even as the indigenous population of Latin America started out before 1492 as much larger than its counterpart in North America, European migrants to Latin America have had a tremendous impact on Latin American culture, larger than the impact that indigenous people have (with a few exceptions). The main destinations for overseas migrants included Argentina, Brazil, Cuba, Uruguay, and Chile, ranging from about four million migrants in Argentina to 300,000 in neighboring Uruguay.[4] The major "push" of immigrants occurred in Latin America simultaneously with the United States, for both similar and different reasons. Similarly, in both regions, there was a desire for inexpensive labor. The differences in desire for immigrants, however, are more significant. In the United States, a relatively open immigration policy in the late nineteenth and early twentieth centuries was in the interest of large, industrial corporations that wanted inexpensive labor, and thus immigration fueled industrialization. In Latin America, however, immigration was promoted out of a positivist desire to import more European culture to Latin America. In some parts of Latin America, European migrants were seen, in a racist way, as important because (it was thought) the migrants would bring in European culture to the parts of Latin America in which there were many African slaves.

During times of economic hardship in the United States, anti-immigrant sentiment (which has existed since the early nineteenth century) flares up. Clearly, the impetus behind immigration policy comes from both domestic, internal political forces, and international ones. Indeed, migration is an important component of the process of globalization. As such, immigration policy, in the United States and elsewhere, is a classic "intermestic" issue— both international and domestic at the same time.

Although the desire of the citizen of one nation to enter another has, of course, existed since the beginning of the nation-state system, it is a truism that with more easily available and less expense international travel options, migration has dramatically increased since the Second World War. As the crossing of international borders has increased, the cultures of many nations have become more multicultural. Not surprisingly, with the rise of this type of multiculturalism has come an anti-immigrant backlash in many countries.

Both nations and migrants focus on two key motives in their desire to move (in the case of migrants) and their desire to control/resist immigration (in the case of countries where migrants want to enter). These motives are security and economics. If immigrants feel their personal security is threatened or want better economic opportunities, they of course want to move. On the part of nations, if they feel threatened by a potential influx of foreigners, it is often because they fear these foreigners will not assimilate into the "national culture" of their new nation. With regard to how nations view an influx of immigrants in economic terms, it is contradictory. For their part, employers in the host nation often want to hire immigrants because they are willing to work for less money than native-born workers or are willing to do work considered drudgery—and work that most native-born workers refuse to do. However, these same employers don't want immigrant workers to maintain their culture from the "old country," which is often perceived by members of the nation that the immigrants migrated to as inferior. For example, in some country clubs, Spanish-speaking immigrants are hired to work in the kitchen, but are forbidden to speak Spanish within earshot of the patrons. Wage earners in the nations where immigrants are migrating to not surprisingly fear that a large influx of immigrants will drive down wages.

US immigration policy and the Cold War

The United States opened up its immigration policy in the mid-1960s, with the Immigration and Nationality Act of 1965, which reformed US immigration law. The United States would now become more open to immigrants. The authors of this act wanted to make it clear that the United States had fully rejected the system of restrictive quotas placed on immigration by the National Origins Act of 1924—a system that privileged Northern Europeans and was disadvantageous to those who were not of European background. The Act reflected the racism of the time.

A key motive of US immigration reform was to "score points" against its communist adversaries in the Cold War—which was of course not only a diplomatic standoff and military confrontation but also an ideological battle (a "battle for ideas"). This battle for ideas was multifaceted in that the noncommunist and communist worlds clashed in the areas of political system (representative government vs. authoritarian) and economic system (free-market capitalism vs. state-controlled economy). From the point of view of the noncommunist world, the communist world was symbolically a prison camp, and communism enslaved its people. What better way to emphasize and disseminate this characterization than by opening up US immigration policy and then making it clear to the world that migrants wanted to come to the United States? People did not, as US officials stated, want to move to the communist nations. What was even worse, some communist nations prevented some of its citizens from emigrating. What clearer evidence was needed, the United States concluded, that the noncommunist world's political and economic systems were far superior to those of the communist world?

Interestingly, the Immigration Act of 1965, even as it opened up US immigration policy in general, put the first quotas on immigration from Latin America in US history. The restrictive National Origin Act did not place any limit on Latin American immigration, largely because large farmowners in the United States relied on migrant (mainly Mexican) labor, and these powerful farmowners wanted their work force to be able to migrate relatively freely across the border between the United States and Mexico.

Two points are important here. First, before 1965, although there were no overall quotas on Latin American immigration, there were time periods in which in effect immigration from Latin America was severely curtailed. At times, US officials would declare immigrants from Mexico as a public health problem and subject them to fumigation. This inhuman treatment caused immigration to be severely diminished.

Second, the quotas introduced in 1965 gave US policy makers a key lever for curtailing Latin American immigration. When the US public wanted to restrict immigration, usually during times of economic hardship for the poor and working classes in the United States, the quotas were lowered. Another aspect of the immigration system was asylum. Asylum could be granted to migrants who made the case that they were suffering political persecution. During the Cold War, asylum grantees went of course to Cuba (in which all migrants were accepted) and to Sandinista Nicaragua (1979–1990) which, although its polity could best be described as mixed socialism, was viewed by the Reagan (1981–1989) and George H.W. Bush (1989–1993) administrations as communist. Migrants from anticommunist, repressive right-wing regimes, which were friendly toward the United States, were not granted asylum.

Immigration and the inter-American system

Going back to the early Cold War, interestingly and importantly, US immigration policy toward Latin America ran parallel to its interests with regard to inter-American relations more generally. Both with immigration and other aspects of US-Latin American relations, ideology, security, and economics dictated US policy. Ideologically, as noted above, the United States aimed to use its immigration policy to bulwark its mission of promoting stable democracies in the Americas. It aimed to portray itself as a more open society when compared to the Soviet Union and People's Republic of China. Further, US officials perceived that US immigration policy was a "safety valve." That is, if Washington eased restrictions on immigration from a particular country during a particularly difficult and divisive time in that nation's history, it would foster political stability and (hopefully) eventually democracy in that country. And, of course, the United States was particularly clear that it did not want another Castro-type regime in Latin America, in particular in the Caribbean.[5]

Second, the United States aimed to use its immigration policy to punish communist nations as well as support noncommunist nations. For example, to embarrass the communist regime of Fidel Castro in Cuba, it allowed any

Cuban that wanted to come to live in the United States to do so. As flows of Cubans arrived in the United States, US officials could proclaim they were leaving a "prison camp" society for freedom. However, even though many of the Guatemalan dictatorships were very repressive, US leaders did not want to open US doors to Guatemalans fleeing their repressive government because those governments were US-backed. And finally, an open immigration policy went hand in hand with an open policy toward accessing a Latin American nation's market.[6]

The situation was similar in the post–Cold War era. Neoliberalism and globalization in the 1990s had a big influence on the increase in the flow of Latin American migrants, legal and otherwise, to the United States. The logic is straightforward. With neoliberal globalization in Latin America, the disparity of wealth between the wealthiest and the nonelites, already the most unequal society in the world, grew ever larger. As such, many on the bottom rungs of Latin American society, facing economic deprivation and ghastly living conditions in the large swaths of slums that mushroom out from most of Latin America's major cities, see their only hope as moving to the United States.[7]

Transnationalism—and controversy

As flows of migrants have increased, the United States has become a more transnational country. Two divergent phenomena have occurred within the United States. First, as the flows of Latin Americans into the United States have swollen, Latin American culture has become popular in the United States, even outside of the "traditional" areas where Latin Americans had lived in the United States in the past, such as Florida and the Southwest. One interesting statistic is that recently sales of salsa outpaced sales of catsup in the United States for the first time. The second tendency is that anti-immigrant sentiment in the United States has sharply increased since the 1990s. A good example was Proposition 187 in California that voters approved at the ballot box in 1994, which stripped some legal immigrants of some of their benefits. (A few years after it passed, the US Supreme Court struck down significant parts of the law.)

Of course, one reason why immigration from Latin America has proven controversial is that there is a fear in the United States that immigrants will drive down wages or displace workers. A second major fear is that many immigrants from Latin America come into the United States illegally. Some observers have even concluded that with regard to Latin American immigration to the United States, the number of illegal immigrants is as large as the number of legal immigrants.[8] In recent years, millions of US government dollars have flowed into the Border Patrol, and there is discussion of "militarizing" the Patrol so it has the option of using deadly force against illegal immigrants. Fearing a lack of control over their borders and a threat to their identity, a segment of the conservative Republican Party in the United States calls for lower immigration quotas from Latin America as well as broader anti-immigrant policies.

Conclusion: International meets national in the Western Hemisphere

Importantly, the study of US immigration policy and how it changes over time tells us a great deal about how in the future the boundaries and barriers between "domestic" and "international" issues will begin to dissolve. In Latin America, there has been a fear that international economic activity will cause its economy to be controlled by outsiders—hence, the intense interest in economic nationalism (as discussed in Chapter Seven). Also, as scholar Juan Gonzáles has argued, US and European economic policy toward Latin America has had a big impact on Latin American history and identity. Since the late nineteenth century, as discussed in Chapter Five, Latin American economic policy has largely focused on export-oriented agriculture and production to the industrialized world. This policy was fostered by US and European capital investment. But, when the market for exports collapsed, many in Latin America were left without work, so they immigrated to the United States. Learning English and picking up the ways of the North Americans, the identity of these migrants became over time more cosmopolitan. Gonzáles argues that US economic expansion flowed directly from US Manifest Destiny (discussed in Chapter Three). Further, he argues there is a direct connection between US foreign policy and Latin American immigration. In turn, the process of migration changes the nature of the country where the immigrants reside (in Latin America, mainly the United States) and causes the identity of the migrants to become divided between North and South America and thus more complex.

If there is little contact/connection between nations, it is fairly straightforward for nations to divide policy issues into domestic and international columns. Welfare policy would be domestic; foreign trade would be international. But immigration policy is "intermestic"—it simultaneously impacts both traditionally domestic and international policies. As globalization advances, more and more issues will be "intermestic," defying the traditional boundaries between domestic and international.

Study Questions

1. How has the migration of people from Latin America affected people in other parts of the world?
2. Discuss the connections you see between immigration and neoliberalism, if any.
3. Discuss the importance of migration of Latin Americans to other nations for Latin America.
4. How would you define "intermestic"? What is its significance for Latin American identity?

For Further Reading

Gonzáles, Juan. *Harvest of Empire—A History of Latinos in America*, 2nd ed. New York: Penguin Press, 2011.

Holloway, Thomas H. *Immigrants on the Land—Coffee and Society in Sao Paulo, 1886–1934*. Chapel Hill: The University of North Carolina Press, 2012.

Mitchell, Christopher, ed. *Western Hemisphere Immigration and United States Foreign Policy*. University Park: Pennsylvania State University Press, 1992.

CHAPTER EIGHTEEN

Globalization, Nationalism, and Inter-American Relations

[The United States] appears destined by Providence to plague America with miseries in the name of Freedom.

SIMÓN BOLÍVAR AS QUOTED IN BUSHNELL AND LANGLEY[1]

Introduction

The idea of Latin America as a distinct cultural entity began to become more prominent as the United States increased its economic and military power, in particular in the late nineteenth century. Obviously, Spain and Portugal had exerted and exert tremendous cultural impact on the region, in particular through language, institutions, and religion. But, as we move into the twentieth century, the economic, political, and cultural impact of the United States has been and continues to be tremendous. How Latin Americans responded to the 900 lb. US gorilla has of course changed over time. But, in general, as soon as the United States exerted significant economic influence over the region starting in the twentieth century, Latin Americans' attitudes were divided. Although many Latin Americans admired US culture and the US people, they disliked US military and political interference in their nations. In the end, to understand how globalization affected Latin America, one must examine how globalization has historically interacted with inter-American relations. Once we understand this relationship, it will be easier to assess the impact of globalization on inter-American relations and Latin American nationalism today.[2] Significantly, in order to understand the US globalization "project" in the world of the twenty-first century and thus to understand globalization today, one must dip back into the history of US policy toward Latin America in the early nineteenth century. US leaders had a "reform project" for Latin America—to make it more like the United States. As such, Latin America was in a sense a "laboratory" for the US globalization efforts of the twentieth century.[3]

The initial foray of the United States in Latin American affairs came with the famous Monroe Doctrine of 1823. Although many surveys of US history incorrectly state that the United States stated in the Monroe Doctrine that the United States aimed to force the Europeans out of the Western Hemisphere, Monroe's famous statement was more modest. It was in essence the first containment policy of the United States. Monroe stated that the United States would not tolerate the expansion of already existing European colonies, and more broadly influence, in the region. The United States feared that the powerful European countries would use their colonies as springboards to extend and deepen their influence in the region to the detriment of Latin America and the United States. The young United States did not have the military power to back up the Doctrine, but the Doctrine proved to be an important precursor.

Expanding US power in the hemisphere: Crucible of globalization

Although the United States has been an expansionary nation in physical, cultural, economic, and political terms since its beginning in 1776, the expansion leapt beyond the confines of North America starting in 1898 with the Spanish-American War. About the same time, the United States began to exert influence in the circum-Caribbean region in a more systematic way and in South America for the first time. In South America, when it appeared that a coup would oust the young Brazilian Republic in 1893, the United States sent warships to the harbor in Rio to support the Republic. Fearing an expansion of British power in the region in the period 1894–1895, the United States intervened in a border dispute between British Guyana and Venezuela. The United States told Great Britain, in no uncertain terms, that the United States wanted the British to submit the boundary dispute to a (US controlled) arbitration board. The border dispute was resolved in favor of the Venezuelans. In a paternalistic fashion, the United States did not consult with the Venezuelans during the entirety of the dispute; the United States assumed a paternalistic hegemony over Latin America.

The intensifying interest of the United States in Latin American affairs was due in large part to the simultaneously rapidly industrializing yet depression-wracked US economy. As the increasingly efficient US factories churned out more and more goods, and the middle class did not have the purchasing power to buy them (working-class people did not have significant disposable income in that time to be much of a market), a consensus emerged in the US military, government, and larger businesses that the US government needed to exert significant effort to facilitate the sale of US products overseas. Indeed, the famous "Open Door" policy of the United States toward China, which looked like it was devolving into chaos in the late nineteenth century and would be partitioned by the European powers and Japan, was based on similar logic.

Summarized as "a fair field and no favor," the Open Door policy ultimately aimed to make all of China available to outside, private sector foreign investment and trade. US officials thought that if foreigners bought US goods, it would benefit not only US capitalists but also the foreign purchasers. When foreigners purchased US goods, they would also psychologically imbibe US notions of progress, which would redound to their benefit in the future. Although US exports in the 1890s were small, they were growing quickly. US leaders had high hopes that in the future US exports would prove to significantly contribute to overall US economic growth. Therefore, US leaders' interest in economic expansion in the late nineteenth century was understandably intense.

The notion that the United States had a duty (along the lines of famous British writer Rudyard Kipling, who advocated the "white man's burden") to uplift the nonwhite peoples of the world was an important impulse behind US-Latin American relations in the late nineteenth and early twentieth centuries. Although the ideal of exporting US-style progress (economic, social, and political) to Latin America went back to the founding of the United States, the intensity of the urge to remake the world in the image of the United States increased dramatically in the early twentieth century. The US Progressive movement is key here.

There were three main Progressive era presidents, such as T. Roosevelt, Taft, and Wilson, whose terms spanned from 1901 to 1921. Although Roosevelt and Wilson were more intent on exporting the US system to Latin America than Taft, all three exemplified the ideal that the United States had to in effect take over from the British (whose imperial power was fading) the important goal of exporting Western-style notions of progress around the world. Of course, the United States had the most ability to export such notions to Latin America because of the proximity of Latin America and the asymmetrical power relationship between the United States and its southern "neighbors." Before we delve into this formative period of the creation of what came to be known as the "inter-American system," it is important to investigate the roots of US interest in reforming Latin America in its own image.

Pan-Americanism: Seed of globalization in Latin America?

One of the roots of globalization in Latin America is the Pan-American movement. The lofty ideals of Pan-Americanism stretch back to the era of the Monroe Doctrine, in which the peoples of the Americas viewed themselves as superior to Europe when it came to conflict resolution. Whereas Europeans solved problems by resorting to violence and war, the peoples of the Americas avoided conflict to an extent through meetings of North and Latin American officials. The first such meeting was the Congress of Panama in 1826. Pan-Americanism, however, became an enduring feature of inter-American relations in the late nineteenth century due to the efforts of James G. Blaine and the formation of the Pan-American union, which culminated in the building of an ornate home for the Union in Washington, DC (paid for by US industrialist Andrew Carnegie).

James G. Blaine, known informally as the "Plumed Knight" from Maine, was Secretary of State in 1881 and 1889–1892. His Pan-American vision, shared by some in Latin America, was for there to be in a sense a "common American home" for the peoples of the Americas. As such, agreements would be hashed out, including a customs union, which would facilitate economic intercourse between North and South America. Impressively, Blaine organized a meeting in the United States of some of the foreign ministers of Latin America. Although his vision for inter-American unity remained notional until the twentieth century, Blaine set forth the parameters of Pan-Americanism.

To the extent that the United States in the late nineteenth century had a policy toward the industrializing world, it was encapsulated in the "Open Door" policy, originally promulgated with regard to China in 1899–1900, as noted above. However, considering that "great powers" often secure a "sphere of interest" in the smaller, less powerful nations on their border or near them, it is not surprising that the United States carved out the circum-Caribbean region of Latin America (the "Greater Caribbean," including the eastern coast of Central America and the northern tier of South America) as an exception to the Open Door. The United States worked to exclude extra-hemispheric powers from exerting influence in this "strategic area" for the United States. Once the United States quietly worked to sever Panama, a province of Colombia, from that nation in 1903, and then build the Panama Canal, the United States had a tangible reason for its general goal of keeping powerful, non-Western Hemisphere nations out of the circum-Caribbean.

A bridge from the nineteenth-century era, when the United States was not overly concerned with Latin America, to the early twentieth century period, when it became very important for the United States in its overall foreign policy, was Elihu Root. Root was one of the more influential foreign policy makers in twentieth-century US foreign policy. One of the more impressive legal minds of his era, he served as secretary of war from 1899 to 1904 and Secretary of State from 1905 to 1909. He relished the opportunity to help the United States exert itself on the world stage. Although Root showed less interest in Latin America than did Blaine, Root did see Latin America as important. Sharing the prejudices of many in the United States at the time, Root viewed Latin America in a paternalistic way that supported US interests. In an influential 1907 talk, Root stated that the Latin American and North American nations complimented each other perfectly. The North Americans were thrifty whites; the brown and black-skinned Latin Americans were spendthrifts. As such, the North Americans needed both outlets for private sector capital investment and markets for the goods churned out by their amazingly productive factories. Lacking the capital, knowledge, and overall ability to produce industrialized (finished) goods, the Latin peoples would necessarily purchase them from the United States.[4]

Understanding the new US interventionism of the early twentieth century

Before the Spanish-American War, with few exceptions, the United States avoided direct military intervention in Latin America. The main reason was that the United States lacked the military might to back up its will in the region. Good evidence of this lack of military muscle is that when a dispute between the United States and Chile in 1891 seemed poised to erupt into violent conflict, some observers concluded that the Chilean military might best the US military. Although the US military grew rapidly in size and power in the 1890s, US leaders were wary of using it unless absolutely necessary—and it appeared the United States would win.

As such, US leaders used economic ties (mainly private sector US investment) to purse its goals of a pro-US, politically stable, and potentially reformable (in the US image) Latin America. US investment in Latin America before 1898 was uneven. The one country (actually a colony of Spain at the time) that did have significant US investment was Cuba, the recipient of a large flow of US investment in sugar plantations. When a civil war broke out in Cuba between pro-independence forces and those loyal to Spain, it appeared that US investment would be consumed in the maelstrom. To avoid this fate and to protect the lives of US citizens in Cuba, the McKinley Administration declared war on Spain. McKinley's vision, however, was broader than Cuba. He aimed to ensure that the US Navy had good ports in the Pacific as well and ordered the US Navy to defeat the Spanish in the Philippines, turning the Philippines (and their stellar ports, right off the coast of China) into a US colony.

The cost was high for the United States in the Philippines compared to Cuba. In the Philippines, the US military experienced many casualties. Nationalistic Filipinos, incensed at becoming a US colony, fought back, precipitating the first US guerrilla war in what would become the Third World. In terms of the sacrifice of principles, Filipinos would not be US citizens but instead be in effect subjects and not enjoy the civil rights enshrined in the Bill of Rights which supposedly applied to all Americans.

Anti-American nationalism and US reformism

Significantly, US leaders never "threw in their lot" with the pro-independence forces in Cuba to the extent that US leaders wanted an independent Cuba. Instead, US forces fought parallel to the independence fighters, and US leaders maintained their traditional US freedom of action—probably the most hallowed principle of US foreign policy.[5] When the Spanish and their Cuban loyalists were defeated, the United States, instead of offering official diplomatic recognition to the pro-independence forces, placed a protectorate over Cuba. The majority of Cubans disagreed with this policy, but assented to it, recognizing that they had no choice in the matter given overweening US power on the island. US leaders, in placing a protectorate over Cuba, controlled its foreign policy and asserted the right to intervene in Cuba's internal affairs if it deemed necessary. US military troops occupied the island on a number of occasions in the early twentieth century. In the early years of the US protectorate, US officials attempted to modernize the infrastructure of the island, seen as necessary not only for helping the Cuban people but also in creating a propitious environment for US private sector investment, redounding to the benefit of both US capitalists and some wealthier Cubans as well.

It is important to note that the US reformist impulse was formulated by, articulated by, and implemented by upper-class American males, who saw such efforts as reflective of males of their social stature. Many upper-class Americans were imbued with a sense of "noblesse oblige," that is, that their exalted social standing required them to help out those less fortunate, especially the poor in the United States and nonwhites overseas. "Noblesse oblige" of course dovetailed with the "white man's burden." Further, some US males, fearing that urban, rapidly industrializing US society was "softening" upper-class urban males in particular, vowed to reverse this trend. Theodore Roosevelt is a good example of a US leader with a strong sense of "noblesse oblige" who forcefully argued that US males needed to exert themselves in reformist efforts, in particular in poorer nations overseas, to prevent themselves from becoming flabby of body and mind.[6]

Presidents Woodrow Wilson and Franklin D. Roosevelt emphasized Pan-Americanism more than any other US presidents up through 1945. US leaders of course defined Pan-Americanism and set up the inter-American system to benefit the United States. As outlined by Root in his remarkable 1906 speech, it was a racist-paternalist system. This racist-paternalist system was set up, of course, to benefit North Americans. Importantly, this racist-paternalist system called for reform of Latin American economic, social, and political institutions—in effect, attempting to reform Latin America in the image of the United States. Not only did US leaders see this US-style reform as benefiting the Latin Americans, but also they saw it as imperative in the goal of building up the middle class in Latin America. In the minds of US officials, a larger middle class necessarily lead to pro-US stability in the long run.

One of the more interesting historical convergences in the history of inter-American relations occurred in the early twentieth century. It featured the growth of US direct investment in the circum-Caribbean region (including the eastern part of Mexico, Central America, and the "northern tier" countries in South America), increased US military intervention in parts of this region, and the rise of Pan-Americanism. These three trends are connected. US investment in Central America, especially propelled by "el pulpo" (the octopus), the Boston-based United Fruit Company, created an enclave economy which only benefitted a small slice of Central America's society. Yet, US leaders saw US private foreign investment as key to promoting economic, social, and ultimately political reform in the region. Meanwhile, US sugar companies increased their stake in the Caribbean, and US oil companies drilled for oil in Venezuela and Mexico.

Globalization was rapidly occurring in early twentieth-century Caribbean as European powers clung to their colonies and wanted to maintain their influence as a rising United States wanted to be the hegemonic power to "call the shots." Fearing that instability in the circum-Caribbean region would draw in European troops and crowd out US influence in an area considered vital to US security, the United States sent in its own troops to maintain a pro-US order in the region. Theodore Roosevelt legitimized this exertion of force stating that it was the responsibility of the United States to maintain order in the region. Behind his assertion of the United States as the self-appointed policeman of the Caribbean lay a racist paternalism. The nonwhite peoples of the region needed to be taught how to run a country at the point of a gun if necessary. It was the duty of the United States, as the most powerful nation in the Western Hemisphere, to ensure these reforms took place in a timely and efficient manner—backed up by the threat or exertion of US force. Significantly, US military incursions occurred where there was quite a bit of US investment (along with US personnel) that the US government saw as its duty to protect.

Finally, US military intervention squared with Pan-Americanism in that in the long-run US military efforts would help to promote the reform of Latin American society. Indeed, US leaders saw the interventions as in a sense "necessary evils"—a crisis situation demanded a forceful, short-term response. In theory, once the Latin American nations reformed themselves, US troops would not be necessary. In the long run, if Latin American nations accepted US values, the ideals of Pan-Americanism (in particular inter-American unity) would prevail.

Depression, "hot" war, and the Cold War

By the middle twentieth century, US leaders would at least rhetorically describe the system in less racist terms and assert that in the Organization of American States (1948) all nations were equal. It was in US interests to make the system seems more egalitarian because US leaders wanted Latin American "buy-in" in the US global fight against communism. Not surprisingly, Latin Americans began to realize that their participation in the system as described by Root necessarily meant that the United States would benefit from it more than they. As such, by the 1950s, some Latin Americans formulated the dependency critique of the system in the 1950s and 1960s, expressed most articulately by the US Economic Commission for Latin America (ECLA) under the leadership of Argentine economist Raul Prebisch.

ECLA realized that because the terms of trade of the Latin American nations were declining relative to those of the United States, it would be impossible for them to ever accumulate significant foreign exchange to industrialize/diversify their economies. US leaders had little time for ECLA criticisms, which were similar to the dependency theorists' criticisms of modernization theory (discussed at the end of Chapter Nine).

With the rise of Castro's Cuba in 1959, multiple forms of political globalization competed for the hearts and minds of the developing, or nonindustrialized, (Third) world. Soviet-style communism was one answer for the nonelite members of the Third World—a top-down style of development. Agrarian revolution in the countryside, along the lines of Communist China and Cuba, offered another set of answers to those nations in the nonindustrialized world that yearned for development. The United States, with its Alliance for Progress, announced in 1961 as a response to Castro, offered a free-market, representative government model (even as anticommunist US leaders would aid authoritarian regimes in Latin America if they were firmly anticommunist). As the Cold War wound down, the US administrations of Jimmy Carter and Ronald Reagan in different ways worked to promote democracy in Latin America. Tired of authoritarian rule with militaries that were themselves tired of ruling, democracy became more prevalent. However, with the rise of neoliberalism (discussed in Chapters Twelve and Fourteen) inequality became more of a concern, in some cases leading to a new rise of populism. The governments of Rafael Correa in Ecuador, Evo Morales in Bolivia, and Hugo Chávez and his successor Nicolás Maduro in Venezuela are examples. These populist leaders proved to be more anti–United States than other Latin American leaders and also more economic nationalist than Latin American leaders had been since the 1940s and 1950s.

Conclusion

With the waning power of the United States, at least in economic terms, after the 2008 financial crash, globalization in Latin America seemed to be driven by more non-US actors than ever before. Many Latin American nations reached out to China for investment and markets; China, to feed its growing population, aimed to make trade agreements with Latin America. Latin American nations that aimed to show the world they were not living in the shadow of US hegemony, such as Venezuela's Chávez, reached out to Iran.

Although many observers have viewed US-Latin American relations as apart from the rest of the world, globalization has always been an important factor both in US-Latin American relations and in Latin America. As this brief overview of Latin American nationalism in the context of globalization draws to a close, it is important to focus on an important theme in this narrative—that of identity. The big question for Latin America is whether the traditional sense of nationalism, based in the nation-state that stretches back to the nineteenth-century Wars for Independence, will significantly impact Latin American individuals' identity over the long run.

Certainly the strength of the Indian movements in the Andes and Guatemala will continue apace, but it is an open question how much influence they will have over their respective polities. Certainly, also, Latin American leaders of different political stripes will use the memory of Bolívar in particular, and Latin American nationalism more generally to build up a sense of nationalist pride and thus unity. However, the pitfalls of attempting to build a Latin American regional nationalism (meta-nationalism) from the building blocks of nation-state nationalism are profound. Hugo Chávez tried to promote his "Bolivarian Republic" idea, basically a return to the Gran Colombia idea of the early nineteenth century of unifying the "northern tier," the northern nations of South America. Of course, Chávez envisioned this regional organization be directed/led by his Venezuela. His demand for leadership of the Bolivarian Republic caused disputes over leadership to pop up, inhibiting the formation of this regional pact. It is not surprising that Chávez would invoke the Liberator, Simón Bolívar, because few in Latin America criticize the hallowed Bolívar. But attempting to use the past to address the problems of the present has its pitfalls. Although farcical, the 2002 movie *Bolivar soy yo* (I am Bolívar) clearly displays the problems when one tries to move from an apolitical form of Bolívar admiration to invoking his political wishes to correct the wrongs of the present as part of a political agenda. In the movie, an actor who plays Bolívar assumes the Liberator's persona, and attempts, through force, to get the leaders of Latin America to focus on the region's ills—to no avail.

In the end, it is clear that growing and deepening globalization will facilitate a feeling of loss of control on the part of many Latin Americans. Nationalism (in all its complex, multifaceted senses) has and will become a potent force repelling such intrusions. As such, national identity will be a key aspect of the identity of the vast majority of Latin Americans. Based on current trends, nationalism will continue to be a prominent feature of Latin Americans' identity. It deserves future, more in-depth research than this book can provide.

Study Questions

1. What are the most important points of conflict between the United States and Latin America?
2. What are US interests in Latin America? How can one determine if the United States will pursue its interests in a nonmilitary fashion in one instance but use military force in other instances?
3. How has US power facilitated globalization in the Western Hemisphere? How has US power helped to shape the type of globalization that has occurred in the Western Hemisphere?

For Further Reading

Joseph, Gilbert M., Catherine LeGrand, and Ricardo Salvatore, eds. *Close Encounters of Empire: Writing the Cultural History of U.S.-Latin American Relations*. Durham, NC: Duke University Press, 1998.

Loveman, Brian. *No Higher Law: American Foreign Policy and the Western Hemisphere since 1776*. Chapel Hill: University of North Carolina Press, 2010.

O'Brien, Thomas F. *Making the Americas: The United States and Latin America from the Age of Revolutions to the Era of Globalization*. Albuquerque: University of New Mexico Press, 2007.

Rosenberg, Emily. *Spreading the American Dream: American Economic and Cultural Expansion, 1890–1945*. New York: Hill and Wang, 1982.

CHAPTER NINETEEN

Conclusion

Globalization is not so much an issue for debate as it is a force of nature. The people of the world are clearly intent on knitting themselves together. The issue is not globalization; rather, it is the rules the govern it, as well as who makes those rules and who benefits from them.

JIM SHULTZ AND MELISSA DRAPER[1]

Introduction: The elusive turning points of globalization

Although it is easy to fall into the assumption that as globalization advances, nationalism automatically erodes in lockstep fashion, the historical record does not bare this assumption out. Often, as discussed previously, as globalization strengthens and deepens, nationalists fear that they will lose their national identity and thus strengthen their nationalism as a "shield" against increasingly powerful outside actors.

Establishing the turning points in the process of globalization can be tricky. However, clearly the early 1970s were an important turning point. Not only was there the decline and fall of the Bretton Woods system, the early 1970s also saw the rise in importance of instant electronic and communication networks and the rise of the world environmental movement. What is fascinating is that these two phenomena reinforced each other. As people became interlinked through communications, they began to have a deeper understanding of the interconnectedness of global life.[2] Indeed, since of course the natural environment does not know national boundaries, environmental crises, to be effectively dealt with, require an international (not solely national) response. Should nations shun an international response to environmental issues, conflict will most certainly ensue. One example is the issue of Mexico's access to water from rivers that flow into it from the United States. With the US population using increased water, less and less is available to Mexico, which of course has made Mexicans unhappy.

Illicit trade, globalization, and Latin American nationalism

One of the downsides of increased global interconnectedness is that increasingly people have access to illegal substances from far-flung parts of the world. Trade in illicit items has been, and is, of course an important driver of globalization. Since the opium wars in China in the nineteenth century, and probably before, societies have tried to prevent illegal drugs from flowing into their countries. Once addiction occurs and illegal drug networks coalesce to maximize profits from the enterprise, stopping the flow of illegal substances proves extremely difficult. Seemingly, the only thing that reduces the flow of illegal substances is the changes of users' tastes/preferences for drugs.

However, politicians in general, and in the United States in particular, cannot wait for preferences to change. Their societies demand immediate action to end the drug trade and end drug addiction. Such efforts become imperative of course once US officials define ending the drug trade as a "national security" issue. It is understandable how most, or at least many, would view addiction in this light, as addicted members of society cannot be contributing members of society and need treatment in order to function or even survive. Once "national security" is the lens through which drug suppression/interdiction efforts are viewed, it's but a small step to declaring a "war on drugs." And once war is declared, the consequences of losing such a war are substantial.

Two different categories of solutions exist for ending the trade in illegal narcotics. First, there are demand-side solutions. If a society, through education/treatment, minimizes addiction, the theory goes that those who supply the illegal product will stop producing it. Of course, demand-side solutions, even though more long lasting, are also expensive for the country with the drug problem and take a long time to succeed. A second category of solutions lie on the supply side: using coercion, the country with the addiction problem tries to suppress production/supply of the illegal drug. These solutions are politically expedient for the producing country. First, once money is allocated, then concrete data can quickly be collected on the reduction of the number of hectares of coca produced and amount of cocaine interdicted. With such concrete data, it is easy to show that a "solution" is "working," and thus get politicians to allocate more funds for the war on drugs. Second, and most importantly, the costs of the supply-side tactics are borne by people outside of the "user" country. Moreover, the vast majority of those producing and distributing the drugs are nonwhite, poor, and live a long way from the user country. Of course, they have virtually no political constituency in the user country.

But supply-side solutions are doomed to fail, since once users are "hooked," there is a lot of money to be made producing illegal drugs. Even if the user country manages to suppress the trade in drugs in one country, because of economic incentives, other countries will pick up the slack. (This is known as the "balloon theory"—if you squeeze a long, thin balloon on one side, the other side will expand.) As such, although multiple analyses over the years have shown that the resources spent by the user country to suppress drug production and international distribution, user countries continue to implement ultimately futile supply-side tactics.

Latin America provides an excellent example of the long-term failure of supply-side attempts to reduce the flow of illegal narcotics. Most importantly for the argument of this book, in the case of Latin America, the illegal drug trade has simultaneously brought Latin America more directly into a rapidly globalizing world in the twentieth century while both strengthening some of the nations' economies and weakening a sense of nationalism.

The first main recipient of illegal narcotics from Latin America was of course the United States. In the early twentieth century, US government officials, in particular the US Federal Bureau of Investigation (FBI), aimed to stem the flow of marijuana from Mexico to the United States as well as alcohol from the Caribbean. (In the United States, production and consumption of alcohol was prohibited from 1919 to 1933.) Starting in the 1970s, US concerns about cocaine trumped those of marijuana as the popularity of the drug increased dramatically in the 1980s and began becoming popular in Europe (as well as parts of Latin America) as well.

The cocaine trade, focused in the Andes where the coca leaf, the main raw material for the substance, is prolific in some areas, strengthened some economies, in particular in the 1980s, a crucial time in Latin America's recent economic history. As discussed in a previous chapter, the 1980s was a "lost decade" for many Latin American nations as many groaned under unsustainable debt burdens, and primary products exporters saw their foreign exchange earnings dry up as prices for their key exports dropped. Yet the drug trade flourished, not only providing crucially important income for many in the region, including the poor, but the prosperous economies helped to bulwark a sense of nationalism. In addition, some Latin Americans in the nations that produced the illegal drugs but did not (in general) consume them saw their nation as superior in a sense to that of the consuming, user nations. The idea was that "we here in the Andes may be poor, but at least we're not a bunch of drug addicts like in the United States." But the drug trade as well meant that powerful leaders of the drug cartels ("drug kingpins") used their vast resources to buy influence with powerful political leaders. This eroding away of the faith of the populace in the Andean nations in their governments of course diminishes national pride and thus nationalism.

Even as there was cynicism in the drug-producing countries with regard to the corruption-induced problems with their political systems, the drug-producing nations still exhibited a strong sense of nationalism. For example, anger boiled over with the infringement of national sovereignty demanded by the United States in its efforts (ultimately futile I would argue) to squelch production of coca leaves and cocaine in its supply-side-driven antidrug policies. The people of the Andean nations where coca leaves are produced and cocaine is processed and shipped to users in other countries dislike how the United States has militarized the drug war. US advisers train the police and military to more efficiently suppress the production of coca leaves and cocaine, leading to social conflict.

The US government has used the fact that Bolivians would like to have access to the big US market to coerce Bolivia to "toe the line" with regard to supporting the "war on drugs." The US government has given Bolivia trade preferences to allow it to export textiles to the big US market with lower tariffs compared to other exporters. But, in exchange, Bolivia has to maintain its vigilance on the drug war—which includes a major infringement on its sovereignty. The Bolivian justice system has set up special tribunals for offenders of the antidrug laws which prescribe harsh penalties. In sum, the powerful actors in the world economy have attempted to control the trade in "controlled substances" (often viewed as "illicit") to prevent those substances from entering the nations of the developed world.

Toward a new nationalism: The economic crisis spawned by neoliberalism, and Latin America's nationalistic response

In Chapters Thirteen and Fifteen, the reasons behind the growing power of neoliberalism and the concomitant declining power of the state were discussed. But, as the state declined, many Latin Americans feared that a neoliberal policy would lead to a systematic draining of resources from the continent. Their fears were warranted. According to the Comisión Económica de America Latina (CEPAL, or Economic Commission of Latin America), Latin America as a whole went from a net inflow of financial resources in 1998, $27.3 billion, to a net *outflow* in 2006 of $10.2 billion—in less than a decade.[3] This outflow was the result of a number of factors, including lower prices for primary good exports, increased imports of finished goods from overseas, and the shifting of investment capital from Latin America to other parts of the world.

The response of Latin America to this shocking reversal of economic fortune and systematic draining of resources was, not surprisingly given Latin American history for the last two centuries, to turn toward nationalism. Stronger national economies, a majority of Latin Americans concluded, would mean less of an outflow of financial resources overseas. As such, nationalistic leaders such as Venezuela's Hugo Chávez, Bolivia's Evo Morales, and Ecuador's Rafael Correa arose in the late 1990s and early 2000s. Typically, they put controls on foreign companies' activities in their nation as well as raising taxes on foreign economic activity.[4] Some observers might conclude that such actions would facilitate capital flight, worsening the problem of outflows of financial resources abroad. However, until the mid-2010s, a majority of Latin Americans thought this shift to the left politically, as well as a strengthening of the nation, was warranted to "stem the tide" of the massive outflow of financial resources.

Ending on a positive note: The sound of nationalistic/globalizing music

Latin American culture, which originally emanated from individual nations or Latin America as a region, has gone global. One of the best ways to see this is through music. The mournful music of the Andes, which partially comes out of the Indian tradition in that part of South America and in which some of the lyrics are in Aymara or Quechua, was of course also influenced by the Spanish. The mournful sound, with its minor keys, is popular the world over. Musical groups playing "traditional" Andean music have become a regular feature on street corners from Japan to Europe. Some of the more popular Andean musical groups spend more time playing overseas than in the Andes. Moreover, the world has, musically, come to the Andes. The popular group the Kjarkas, from Cochabamba, Bolivia, has a Japanese musician in the group. In previous years, having a non-Bolivian member of the group would be unthinkable. Thus as the Kjarkas reach a global audience, their makeup has become global as well.

Yet, the Kjarkas are nationalist as well. While playing some of their songs, they sometimes play video clips on an enormous screen in the back of the stage. Some of the video clips feature scenes of the antineoliberal protests in late 2003, after the government of Sánchez de Lozada made the controversial decision to sell Bolivian natural gas to Bolivia's archenemy Chile. Fearing that selling gas to Chile would be the first step in the Chileans draining Bolivia of their nonrenewable—and valuable—natural resources, Bolivians took to the streets in large numbers.

Interestingly, the Kjarkas' foreign member is from Japan. Although the archeological evidence is not ample enough for us to know the precise time period and the number of migrants, what we know from the archeological evidence is that the first Americans, who became the indigenous peoples of the Americas, came across the Bering Strait about 25,000 years ago—from Asia. So, perhaps, we have come full circle. Asiatic peoples might form the basis of the first civilizations in the Americas. Now, in an age of globalization, a musical group that plays music that is seen as deeply imbedded in the cultures of the Andes, has an Asian musician. The two entities, nations and globalization, have and will continue to interact in new and fascinating—and historic—ways.

Study Questions

1. How do globalization and nationalism reinforce each other?
2. How do globalization and nationalism work against each other?
3. What are the connections, if any, between economic globalization and cultural globalization?

For Further Reading

Ali, Tariq. *Pirates of the Caribbean: Axis of Hope*. London: Verso, 2006.
Shultz, Jim and Melissa Crane Draper, eds. *Dignity and Defiance: Stories from Bolivia's Challenge to Globalization*. Berkeley: University of California Press, 2009.
Walker, William O. III, ed. *Drugs in the Western Hemisphere—An Odyssey of Cultures in Conflict*. Wilmington, DE: Scholarly Resources, 1996.

NOTES

Chapter 1

1   E. Bradford Burns, *Nationalism in Brazil* (New York: Praeger, 1968), 3.
2   Michael Billig, *Banal Nationalism* (Thousand Oaks, CA: SAGE Publications, 1995), 1.
3   Michael Goebel, "Globalization and Nationalism in Latin American, c. 1750–1950," *New Global Studies* 3 (2009): 4, 5.
4   Don H. Doyle and Marco Antonio Pamplona, eds., *Nationalism in the New World* (Athens: University of GA Press, 2006), xx.
5   Gerhard Masur, *Nationalism in Latin America—Diversity and Unity* (New York: Macmillan, 1966).
6   John Hutchinson and Anthony D. Smith, eds., *Nationalism* (Oxford: Oxford University Press, 1994), 4.
7   José Enrique Rodó, *Ariel* (Barcelona: Linkgua Ediciones, 2008).
8   Jorge J. E. Gracia, "Race, Ethnicity, and Nationality in Hispanic American and Latino/a Thought," in *Forging People—Race, Ethnicity and Nationality in Hispanic American and Latino/a Thought*, ed. Jorge J. E. Gracia (Notre Dame, IN: Notre Dame University Press, 2011), 6.
9   Peter Lambert, "Myth, Manipulation, and Violence: Relationships between National Identity and Political Violence," in *Political Violence and the Construction of National Identity in Latin America*, eds. Will Fowler and Peter Lambert (New York: Palgrave, 2006), 19.
10 Gracia, "Race, Ethnicity, and Nationality in Hispanic American and Latino/a Thought," 24.
11 Gracia, "Race, Ethnicity, and Nationality in Hispanic American and Latino/a Thought," 24–25.
12 Will Fowler, "The Children of the Chingada," in *Political Violence and the Construction of National Identity in Latin America*, eds. Will Fowler and Peter Lambert (New York: Palgrave, 2006), 9.
13 Lambert, "Myth, Manipulation, and Violence: Relationships between National Identity and Political Violence," 26.
14 Anton Allahar, *Ethnicity, Class and Nationalism: Caribbean and Extra-Caribbean Dimensions* (Lanham, MD: Lexington Books, 2005), xii.
15 Antonio Carlos de Souza Lima, "On Indigenism and Nationality in Brazil," in *Nation- States and Indians in Latin America*, eds. Greg Urban and Joel Sherzer, 2nd ed. (Tucson, AZ: Hat's Off Books, 2001), 238
16 Miguel A. Centeno and Agustin E. Ferrero, eds., "Introduction," in *State and Nation Making in Latin America and Spain* (New York: Cambridge, 2013), 10–13.

17   Benedict Anderson, *Imagined Communities – Reflections on the Origins and Spread of Nationalism*, 2nd ed. (London: Verso, 1991).

18   Nicola Foote and René D. Harder Horst, eds., *Military Struggle and Identity Formation in Latin America: Race, Nation, and Community during the Liberal Period* (Gainesville: University Press of Florida, 2010), 6.

19   Sarah Castro-Klaren, "The Nation in Ruins—Archeology and the Rise of the Nation," in *Beyond Imagined Communities—Reading and Writing the Nation in Nineteenth-Century Latin America*, eds. John Chasteen and Sarah Castro-Klaren (Washington and Baltimore: Woodrow Wilson Center Press and Johns Hopkins University Press, 2003), 161–95.

20   Two often-cited works on dependency theory include Enrique Cardoso and Enzo Faletto, *Dependency and development in Latin America* (Berkeley: University of California Press, 1979); Andre Gunder Frank, *Capitalism and Underdevelopment in Latin America: Historical Studies of Chile and Brazil* (New York: Monthly Press, 1967).

21   Claudia Zapata, "Discursos de la resistencia: Los indígenas frente al Estado mexicano a partir de los 1970s," in *Identidad y Nación en América Latina*, eds. M. Eva Muzzopappa, Alicia Salomone, Pamela Tala, and Claudia Zapata (Santiago: Facultad de Filosofiía y Humanidades, Universidad de Chile, 2002), 364.

22   Nicola Miller, *In the Shadow of the State—Intellectuals and the Quest for National Identity in Twentieth-Century Spanish America* (London: Verso, 1999), 20.

23   Miller, *In the Shadow of the State*, 35.

24   Fernando López-Alves, "Visions of the National—Natural Endowments, Future, and the Evils of Men," in *State and Nation Making in Latin America and Spain*, eds. Miguel A. Centeno and Agustin E. Ferrero, (New York: Cambridge, 2013), 298.

25   Miller, *In the Shadow of the State*, 23.

26   Mark Lilla, "Our Illegible Age—How We Declined into Libertarianism," *The New Republic* 245 (June 30, 2014): 45.

27   Michael Goebel, "Globalization and Nationalism in Latin American, c. 1750–1950," *New Global Studies* 3 (2009): 9–11.

28   Eric Hobsbawm and Terence Ranger, eds., *The Invention of Tradition*, re-issued ed. (Cambridge: Cambridge University Press, 2012).

29   Fernando Vizcaíno, "Estado multinacional y globalización," in *Nación y nacionalismo en América Latina*, ed. Jorge Enrique González (Bogota: Universidad Nacional de Colombia, Facultad de Ciencias Humanas, Centro de Estudios Sociales—CES), 37

30   Claire Charters and Rodolfo Stavenhagen, eds., *Making the Declaration Work: The United Nations Declaration of the Rights of Indigenous Peoples*, Doc. 127 (Copenhagen: International Work Group for Indigenous Affairs, 2009), 27

31   Bruce Mazlish, *The New Global History* (New York: Routledge, 2006).

32   A. G. Hopkins, ed., *Global History—Interactions between the Universal and the Local* (New York: Palgrave, 2006), 4, 5.

33   Alfred E. Eckes, Jr. and Thomas W. Zeiler, *Globalization and the American Century* (Cambridge: Cambridge University Press, 2003), 1.

34 Immanuel Wallerstein, "The Modern World System as a Capitalist World Economy," in *The Globalization Reader*, eds. Frank J. Lechner and John Boli (Malden, MA: Wiley-Blackwell, 2015), 56–62.

35 Angie Hoogvelt, *Globalization and the Post colonial World—The New Political Economy of Development*, 2nd ed. (Baltimore, MD: Johns Hopkins University Press, 2001), 31.

36 John Micklethwait, and Adrian Wooldridge, "The Hidden Promise—Liberty Renewed," in *The Globalization Reader*, eds. Frank J. Lechner and John Boli, 5th ed. (Malden, MA: Wiley-Blackwell, 2015), 11–18.

37 Hoogvelt, *Globalization and the Post colonial World*, 32.

38 Eckes and Zeiler, *Globalization and the American Century*, 185.

39 Néstor García Canclini, *Consumers and Citizens—Globalization and Multicultural Conflicts* (Minneapolis: University of Minnesota Press, 2001), 18.

40 Charles C. Mann, *1493: Uncovering the New World Columbus Created* (New York: Knopf, 2011), 23.

41 Alfred W. Crosby, *The Columbian Exchange: Biological and Cultural Consequences of 1492* (Westport, CT: Praeger, 2003).

42 Canclini, *Consumers and Citizens*, 18, 19.

43 Hoogvelt, *Globalization and the Post colonial World*, 162.

Chapter 2

1 Samuel Baily, *Nationalism in Latin America* (New York: Knopf, 1970), 13–14.

2 Sheldon B. Liss and Peggy K. Liss, *Man, State, and Society in Latin American History* (New York: Praeger, 1972), 13.

3 Simón Bolívar, comp. Vicente Lecuna, ed. Harold A. Bierck, Jr., trans. Lewis Bertrand, *Selected Writings 1810–1830* (New York: Colonial Press, 1951), 567–70.

4 John Lynch, "Spanish-American Independence in Recent Historiography," in *Independence and Revolution in Spanish America: Perspectives and Problems*, eds. Anthony McFarlane and Eduardo Posada-Carbo (London: Institute of Latin American Studies, 1999), 38.

5 Aimes McGuiness, "Searching for 'Latin America': Race and Sovereignty in the Americas in the 1850s," in *Race and Nation in Modern Latin America*, eds. Nancy P. Applebaum, Anne S. Macpherson, and Karin Alejandra Rosemblatt (Chapel Hill: University of North Carolina Press, 2003), 88.

6 David Brading, "Nationalism and State-Building in Latin American History," in *Wars, Parties and Nationalism: Essays on the Politics and Society of Nineteenth-Century Latin America*, ed. Eduardo Posada-Carbo (London: Institute of Latin American Studies, 1995), 95.

7 Miguel A. Centeno, *Blood and Debt—War and the Nation-State in Latin America* (University Park: Pennsylvania State University Press, 2002), 1–31.

8 Jose Antonio Aguilar Rivera, "Men or Citizens? The Making of Bolivar's *Patria*," in *Forging People—Race, Ethnicity and Nationality in Hispanic*

American and Latino/a Thought, ed. Jorge J. E. Gracia (Notre Dame, IN: Notre Dame University Press, 2011), 58.

9   Rivera, "Men or Citizens? The Making of Bolivar's *Patria*," 58.

10   Brading, "Nationalism and State-Building in Latin American History," 98.

11   Richard Morse, *New World Soundings—Culture and Ideology in the Americas* (Baltimore, MD: Johns Hopkins University Press, 1989), 114–15.

12   David Maybury-Lewis, "Becoming Indian in Lowland South America," in *Nation-States and Indians in Latin America*, eds. Greg Urban and Joel Sherzer, 2nd ed. (Tucson, AZ: Hat's Off Books, 2001), 207–18; Simon Collier, *Ideas and Politics of Chilean Independence, 1808–1833* (Cambridge: Cambridge University Press, 1967), 212–15.

13   Greg Urban, "The Semiotics of State-Indian Linguistic Relationships: The Cases of Peru, Paraguay and Brazil," in *Nation-States and Indians in Latin America*, eds. Greg Urban and Joel Sherzer, 2nd ed. (Tucson, AZ: Hat's Off Books, 2001), 312–15.

14   Baily, *Nationalism in Latin America*, 13–14.

Chapter 3

1   Jeffrey Lesser, *Immigration, Ethnicity, and National Identity in Brazil, 1808 to the Present* (Cambridge: Cambridge University Press, 2013), 2–3.

2   E. Bradford Burns, *Nationalism in Brazil—A Historical Survey* (New York: Frederic A. Praeger, 1968), 7.

3   José Maurício Domingues, "Nationalism in South and Central America," in *The SAGE Handbook of Nations and Nationalism*, eds. Gerard Delanty and Krishan Kumar (Thousand Oaks, CA: SAGE Publications, 2006), 541–54.

4   Frank Safford, "The Construction of Nation States in Latin America, 1820–1890," in *State and Nation Making in Latin America and Spain*, eds. A Miguel Centeno and Agustin E. Ferrero (New York: Cambridge, 2013), 41.

5   Safford, "The Construction of Nation States in Latin America, 1820–1890," 40.

6   Bradford, *Nationalism in Brazil*, 38.

7   Walter LaFeber, "United States Depression Diplomacy and the Brazilian Revolution, 1893–1894," *The Hispanic American Historical Review* 40 (1960): 107–18.

8   Thomas Holloway, *Immigrants on the Land: Coffee and Society in São Paulo, 1886–1934* (Chapel Hill: University of North Carolina Press, 1980).

9   Safford, "The Construction of Nation States in Latin America, 1820–1890," 36–38.

10   Rachel Price, *The Object of the Atlantic—Concrete Aesthetics in Cuba, Brazil, and Spain, 1868–1968* (Evanston, IL: Northwestern University Press, 2014), 8.

11   G. Reid Andrews, *Blacks and Whites in Sao Paulo Brazil, 1888–1988* (Madison: University of Wisconsin Press, 1991).

12   Lesser, *Immigration, Ethnicity, and National Identity in Brazil*, 2, 3.

13   David Brading, *The Origins of Mexican Nationalism* (Cambridge: Centre for Latin American Studies, 1985), 55.

14   Gilbert Joseph, *Revolution from Without—Yucatan, Mexico, and the United States, 1880–1924* (Cambridge: Cambridge University Press, 1982), 33–89.

Chapter 4

1 Franklin Knight, *The Caribbean: Genesis of a Fragmented Nationalism*, 3rd ed. (New York: Oxford University Press, 2011), 204.
2 Rachel Price, *The Object of the Atlantic—Concrete Aesthetics in Cuba, Brazil, and Spain, 1868–1968* (Evanston, IL: Northwestern University Press, 2014), 4.
3 Jerome Teelucksingh, *Caribbean Liberators—Bold, Black Personalities and Organizations, 1900–1989* (Palo Alto, CA: Academia Press, 2013), ixx–6.
4 Ralph Lee Woodward, *Central America—A Nation Divided*, 3rd ed. (New York: Oxford University Press, 1999), 40–41.

Chapter 5

1 Juan Gonzales, *Harvest of Empire—A History of Latinos in the United States*, 2nd ed. (New York: Penguin Books, 2011), 307.
2 Samuel L. Baily, *Nationalism in Latin America* (New York: Alfred A. Knopf, 1970), 6.
3 Anthony D. Smith, *The Ethnic Origins of Nations* (Oxford: Basil Blackwell, 1986), 130–33.
4 José Antonio Ocampo and Juan Martin, *Globalization and Development—Latin American and Caribbean Perspective* (Santiago: UN Commission for Latin America and the Caribbean, 2003), 19.
5 Florencia Mallon, *Peasant and Nation: The Making of Postcolonial Mexico and Peru* (Berkeley: University of California Press, 1995), 22–62 and 176–219.

Chapter 6

1 Samuel Baily, *Nationalism in Latin America* (New York: Knopf, 1970), 121.
2 Sarah Castro-Klaren, "The Nation in Ruins: Archeology and the Rise of the Nation," in *Beyond Imagined Communities: Reading and Writing the Nation in 19th Century Latin America*, eds. Sarah Castro-Klaren and John Chasteen (Baltimore, MD: Johns Hopkins University Press, 2003), 161–95.
3 Jorge J. E. Gracia, "Race, Ethnicity, and Nationality in Hispanic American and Latino/a Thought," in *Forging People—Race, Ethnicity and Nationality in Hispanic American and Latino/a Thought*, ed. Jorge J. E. Gracia (Notre Dame, IN: Notre Dame University Press, 2011), 24.
4 Special Collections, Bodleian Library, Rhodes House, Anti-Slavery Society Papers, *MS British Empire* 22 (1911): G219–30. Argentina, Bolivia, Peru, early 1900s.
5 Jon Lee Anderson, "The Distant Shore—In Peru, a Killing Brings an Isolated Tribe into Contact with the Outside World," *The New Yorker* 92 (Aug 8–15): 42.
6 John E. Kicza, ed., *The Indian in Latin American History: Resistance, Resilience, and Acculturation* (Wilmington, DE: Scholarly Resources, 1993), xxiv.

7   Laura Gotkowitz, *Revolution for Our Rights—Indigenous Struggles for Land and Justice in Bolivia, 1880–1952* (Durham, NC: Duke University Press, 2007), 193–232.

8   Blanca Muratorio, "Images of Indians in the Construction of Ecuadorian Identity at the End of the Nineteenth Century," in *Latin American Popular Culture since Independence—An Introduction*, eds. William H. Beezley and Linda A. Curcio-Nagy, 2nd ed. (Lanham, MD: Rowan/Littlefield, 2012), 121–36.

9   William Robinson, *Latin America and Global Capitalism—A Critical Globalization Perspective* (Baltimore, MD: Johns Hopkins University Press, 2008), 12.

Chapter 7

1   Duncan Green, *Silent Revolution: The Rise and Crisis of Market Economics* (New York: Monthly Review Press; London: Latin American Bureau, 2003), 46.

2   Laurence Duggan, Secretary of State for American Reps Affairs, in his *The Americas—The Search for Hemisphere Security* (New York: Henry Holt and Company, 1949), 147.

3   Gilbert M. Joseph, *Revolution from Without: Yucatan, Mexico, and the United States, 1880–1924* (Durham, NC: Duke University Press, 1987).

4   Manuel Ugarte, J. Fred Rippy, and Catherine Alison Phillips, eds., *The Destiny of a Continent* (New York: AA Knopf, 1925), 139–48.

5   Paul W. Drake, *The Money Doctor in the Andes: U.S. Advisors, Investors, and Economic Reform in Latin America from World War I to the Great Depression* (Durham, NC: Duke University Press, 1989), 13.

6   Elsie Rockwell, "Schools of the Revolution: Enacting and Contesting State Forms in Tlaxcala, 1910–1930," in *Everyday Forms of State Formation: Revolution and the Negotiation of Rule in Modern Mexico*, eds. G. M. Joseph and Daniel Nugent (Durham, NC: Duke University Press, 1994), 199.

7   Nelson Werneck Sodre quoted in E. Bradford Burns, *Nationalism in Brazil—A Historical Survey* (New York: Frederic A. Praeger, 1968), 11

Chapter 8

1   Piero Gleijeses, *Shattered Hope—The Guatemalan Revolution and the United States, 1944–1954* (Princeton: Princeton University Press, 1991).

2   Angie Hoogvelt, *Globalization and the Post colonial World—The New Political Economy of Development*, 2nd ed. (Baltimore, MD: Johns Hopkins University Press, 2001), xi–xvi.

3   José Maurício Domingues, "Nationalism in South and Central America," in *The SAGE Handbook of Nations and Nationalism*, eds. Gerard Delanty and Krishan Kumar (Thousand Oaks, CA: SAGE Publications, 2006), 542.

4   Gleijeses, *Shattered Hope*.

5   Juan José Arévalo, *The Shark and the Sardines*, trans. June Cobb and Dr. Raul Osgueda (New York: Lyle Stuart, 1961), 9–13.

6   Kenneth Lehman, *Bolivia and the United States—Limited Partnership* (Athens: University of Georgia Press, 1990); James F. Siekmeier, *The Bolivian Revolution and the United States, 1952–Present* (University Park: Pennsylvania State University Press, 2011).

7   Lars Schoultz, *That Infernal Little Cuban Republic: The United States and the Cuban Revolution* (Chapel Hill: University of North Carolina Press, 2009).

8   Stephen G. Rabe, *U.S. Intervention in British Guiana: A Cold War Story* (Chapel Hill: University of North Carolina Press, 2005).

9   Phyllis R. Miller, *Brazil and the Quiet Intervention* (Austin: University of Texas Press, 1964); Ruth Leacock, *Requiem for Revolution: The United States and Brazil, 1961–1969* (Kent, OH: Kent State University Press, 1990).

10 Michael L. Conniff, *Panama and the United States: The End of the Alliance* (Athens: University of Georgia Press, 2012).

11 Tanya Harmer, *Allende's Chile and the Inter-American Cold War* (Chapel Hill: University of North Carolina Press, 2011); William F. Sater, *Chile and the United States: Empires in Conflict* (Athens: University of Georgia Press, 1990).

12 Lawrence A. Clayton, *Peru and the United States: The Condor and the Eagle* (Athens: University of Georgia Press, 1999).

13 Karl Bermann, *Under the Big Stick: Nicaragua and the United States since 1848* (Boston: South End Press, 1986); Thomas W. Walker and Christine J. Wade, *Nicaragua: Living in the Shadow of the Eagle* (Boulder, CO: Westview Press, 2011).

Chapter 9

1   José Antonio Ocampo and Juan Martin, *Globalization and Development—A Latin American and Caribbean Perspective* (Santiago: UN Commission for Latin America and the Caribbean, 2003), xiii.

2   Amy L. Sayward, *The Birth of Development: How the World Bank, Food and Agriculture Organization, and World Health Organization Changed the World, 1945–1965* (Kent, OH: Kent State University Press, 2009), 4–7.

3   Richard Gardner, *Sterling-Dollar Diplomacy in Current Perspective*. New York: Columbia University Press, 1980.

4   Eric Helleiner, *Forgotten Foundations of Bretton Woods—International Development and the Making of the Postwar Order* (Ithaca, NY: Cornell, 2014), 156–207.

5   Walter LaFeber, "The Alliances in Retrospect," in *Bordering on Trouble—Resources and Politics in Latin America*, eds. Andrew Maguire and Janet Welsh Brown (Bethesda, MD: Adler and Adler Publishers, 1986), 337–88. For a summary of the covert US Assistance to Latin America in the 1960s for two nations where the Central Intelligence Agency was particularly active, Bolivia and Chile, see US Department of State, *Foreign Relations of the United States, 1964–1968*, vol. XX, *South America and Mexico*, Editorial Note, Documents 147 and 248. See also *Foreign Relations of the United States, 1964–1968*,

vol. XXXII, *Dominican Republic; Cuba; Haiti; Guyana*, "Note on U.S. Covert Actions," xxxi.

6   Joel C. Christenson, 'From Gunboats to Good Neighbors: U.S. Naval Diplomacy in Peru, 1919–1942'. Ph.D diss. Department of History, West Virginia University, 2013.

7   Robert O. Kirkland, *Observing our hermanos de armas: U.S. military attachés in Guatemala, Cuba, and Bolivia, 1950–1964* (New York: Routledge, 2003), 27–54.

8   Arthur Schlesinger, Jr. *A Thousand Days: John F. Kennedy in the White House* (Boston: Houghton Mifflin, 1965), 769.

9   David Sheinin, *Argentina and the United States—An Alliance Contained* (Athens: University of Georgia Press, 2007), 122, 123.

10 Riordan Roett, *The Politics of Foreign Aid in the Brazilian Northeast* (Nashville, TN: Vanderbuilt University Press, 1972), 6.

11 Bevan Sewell, *The United States and Latin America: Eisenhower, Kennedy and Economic Diplomacy in the Cold War* (London: I. B. Tauris, 2015).

Chapter 10

1   Quoted in Jorge J. E. Gracia, *Forging People—Race, Ethnicity, and Nationality in Hispanic American and Latino/a Thought* (Notre Dame, IN: University of Notre Dame Press, 2011), 66. Pardos were people of mixed European and African extraction; what Bolívar meant by *par docracia* was mob rule by mixed-race or non-white peoples.

2   Quoted in Leopoldo Zea, *Discurso desde la marginación y la barbarie* (Mex, DF: Fondo de Cultural Económica, 1990), 102. Translation by the author.

3   Jorge J.E. Gracia, "Preface," in *Forging People—Race, Ethnicity and Nationality in Hispanic American and Latino/a Thought*, ed. Jorge J. E. Gracia (Notre Dame, IN: Notre Dame University Press, 2011), xiv.

4   Gracia, "Preface", xv.

5   Ibid., xiii.

6   Ibid ., xiv.

7   Gracia, "Race, Ethnicity, and Nationality in Hispanic American and Latino/a Thought," 4.

8   Nataniel Aguirre, *Juan de la Rosa—Memoirs of the Last Soldier of the Independence Movement* (Oxford: Oxford University Press, 1998), xiii, 230–45.

9   John J. Johnson, *Latin America in Caricature* (Austin: University of Texas Press, 1980).

Chapter 11

1   Daniel Cosío Villegas, "Nationalism and Development," Special Collections, Bodleian Library, William Clark, box 137, folder 1 [Latin American nationalism], 5. Oxford University, Oxford, England.

2   Riordan Roett, *The Politics of Foreign Aid in the Brazilian Northeast* (Nashville, TN: Vanderbuilt University Press, 1972), 158–59.

3   Guillermo A. O'Donnell, *Modernization and Bureaucratic-Authoritarianism—Studies in South American Politics* (Berkeley: Institute of International Studies, University of California, 1973), 51–111.

4   David Sheinin, *Argentina and the United States—An Alliance Contained* (Athens: University of Georgia Press, 2007), 122, 136.

5   Roberto de Oliveira Campos, "United States-Latin American Relations," Special Collections, Bodleian Library, William Clark, box 137, folder 1 [Latin American nationalism], 1.

6   de Oliveira Campos, "United States-Latin American Relations," 8.

7   Ibid., 9.

8   Ibid., 10.

9   Ibid., 11, 12.

10 Ibid., 14.

11 Villegas, "Nationalism and Development," 3, 5.

12 Ibid., 6.

13 Ibid., 7.

14 Ibid., 8, 9.

15 Ibid., 10.

16 Ibid., 11.

17 Ibid.

18 José Figueres, "The commerce between rich and poor countries as a source of tensions," Special Collections, Bodleian Library, William Clark, box 137, folder 1 [Latin American nationalism], 2.

19 Figueres, "The commerce between rich and poor countries as a source of tensions," 2.

20 Ibid., 3, 8.

21 Ibid., 2, 4, 6.

22 Ibid., 2, 8, 11.

23 Villegas, "Nationalism and Development," 8, 11.

24 Juan José Arévalo, Special Collections, Bodleian Library, William Clark, box 137, folder 1, [Latin American nationalism], 8, 11.

25 Stephen Rabe, *The Killing Zone—The United States Wages Cold War in Latin America* (New York: Oxford, 2012), xxvii.

26 Rabe, *The Killing Zone*, xxvi.

27 Peter Kornbluh, *The Pinochet File: A Declassified Dossier on Atrocity and Accountability*, 2nd ed. (New York: The Free Press, 2013).

28 James Dunkerley, *Rebellion in the Veins—Political Struggle in Bolivia 1952–1982* (London: Verso, 1984).

Chapter 12

1   Anatoly Glinkin, *Inter-American Relations—From Bolivar to the Present* (Moscow: Progress Publishers, 1990), 15.

2   President Ernest Geisal of Brazil quoted in *Reseñha de política exterior do Brasil* (Review of Brazil's foreign relations) 4 (1975): 8.

3   Centeno, *Blood and Debt*, 11.

4   Ibid., 16.

5   Ibid., 23.
6   Brian Loveman, *For la patria—Politics and the Armed Forces in Latin America* (Wilmington, DE: Scholarly Resources, 1999), 59.
7   Centeno, *Blood and Debt*, 56.
8   Loveman, *For la patria*, 236.
9   Ibid., 239, 241, 244.
10 Nicola Foote and Michael Goebei, eds., *Immigration and National Identities in Latin America* (Gainesville: University of Florida Press, 2014), 6.
11 Frederick Pike, *The United States and the Andean Republics* (Cambridge, MA: Harvard University Press, 1978), 1–23.
12 Gracia, "Race, Ethnicity, and Nationality in Hispanic American and Latino/a Thought," 13.
13 Jason Parker, "The Failure of the West Indian Confederation," in *Ultimate Adventures with Britain—Personalities, Politics, and Culture in Britain*, ed. William Roger Louis (London: I. B. Tauris, 2009), 235–45.
14 Virginia Bouvier, ed., *The Globalization of U.S.-Latin American Relations—Democracy, Intervention, and Human Rights* (Westport, CT: Praeger, 2002), 2.
15 Centeno, *Blood and Debt*, 277.

Chapter 13

1   Quoted in www.goodreads.com (accessed January 25, 2017).
2   Benjamin Stephansky, "Latin America: Towards a New Nationalism," *Headline Series* 211, Foreign Policy Association (June 1972): 1718.
3   Centeno, *Blood and Debt*, 14, 15.
4   Robinson, *Latin America and Global Capitalism*.
5   Loveman, *For la patria*.
6   Frederick A. Von Hayek's *The Road to Serfdom* (Chicago: University of Chicago Press, 1944) proved very popular in both Europe and the United States.
7   Peter J. Katzenstein, *Small States in World Markets: Industrial Policy in Europe* (Ithaca, NY: Cornell University Press, 1985), 199–204.

Chapter 14

1   Erick D. Langer and Elena Muñoz, eds., *Contemporary Indigenous Movements in Latin America* (Wilmington, DE: Scholarly Resources, 2003), xiv.
2   Kevin Healy, *Llamas, Weavings, and Organic Chocolate: Multicultural Grassroots Development in the Andes and Amazon of Bolivia* (Notre Dame, IN: Notre Dame University Press, 2001).
3   Jim Shultz and Melissa Crane Draper, eds., *Dignity and Defiance—Stories from Bolivia's Challenge to Globalization* (Berkeley: University of California Press, 2009), 174.
4   Shultz and Draper, *Dignity and Defiance*, 16–26.
5   James C. Cockroft, *Latin America—History, Politics, and U.S. Policy*, 2nd ed. (Chicago: Nelson-Hall Publishers, 1998), 32–36.

6   Gian Luca Gardini, *The Origins of Mercosur: Democracy and Regionalization in South America* (New York: Palgrave Macmillan, 2010), 6, 7.

7   Joseph S. Tulchin and Meg Ruthenburg, eds., *Citizenship in Latin America* (Boulder, CO: Lynne Rienner, 2007), 43–52.

Chapter 15

1   Quoted in www.goodreads.com (accessed January 25, 2017).

2   J. Roddick, *The Dance of the Millions: Latin America and the Debt Crisis* (London: Latin America Bureau, 1988), 24–30.

3   Roddick, *The Dance of the Millions*, 53–57; 63–68.

4   Shultz and Draper, *Dignity and Defiance*, 119.

5   Helleiner, *Forgotten Foundations of Bretton Woods*, 156–83.

6   Shultz and Draper, *Dignity and Defiance*, 153–58.

7   Roddick, *The Dance of the Millions*, 45–47; 81–104; Shultz and Draper, eds., *Dignity and Defiance*, 142–43.

8   Carlos Andrés Pérez, "The Latin America Debt Crisis," adapted from the Henry E. and Nancy Horton Bartels World Affairs Fellowship Lecture given at Cornell University on September 18, 1989 (Ithaca, NY: Cornell University, Office of Publication Services, 1989), 16.

9   Martha Alicia Duque G., "Colombia en subasta. Recursos estrategicos, bioversidad, y TLC [Tratdo Liberal de Comercio]: la nueva amenaza," in *La insertacion de America Latina en la economia internacional*, ed. Jaime Estay (Buenos Aires: Clasco, 2008), 167.

Chapter 16

1   Quoted in A. Campomar, "Latin American football: the antidote to politics," *Telegraph*, May 29, 2014. Available online: www.telegraph.co.uk/culture/hay-festival/10848592/Latin-American-football-the-antidote-to-politics.html (accessed January 25, 2017).

2   Billig, *Banal Nationalism*, 6.

3   Billig, *Banal Nationalism*, 174–77.

4   Castro-Klaren, "The Nation in Ruins—Archeology and the Rise of the Nation," 170–71, 194.

5   Jeffrey M. Pilcher, *Que Vivan Las Tamales!—Food and the Making of Mexican Identity* (Albuquerque: University of New Mexico Press, 1998), 154.

6   Regina A. Root, *The Latin American Fashion Reader* (New York: Berg, 2005).

7   Gabrielle Kuenzli, *Acting Inca—National Belonging in Early Twentieth-Century Bolivia* (Pittsburgh: University of Pittsburgh Press, 2013).

Chapter 17

1   Juan Gonzales, *Harvest of Empire—A History of Latinos in America*, 2nd ed. (New York: Penguin Press, 2011), 307–8.

2   Azam Ahmed and Sandra E. Garcia, "Dominican Plans to Expel Haitians Test Close Ties," *New York Times*, July 5, 2015, 8.

3   Christopher Mitchell, ed., *Western Hemisphere Immigration and United States Foreign Policy* (University Park: Pennsylvania State University Press, 1992), 90.

4   Foote and Goebel, *Immigration and National Identities*, 2.

5   Mitchell, *Western Hemisphere Immigration*, 90, 91.

6   Ibid., x.

7   Thomas F. O'Brien, *Making the Americas—The United States and Latin America from the Age of Revolutions to the Era of Globalization* (Albuquerque: University of New Mexico Press, 2007), 12.

8   Mitchell, *Western Hemisphere Immigration*, 12–16.

Chapter 18

1   David Bushnell and Lester D. Langley, *Simón Bolívar: Essays on the Life and Legacy of the Liberator* (Lanham, MD: Rowman and Littlefield, 2008), 135.

2   Peter N. Stearns, *Globalization in World History* (New York: Routledge, 2010), 3.

3   O'Brien, *Making the Americas*, 1.

4   Emily S. Rosenberg, *Spreading the American Dream: American Economic and Cultural Expansion, 1890–1945* (New York: Hill and Wang, 1982).

5   Brian Loveman, *No Higher Law—American Foreign Policy and the Western Hemisphere since 1776* (Chapel Hill: University of North Carolina Press, 2010).

6   O'Brien, *Making the Americas*, 4.

Chapter 19

1   Shulz and Draper, *Dignity and Defiance*, 2.

2   Rachel Price, *Planet Cuba—Art, Culture, and the Future of the Island* (London: Verso, 2015), 9.

3   Jaime Estay Reyno, "Situacion Reciente de los procesos Latinamericanos de integracion," in *La insertacion de America Latina en la economia internacional*, ed. Jaime Estay Reyno (Buenos Aires: Consejo Latinoamericana de Ciencias Sociales [Clasco], 2008), 214–29.

4   Tariq Ali, *Pirates of the Caribbean: Axis of Hope* (London: Verso, 2006), 96, 138, 222, 230.

SELECT BIBLIOGRAPHY

Alba, Víctor. *Nationalists without Nations: The Oligarchy versus the People in Latin America*. New York: Praeger, 1968.

Ali, Tariq. *Pirates of the Caribbean: Axis of Hope*. London: Verso, 2006.

Allahar, Anton. *Ethnicity, Class and Nationalism: Caribbean and Extra-Caribbean Dimensions*. Lanham, MD: Lexington Books, 2005.

Andrews, G. Reid. *Afro-Latin America, 1800–2000*. Oxford: Oxford University Press, 2004.

Appelbaum, Nancy P., Anne S. Macpherson, and Karin Alejandra Rosemblatt. *Race and Nation in Modern Latin America*. Chapel Hill: University of North Carolina Press, 2003.

Baily, Samuel. *Nationalism in Latin America*. New York: Knopf, 1970.

Billig, Michael. *Banal Nationalism*. Thousand Oaks, CA: SAGE Publications, 1995.

Centeno, Miguel A. *Blood and Debt—War and the Nation-State in Latin America*. University Park: Pennsylvania State University Press, 2002.

Centeno, Miguel A. and Agustin E. Ferrero. *State and Nation Making in Latin America and Spain*. New York: Cambridge University Press, 2013.

Charters, Claire, and Rodolfo Stavenhagen, eds. *Making the Declaration Work: The United Nations Declaration of the Rights of Indigenous Peoples, Doc. 127*. Copenhagen: International Work Group for Indigenous Affairs, 2009.

Chasteen, John and Sarah Castro-Klaren, eds. *Beyond Imagined Communities—Reading and Writing the Nation in Nineteenth—Century Latin America*. Washington: Woodrow Wilson Center Press, 2003.

Clark, Ian. *Globalization and Fragmentation*. Oxford: Oxford University Press, 1997.

Crosby, Alfred W. *The Columbian Exchange: Biological and Cultural Consequences of 1492*. Westport, CT: Praeger, 2003.

Delanty, Gerard and Krishan Kumar, eds. *The SAGE Handbook of Nations and Nationalism*. Thousand Oaks, CA: SAGE Publications, 2006: 541–54.

Doyle, Don H. and Marco Antonio Pamplona, eds. *Nationalism in the New World*. Athens: University of Georgia Press, 2006.

Eckes, Alfred E., Jr. and Thomas W. Zeiler. *Globalization and the American Century*. Cambridge: Cambridge University Press, 2003.

Estay, Jaime, ed. *La insertacion de America Latina en la economia internacional*. Buenos Aires: Clasco, 2008.

Ferguson, Niall, Charles S. Maier, Erez Manela, and Daniel J. Sargent, eds. *The Shock of the Global—The 1970s in Perspective*. Cambridge, MA: Harvard University Press, 2010.

Fitzgerald, David Scott and David Cook-Martin. *Culling the Masses—Democratic Origins of Racist Immigration Policy in the Americas.* Cambridge, MA: Harvard University Press, 2014.

Foote, Nicola and Michael Goebel, eds. *Immigration and National Identities in Latin America.* Gainesville: University Press of Florida, 2014.

Foote, Nicola and René D. Harder Horst, eds. *Military Struggle and Identity Formation in Latin America: Race, Nation, and Community during the Liberal Period.* Gainesville: University Press of Florida, 2010.

Fowler, Will and Peter Lambert, eds. *Political Violence and the Construction of National Identity in Latin America.* New York: Palgrave, 2006.

Galeano, Eduardo. *Open Veins of Latin America—Five Centuries of the Pillaging of a Continent.* New York: Monthly Review Press, 1973.

Gardini, Gian Luca. *Latin America in the 21st Century—Nations, Regionalism, Globalization.* London: Zed, 2009; English translation, 2012.

Gardini, Gian Luca and Peter Lambert, eds. *Latin American Foreign Policies: Between Ideology and Pragmatism.* New York: Palgrave Macmillan, 2011.

Gardner, Richard. *Sterling-Dollar Diplomacy in Current Perspective.* New York: Columbia University Press, 1980.

Goebel, Michael. "Globalization and Nationalism in Latin American, c.1750–1950." *New Global Studies* 3(3), Article 4 (2009), 1–24.

Gracia, Jorge J. E., ed. *Forging People—Race, Ethnicity and Nationality in Hispanic American and Latino/a Thought.* Notre Dame, IN: Notre Dame University Press, 2011.

Green, Duncan. *Silent Revolution: The Rise and Crisis of Market Economics in Latin America.* New York: Monthly Review Press, 2003.

Gunder Frank, Andre. *Capitalism and Underdevelopment in Latin America: Historical Studies of Chile and Brazil.* New York: Monthly Press, 1967.

Hobsbawm, Eric and Terrence Ranger, eds. *The Invention of Tradition*, re-issued ed. Cambridge: Cambridge University Press, 2012.

Hoogvelt, Ankie. *Globalization and the Post colonial World—The New Political Economy of Development*, 2nd ed. Baltimore, MD: Johns Hopkins University Press, 2001.

Hopkins, A. G., ed. *Global History—Interactions between the Universal and the Local.* New York: Palgrave, 2006.

Hutchinson, John and Anthony D. Smith, eds. *Nationalism.* Oxford: Oxford University Press, 1994.

Iriye, Akira. *Global Interdependence: The World after 1945.* Cambridge, MA: Belknap Press of Harvard University, 2014.

Langley, Lester D. *The Americas in the Age of Revolution, 1750–1850.* New Haven, CT: Yale University Press, 1996.

Mann, Charles C. *1493: Uncovering the New World Columbus Created.* New York: Knopf, 2011.

Masur, Gerhard. *Nationalism in Latin America—Diversity and Unity.* New York: Macmillan, 1966.

Mazlish, Bruce. *The New Global History.* New York: Routledge, 2006.

McPherson, Alan. *The Invaded: How Latin Americans and Their Allies Fought and Ended U.S. Occupations.* Oxford: Oxford University Press, 2014.

Miller, Nicola. *In the Shadow of the State—Intellectuals and the Quest for National Identity in Twentieth-Century Spanish America.* London: Verso, 1999.

Nations and Nationalism 12 (2) (April 2006), Special Issue: Nationalism in Latin America.

Ocampo, José Antonio and Juan Martin. *Globalization and Development—A Latin American and Caribbean Perspective.* Santiago: UN Commission for Latin America and the Caribbean, 2003.

Posada-Carbó, Eduardo, ed. *Wars, Parties and Nationalism: Essays on the Politics and Society of Nineteenth-Century Latin America.* London: Institute of Latin American Studies, 1995.

Ritzer, George. *Globalization—The Essentials.* Walden, MA: Wiley-Blackwell, 2011.

Robinson, William. *Latin America and Global Capitalism—A Critical Globalization Perspective.* Baltimore, MD: Johns Hopkins University Press, 2008.

Rosenberg, Emily. *A World Connecting: 1870–1945.* Cambridge, MA: Belknap Press, 2012.

Sassen, Saskia. *Globalization and Its Discontents.* New York: New Press, 1998.

Staples, Amy L. S. *The Birth of Development: How the World Bank, Food and Agriculture Organization, and World Health Organization Changed the World, 1945–1965.* Kent, OH: Kent State University Press, 2006.

Smith, Anthony D. *The Ethnic Origins of Nations.* Oxford: Basil Blackwell, 1986

Smith, Keri E. Iyall. *The State and Indigenous Movements.* New York: Routledge, 2006.

Steger, Manfred B. *Globalization—A Very Short Introduction.* New York: Oxford, 2013.

Tulchin, Joseph S. and Meg Ruthenburg, eds. *Citizenship in Latin America.* Boulder: Lynne Rienner, 2007.

Wallerstein, Immanuel. *World-Systems Analysis: An Introduction.* Durham, NC: Duke University Press, 2004.

White, Christopher. *A Global History of the Developing World.* New York: Routledge, 2014.

Wood, James A., ed. *Problems in Modern Latin American History: Sources and Interpretations,* 4th ed. Lanham, MD: Rowman and Littlefield, 2013.

Woodward, Ralph Lee. *Central America—A Nation Divided,* 3rd ed. New York: Oxford, 1998.

Yergin, Daniel and Joseph Stanislaw. *The Commanding Heights: The Battle between Government and the Marketplace That Is Remaking the Modern World.* New York: Simon and Schuster, 1988.

INDEX

Lightning Source UK Ltd.
Milton Keynes UK
UKOW06n0401110917

308957UK00005B/96/P